PROGRAMED COLLEGE VOCABULARY 3600

Programed College Vocabulary 3600

■ **THIRD EDITION**

George W. Feinstein

Prentice-Hall, Inc., Englewood Cliffs, New Jersey 07632

Editorial/production supervision and
   interior design: *Hilda Tauber*
Cover design: *Wanda Lubelska*
Manufacturing buyer: *Harry P. Baisley*

Printed in the United States of America

10   9   8   7   6   5

ISBN 0-13-729427-1   01

PRENTICE-HALL INTERNATIONAL (UK) LIMITED, *London*
PRENTICE-HALL OF AUSTRALIA PTY. LIMITED, *Sydney*
PRENTICE-HALL CANADA INC., *Toronto*
PRENTICE-HALL HISPANOAMERICANA, S.A., *Mexico*
PRENTICE-HALL OF INDIA PRIVATE LIMITED, *New Delhi*
PRENTICE-HALL OF JAPAN, INC., *Tokyo*
PRENTICE-HALL OF SOUTHEAST ASIA PTE. LTD., *Singapore*
EDITORA PRENTICE-HALL DO BRASIL, LTDA., *Rio de Janeiro*
WHITEHALL BOOKS LIMITED, *Wellington, New Zealand*

Contents

TO THE INSTRUCTOR

Student compositions are not exactly flawless. English teachers have collected clinkers such as "Hester Prynne broke the seventh amendment," "Eugene O'Neill won a pullet surprise," "My doctor said to take some milk of amnesia," and "I took my mother for granite."

Schultz's Law—formulated, it is said, by a professor who later hanged himself—states: "If two words are remotely similar, some students are going to mix them up." Consequently, this third edition includes "Words Often Confused" (Chapters 8 and 9) among its new materials. Students are programed there not to "mix up" words like *complement–compliment*, *decent–descent*, *lose–loose*, *shone–shown*, and *waist–waste*.

Other new chapters include "Computers" and "Foreign Expressions." The section on Latin derivatives has been expanded. Various chapters have been revised or condensed. A few exercises such as those on poetry, drama, and fiction, which in the previous edition seemed a bit too technical for some classes, have now been placed in Appendix B, where they may be assigned, skimmed, or ignored, as the teacher decides.

Accompanying this third edition of *Programed College Vocabulary 3600* is a new Instructor's Manual that provides the teacher with chapter tests and review materials.

Psychologists insist that a student can learn practically anything, including the theory of relativity, if only it is broken down into easy steps. But how does an English instructor find enough class time or conference time to help each student individually with the thousand details of composition? Programed learning offers a possible solution, not of course where value judgments are concerned but where factual data such as vocabulary must be mastered. In recent seasons industrial firms and educators have adopted programed techniques with startling success.

Programed College Vocabulary 3600 has been designed to supplement freshman English. This book differs from most vocabulary textbooks in that (1) it focuses on literary and academic terms, and (2) it is autoinstructional. In short, the approach is pragmatic. *Programed College Vocabulary 3600* stresses those words that are particularly useful to college students, and it elicits from each student a stream of active responses with immediate verification, a process that psychologists call *reinforcement*. Furthermore, hundreds of additional responses are called for in the teacher-administered tests which accompany this book, so that even the reinforcement gets reinforcement. In any case, the system works. The book has now been adopted in more than two hundred colleges and universities, and reports as to the program's effectiveness are extremely encouraging.

Class procedures are flexible. The teacher can leave vocabulary instruction entirely to the programed text itself and simply give chapter tests to the class, as a checkup, at convenient intervals. But the Instructor's Manual includes additional study suggestions as well as tests, and the teacher may wish to devote further class time to enrichment of each chapter. Thus, the freshman English course may take on brave new dimensions.

ACKNOWLEDGMENTS

I am grateful to a galaxy of kind and talented reviewers. Their comments were—to pluck adjectives from Chapters 11 and 12—*candid* and *astute*; their recommendations were *feasible*. In particular, I wish to thank Ellen Bourland, Wallace College; Vivian Brown, Laredo Junior College; Barbara Dicey, Wallace College; Lisa Feinstein, Santa Monica College; Mary Alice Hawkins, Columbia Basin College; Charlene Hawks, Augustana College; Patricia A. McDermott, Northern Essex Community College; Elizabeth Wahlquist, Brigham Young University; and William F. Woods, Wichita State University.

Also I give warm thanks to the English staff of Pasadena City College; Peter Connolly, computer consultant, San Francisco; and Hilda Tauber, production editor, Prentice-Hall, Inc. . . . And to this book of words, let me add a beautiful word—*Edith*.

GEORGE W. FEINSTEIN
Pasadena, California

HOW TO USE THIS MANUAL

1. Cover the answers at the left side of each page with a strip of paper or with your hand.

2. Study carefully the definitions and examples at the beginning of each "frame," or word group.

3. Complete each statement—and immediately verify your answer—throughout the rest of the frame. Fill blanks with word choices, letter choices, or completions as indicated, without looking back to the definitions.

4. After completing each statement, uncover enough of the key at the left to check your answer.

5. If your answer is correct, go on to the next statement.

6. If you have made an error, study the explanations again at the top of the frame, or consult a dictionary, before you go on.

7. Take the quizzes and the review tests when you reach them, but wait until you have completed each quiz or review test before checking or grading your answers to it.

8. Throughout this manual, fill in the blanks completely and with correct spelling. The act of writing, as well as the repetition, will help the learning process.

PRONUNCIATION KEY

a	cat	ê	hero	ô	corn	ū	amuse
ā	hate	ē	lover	o͞o	fool	û	burn
â	rare	i	hit	oo	took	ü	*as in French* vue
ä	far	ī	kite	oi	coil	zh	*for* si *in* vision
e	men	o	hot	ou	out	ə	*for* a *in* alone
ē	evil	ō	note	u	up	ṅ	*nasal, as in French* bon

PART ONE

1

Latin Derivatives

1. *am, amat* - love
2. *ann, enn* - year
3. *aqu* - water
4. *aud, audit* - hear
5. *capit* - head
6. *cent* - hundred
7. *cred, credit* - believe
8. *dic, dict* - say
9. *duc, duct* - lead
10. *fid* - faith
11. *frater* - brother
12. *greg* - flock
13. *litera* - letter
14. *loc* - place
15. *loqu, locut* - talk
16. *mal* - bad
17. *man* - hand
18. *mater, matr, metr* - mother
19. *mit, miss* - send
20. *mor, mort* - death
21. *mov, mot, mob* - move
22. *nov* - new
23. *omni* - all
24. *ped* - foot
25. *pon, posit* - place

Latin derivatives make up at least half of our language. A student without this half of English vocabulary would be like a sprinter with one leg. Luckily you are already familiar with hordes of useful Latin derivatives and by one technique or another you can learn hundreds more. Taking six years of classical Latin is an excellent method, but if that route is inconvenient, you can study common Latin roots and prefixes that have enriched our English language.

Chapters 1 and 2 focus on fifty important Latin roots and their clusters of derivatives. Chapter 3 reviews Latin prefixes.

First, memorize the Latin term and its definition, given at the beginning of each frame. Next, note carefully the example derivatives that follow in italics. Try to understand the connection between each of these derivatives and its Latin root. Then fill in the blanks.

Roots

1. **am, amat:** love.
   Derivatives: *amateur, amative, amatory, amiable, amity, amorist, amours.*

loving

■ Since *amat* means *love*, an *amative* young man is _____ [hostile / loving].

love

■ An *amateur* golfer plays for _____ [love / the fat fees] of the game.

am

■ The two letters in the words *amorist* and *amatory* that suggest *love* are _____ am _____ .

amorist
amatory

■ The Casanova devoted to *love*-making is an _____ [atheist / amorist], and he has _____ [amatory / mandatory] adventures.

amours

■ Cleopatra's *love* affairs are her _____ amours.

amity

■ Warm friendship between nations is international _____ [animosity / amity].

amiable

■ Friendly people are _____ [amiable / alienated].

2. **ann, enn:** year.
   Derivatives: *annals, anniversary, annual, annuity, biennial, centennial, millennium, perennial, superannuated.*

ann

■ The three letters in the words *annals* and *annual* that suggest *year* are _____ ann _____ .

year

■ *Per annum* means per _____ [month / year].

annuity

■ *Yearly* income from a fund is called an _____ [excise / annuity].

super-
annuated

■ A man who has lived many *years* is said to be _____ [superannuated / supercilious].

enn

■ In some words, like *biennial*, *centennial*, and *perennial*, the Latin root for *year* is _____ [ial / enn].

3. **aqu:** water.
   Derivatives: *aquacade, aqualung, aquamarine, aquaplane, aqua regia, aquarium, aquatint, aqua vitae, aqueduct, aqueous humor, aquiculture, subaqueous.*

water

■ To make an *aqueous* solution you dissolve something in _____ [alcohol / water].

aqu

■ The three letters in *aqualung* and *aquiculture* that suggest *water* are ____*aqu*____ .

water

■ An *aquaplane* is towed on _____ [snow / water / rocks].

aquacade

■ A *water* festival which involves swimming and diving is sometimes called an ____*aqua*___cade.

aquarium

■ Small fish may be kept in an _____*aquar*__ium.

Aquarius

■ The sign of the zodiac that represents a *water* bearer is _____ [Aquarius / Taurus].

aqueous

■ The *watery* fluid between the cornea and the lens of the eye is known as _____ [aqueous / amorous] humor.

4. **aud, audit:** hear.
   Derivatives: *audible, audience, audile, audio-frequency, audiophile, audio-visual, audiphone, audit, audition, auditor, auditorium, auditory.*

4

hear	■ You can assume that *auditory* nerves help you to _____ [(hear) / see], since the five-letter Latin root for *hear* is
audit	_____ [ditor / (audit)].
audition	■ After a successful critical *hearing*, or ___*audit*_ion, a singer
audience	might entertain an ___*audience*ce in an ___*auditor*_ium.
auditorium	
hearing	■ An *audiometer* is an instrument which measures sensitivity of _____ [(hearing) / sight].
hi-fi	■ An *audiophile* is enthusiastic about _____ [stamps / (hi-fi)].
adenoids	■ Which word has no business being in the following list? *audible, audiphone, audio-frequency, (adenoids), auditor* _____ .

5. **capit: head.**
   Derivatives: *cap, capital, capitalism, capitate, capitol, caption, decapitate, per capita, recapitulate.*

head	■ *Capit* is a root that means *h_ead_* _____ ; so the *heading*
caption	of a chapter or an article is called a _____ [decoction / (caption)].
head	■ *Capitation* is a tax or fee on each _____ [(head)/ foot].
head	■ A per *capita* tax is assessed as so much per *h_ead_* _____ .
capit	■ The Latin root for *head* is *capit* _____ .
capital	■ In Paris, the ___*capit*_al of France, King Louis XVI
decapitated	got a sovereign cure for headaches—he was *de_capitated_* .
recapitulate	■ Newscasters sometimes *re_capitulate_* the day's news; such a *recapitulation* literally restates the news (a) in full,
(b)	(b) by headings. ( )

Quiz

Write the meaning of each boldface Latin root.

1. **aud**ience _hear_

2. **cap**itol _head_

3. sub**aqu**eous _water_

4. **am**atory _love_

5. **ann**iversary _year_

1. hear
2. head
3. water
4. love
5. year

---

6. **cent**: hundred.
   Derivatives: *cent, centavo, centenarian, centenary, centennial, centigrade, centigram, centiliter, centime, centimeter, centipede, centuple, centurion, century, tercentennial.*

cent
hundred
century

■ The Latin root for *hundred* is _cent_ ; thus, a *centenarian* has lived a _hundred_ years, in other words, an entire _cent_ury.

centigrade

■ There are one *hundred* degrees between the freezing and boiling points of water on the _____ [Fahrenheit / (centigrade)] thermometer.

centimeter

■ One-*hundredth* of a meter is a _____ [(centimeter) / kilometer].

centigram

■ One-*hundredth* of a gram is a _centigram_ .

centiliter

■ One-*hundredth* of a liter is a _centiliter_ .

centennial
hundred

■ A *centenary*, or _centenn_ial, is celebrated after one _hundred_ years.

2076

■ Since *ter* means *three*, the *tercentennial* of the Declaration of Independence should occur in the year _____ [(2076) / 2776]. You are all invited.

---

7. **cred, credit:** believe; trust.
Derivatives: *accredit, credence, credentials, credible, credit, creditable, creditor, credo, credulity, credulous, creed, discredit.*

cred
believable

■ Since the Latin root for *believe* is _____ [(cred)/ crud], a *credible* story is _____ [(believable)/ absurd].

(b)

■ Your *creed*, or *credo*, is what you (a) fight, (b) (believe) in. ( )

believe

■ To give *credence* to a rumor is to _____ [deny / (believe)] it.

accredited
credentials

■ An ac*credited* _____ college hires only those teachers who have proper _____ *credentials*.

believe

■ Your *credulity* is your readiness to _____ [love / (believe)].

incredulous

■ Sometimes news is so amazing that you are _____ [cretinous / (incredulous)].

8. **dic, dict:** say.
Derivatives: *addict, benediction, contradict, dictaphone, dictate, diction, dictograph, dictum, edict, indicative, indict, interdict, jurisdiction, malediction, predicate, predict, valedictorian, verdict.*

dict
say

■ The four-letter Latin root of *dictate* and *dictum* is *dict* and it means s*ay* .

predict

■ To *say* what will happen, or foretell, is to pre*dict* .

edict

■ An order issued by an absolute ruler is an _____ [(edict)/ audit].

7

verdict

■ The judgment of a jury is a *verdict* .

predicate

■ The part of a sentence which *says* something about the subject is the *predicate* .

indicative

■ The mood of a verb that merely states a fact is _____ [subjunctive / (indicative)].

duck

■ *Dictaphone, contradict, indicate, (duck), addict*—which word floated in by mistake? _____

---

9. **duc, duct:** lead.
   Derivatives: *abduct, aqueduct, conducive, conduct, deduce, duchess, duct, ductility, duke, educate, educe, Il Duce, induce, introduce, produce, reduce, reproduce, seduction, traduce.*

duc
lead

■ To *educate* is literally to "lead out." The three-letter root of *education* is *duc* and it means *lead* .

Leader

■ Mussolini was called *Il Duce*, which means "The *lead*er."

dukes

■ Europe has had many princely *leaders* known as _____ [schlemiels / (dukes)], but America's democratic climate is hardly

conducive

conducive to the growth of a crop of *dukes* and their

duchesses

wives, *duchess* es.

aqueduct

■ Water is sometimes *led* into a city through an *aqueduct* .

seducer

■ An innocent girl may be *led* astray by a _____ [(seducer) / centuple].

■ The ability of a metal to be *led* into various shapes is called

ductility

_____ [motility / (ductility)].

---

10. **fid:** faith; trust.
    Derivatives: *affidavit, confidant, confide, confidence, confidential, diffident, fidelity, fiduciary, infidel, perfidious, perfidy.*

faith	■ To *confide* in a stranger is an act of _____ [leading / faith].
fid	■ The Latin root for *faith* is *fid*_____ .
unfaithfulness	■ *Infidelity* means _____ [unfaithfulness / inability to provide].
perfidious	■ In betraying his *trust*, Benedict Arnold did a _____ [perfervid / perfidious] thing.
perfidy	■ In fact, Benedict Arnold committed an act of _____ [perfidy / persiflage].
confident	■ A prizefighter who has *faith* in himself is said to be con*fident* _____ .
diffident	■ A lad who is shy and lacks *faith* in himself is said to be _____ [amative / diffident].

Quiz

Write the meaning of each boldface Latin root.

1. de**duct**ion   *lead*
2. **cent**ury   *hundred*
3. **cred**ential   *believe*
4. af**fid**avit   *faith*
5. bene**dict**ion   *say*

1. lead
2. hundred
3. believe
4. faith
5. say

11. **frater:** brother.
     Derivatives: *confraternity, frater, fraternal, fraternity, fraternize, fratricide.*

brother	■ *Frater* means *brother* .
brotherly	■ *Fraternal* obligations are _____ [fatherly / brotherly].

fraternize

■ To mingle with conquered people in a social or *brotherly* way is to _____ *fratern* nize with them.

fratricide

■ Killing one's own *brother* is called _____ *fratri* cide.

brother

■ A girls' club should not be called a *fraternity* because *frater* means _____ brother .

confraternity

■ A *brotherly* group devoted to charitable work is sometimes called a _____ [fiduciary / (confraternity)].

---

12. **greg:** flock.
   Derivatives: *aggregation, congregate, egregious, gregarious, segregate.*

greg

■ The Latin root for *flock* is g reg .

congregation

■ A minister's *flock* is called a *con* gregation .

segregation

■ Separation from the main group or *flock* is se gregation .

flock
society

■ Since *greg* means f lock , we may assume that *gregarious* people like _____ [solitude / (society)].

egregious

■ Insulting your teacher during examination week might stand out from your *flock* of lesser mistakes as an _____ [(egregious) / diffident] blunder.

aggregation

■ Bismuth is ineligible to play with the football _____ [aggravation / (aggregation)].

---

13. **litera:** letter.
   Derivatives: *alliteration, literacy, literal, literalism, literally, literary, literate, literati, literature, litterateur, transliteration.*

litera
letter

■ The Latin root of the word *literary* is litera , and it means letter .

literal

■ Translating *letter* for *letter* results in a _____ *liter* al translation.

illiterate

■ A person who can't read or write is *unlettered*, or _____ [illegitimate / illiterate].

literate
literature

■ The person who reads and writes is _____ [literate / libelous] and possibly enjoys _____ *literat* ure.

realistically

■ *Literalism* in art means drawing things to the *letter*, that is, _____ [realistically / imaginatively].

(b)

■ A *litterateur* is (a) a man who keeps rabbits, (b) a man of letters. (   )

---

14. **loc:** place.
    Derivatives: *allocate, dislocate, locale, localism, locality, localize, location, locative,* loco citato, *locus, relocate.*

loc

■ A three-letter Latin root that means *place* is *loc* _____ .

place

■ The *locale* of a train wreck refers to the _____ [place / cause].

locality
localism

■ An expression that is used only in a certain *place*, or _____ *locali* ty, is called a [barbarism / localism].

locus
loci

■ In mathematics the set of points or *places* which satisfy a given condition is called the _____ *loc* us. The plural of *locus* is _____ [locusts / loci].

place

■ In footnotes *loco citato* is abbreviated as *loc. cit.* and means "in the *place* _____ cited."

place

■ In Latin and Greek grammar the *locative* case denotes _____ [time / place].

---

15. **loqu, locut**: talk.
   Derivatives: *allocution, circumlocution, colloquial, colloquium, colloquy, elocution, eloquent, grandiloquent, interlocutor, loquacious, prolocutor, soliloquy.*

talkative

■ A *loquacious* child is _____ [sulky / talkative].

colloquial

■ Most people talk informally, that is, in _____ [literary / colloquial] English.

locut

■ In *interlocutor* and *locution* the five-letter root that suggests *talk* is *locut* _____ .

eloquent

■ Webster was an inspired *talker;* in fact, he was often *eloquent* _____ .

grandiloquent

■ A windy orator who uses grand, phony expressions is _____ [magnanimous / grandiloquent].

circumlocution

■ Saying a thing in a roundabout way is known as _____ [circumspection / circumlocution].

soliloquy

■ Hamlet's "To be or not to be," spoken alone on stage, is a _____ [solecism / soliloquy].

Quiz

Write the meaning of each boldface Latin root.

1. letter
2. talk
3. brother
4. place
5. flock

1. **alliter**ation _*letter*_

2. col**loqu**ium _*talk*_

3. **frater**nal _*brother*_

4. dis**loc**ate _*place*_

5. ag**greg**ate _*flock*_

16. **mal:** bad.
    Derivatives: *maladjusted, maladminister, maladroit, malaise, malapropos, malaria, malcontent,* mal de mer, *malediction, malefactor, malevolent, malfeasance, malformed, malice, malign, malignant, malinger, malnutrition, malocclusion, malodorous, malpractice.*

bad

■ *Malfeasance* in office refers to _____ [bad] / admirable] conduct.

bad

■ *Mal* means b*ad* .

malignant

■ The truly *bad* tumors are the _____ [benign / malignant] ones.

(b)

■ To hurl *maledictions* is to fling (a) small rocks, (b) evil words or curses. (   )

malevolent

■ Evil wishers are _____ [benevolent / malevolent].

bad

■ *Malaise* is physical discomfort that hints of _____ [good / bad] health.

maladroit

■ A clumsy child is said to be _____ [maladroit / adroit].

malnutrition

■ A badly nourished child suffers from ___*malnutri*___tion.

malodorous

■ Goats don't smell good; they are _____*mal*___odorous.

17. **man:** hand.
    Derivatives: *amanuensis, manacle, manage, mandate, mandatory, maneuver, manicure, manifest, manifesto, manipulate, manual, manufacture, manumit, manuscript.*

hands

■ *Manacles* are worn on the _____ [eyes / hands].

man

■ The Latin root for *hand* is m*an* .

manicure

■ *Hands* with ugly nails should be given a _____ [(manicure) / pedicure].

hand

■ Both *emancipate* and *manumit* mean to set free, that is, to let go from the *hand* _____ .

hand

■ An *amanuensis* is a copyist—he works with his _____ [jaw / (hand)].

man
manuscript

■ Another word derived from the root *man* _____ , meaning *hand*, is _____ [amnesia / amenity / enema / (manu-script)].

18. **mater, matr, metr**: mother.
　　Derivatives: *alma mater, maternal, maternity, matriarch, matricide, matriculate, matrilineal, matrimony, matrix, matron, metronymic, metropolis.*

matriarch

■ A *mother* who rules a family or tribe is a _____ [(matriarch) / patriarch].

matr
mother

■ In the words *matrix* and *matrimony* the four-letter Latin root is *matr* _____ , and it means m*other* _____ .

matricide

■ Slaying one's own *mother*, an ungrateful business, is known as _____ [uxoricide / (matricide)].

mater
matriculate

■ Our college is our alma m*ater* _____ (fostering mother). To enroll is to ____*matricul*ate.

matron
maternity

■ A hospital _____*matr*on supervises the care of expectant *mothers* in the _____*materni*ty ward.

mother

■ *Matrilineal* descent refers to kinship through the _____ [father / (mother)].

metronymic

■ Henry Cabot Lodge derived his middle name from the maiden name of his mother; therefore for him the name *Cabot* is a _____ [(metronymic) / patronymic].

19. mit, miss: send.
   Derivatives: *admissible, admit, commissary, commit, emissary, emit, intermittent, mission, missionary, missive, omission, permit, premise, promise, remit, submit, transmit.*

miss
send

■ The Latin root in *mission* is ___miss___ and it means s___end___ .

missionary

■ The person we *send* to convert the heathens is called a ___missionary___ .

emissary

■ The diplomat we *send* out is an _____ [(emissary) / auditor].

missive

■ A tourist usually *sends* his home-town friends a _____ [(missive) / missile].

mit

■ Which three letters in *remit* mean *send*? ___mit___

intermittent

■ Shots *sent* out at intervals are said to be _____ [interdicted / (intermittent)].

---

20. mor, mort: death.
   Derivatives: *immortal, moribund, mortal, mortality, mortgage, mortician, mortify, mortuary, post-mortem,* rigor mortis.

death

■ The root *mort* suggests that a *mortician* is concerned with _____ [birth / (death)].

mortuary
mortis

■ The *mortician* operates a funeral home known as a ___mortua___ry and he is, no doubt, acquainted with the *stiffness of death* known as rigor m___ortis___ .

dying

immortal

■ Greeting card sellers complain that the custom of sending valentines is *moribund*—that is, _____ [too lively / (dying)]. If the custom never died, it would be _____ [(immortal) / immoral].

15

■ If you develop gangrene, your flesh *mortifies;* this means that it (a) decays and dies, (b) glows with health. (   )

Quiz

Write the meaning of each boldface Latin root.

1. **man**ual   *hand*

2. **mater**nal   *mother*

3. **mort**gage   *death*

4. **e**mission   *send*

5. **male**factor   *bad*

---

21. **mov, mot, mob:** move.
    Derivatives: *automobile, commotion, demote, emotion, immobile, immovable, locomotive, mobile, mobility, motile, motion, motivation, motor, promote, remote, remove.*

■ Give the root of *movable:* *mov* ; of *motor:* *mot* ; of *mobile:* *mob* . These variant Latin roots mean *move* .

■ From the letters *mot* it's a safe guess that *motile* cells are able to _____ [talk / move].

■ An army's ability to *move* is referred to as its _____ [stability / mobility].

■ Whatever *moves* one to study or marry or assassinate is one's _____ [innovation / motivation].

■ You are often *moved*, or stirred, by _____ [emotions / omissions].

■ Another word derived from the root meaning *move* is _____ [mother / matador / promotion / smote].

---

22. **nov**: new.
    Derivatives: *innovation, nova, Nova Scotia, novel, novelette, novella, novelty, novice, novitiate, novocain, renovate.*

■ The letters *nov* in *novelty* mean *new* .

new

■ An *innovation* is a _____ [crazy / (new)] idea or custom.

new

■ In a religious order a *new* member is called a ____ *nov* ice and the probationary period is a _____ *noviti* ate.

novice
novitiate

■ A *nova* star is (a) a faithful old planet, ((b)) a brilliant new exploding star. (   )

(b)

■ A hint of something *new* also occurs in the word _____ [naval / (novel) / venerable / Navaho].

novel

■ When our landlord promises to _____ *renov* ate our apartment, we hope he knows that the word-root *nov* means _____ [air / (new)].

renovate

new

23. **omni**: all.
    Derivatives: *omniactive, omnibenevolent, omnibus, omniferous, omnipotent, omnipresent, omniprevalent, omniscient, omnium-gatherum, omnivorous.*

■ In the words *omniscient* (all-knowing) and *omnipotent* (all-powerful) the four-letter root that means *all* is *omni* .

omni

■ An *omnium-gatherum* is a collection of _____ [(many) / one or two] different things.

many

■ A tree that produces *all* varieties is _____ [mellifluous / (omniferous)].

omniferous

■ Because *omni* means _____ [(all) / small], we can assume that an *omnivorous* reader reads (a) only the funnies, (b) practically everything. (   )

all

(b)

17

omnibuses

■ To transport loads of students, a school usually buys _____ [compacts / (omnibuses)].

---

24. **ped:** foot.
    Derivatives: *biped, centipede, expedient, expedite, expedition, impediment, pedal, pedestal, pedestrian, pedometer, quadruped, sesquipedalian.*

foot

■ A *pedestrian* travels by _____ [(foot) / jet plane].

ped

■ The three-letter word-root meaning *foot* is p*ed* _____ .

walked

■ A *pedometer* measures the distance _____ [driven / (walked)].

biped

■ A man has two *feet* and so according to Aristotle is a featherless _____ [(biped) / slob].

feet

■ An *impediment* is literally something that obstructs or holds up the _____ [(feet) / meals].

(a)

■ To *expedite* means, in a sense, to free the *feet*, hence, (a) to speed up the action, (b) to snarl things up. (   )

feet

■ Since *sesqui* means "one and a half," a *sesquipedalian* is a word that is supposedly about one and a half _____ [(feet) / years] long.

---

25. **pon, posit:** place.
    Derivatives: *apposite, appositive, component, composition, depose, deposit, dispose, exponent, expose, impose, interpose, juxtapose, opponent, position, positive, postpone, proponent, propose, repository.*

posit
place

■ The words *position*, *deposit*, and *appositive* all contain the five-letter root *posit* _____ , which means p*lace* _____ .

pon

■ Another root that means *place* is _____ [pan / (pon)].

18

components

■ Stereo set parts that must be *placed* together are called _____ [compartments / components].

juxtaposed

■ Objects *placed* alongside each other are _____ [juxtaposed / coincident].

repository
dispose

■ You can *place* old books in a _____ [repertory / repository] or otherwise *dispose* _____ of them.

exponent

■ One who sets forth, or advocates, a doctrine is its _____ [expatriate / exponent].

apposite

■ Appropriate or *well-placed* remarks are said to be _____ [apposite / appellate].

Quiz

Write the meaning of each boldface Latin root.

1. **ped**al   *foot* _____

2. **nov**elette   *new* _____

3. com**posit**ion   *place* _____

4. **omni**present   *all* _____

5. de**mote**   *move* _____

1. foot
2. new
3. place
4. all
5. move

REVIEW TEST

Write *True* or *False*.

_____T_____   1. A *pedestrian* is one who walks.

_____T_____   2. An *innovation* is something newly introduced.

_____F_____   3. A *localism* is a universally popular pet phrase.

_____F_____   4. A *missive* is a small female ballet dancer.

_____T_____   5. A *literal* translation follows the original very closely.

_____T_____   6. In a *matriarchy* the mother rules the family or tribe.

_____F_____   7. A *dictum* is someone injured in an accident.

_____T_____   8. *Loquacity* refers to talkativeness.

_____F_____   9. To *mobilize* means to hypnotize and to stop action.

_____F_____ 10. The name *Il Duce* means the "deuce" or "two-spot."

Write the meaning of each boldface Latin root. The first letter of each answer is given.

11. a **frater**nity of poets   b_rother_

12. guilty of **mal**practice   b_ad_

13. **aqu**atic sports   w_ater_

14. an in**cred**ible plot   b_eleive_

15. a Robert Frost **cent**ennial   h_undred_

16. an **am**orous sonnet   l_ove_

17. the im**mort**al Chaucer   d_eath_

18. an e**greg**ious idiot   f_lock_

19. an illuminated **man**uscript   h_and_

20. dis**posit**ion of funds   p_lace_

Write the letter that indicates the best completion.

(d)   21. An *infidel* is one who has no (a) married parents, (b) schooling, (c) musical ability, (d) religious faith.

(c)   22. An *audible* kiss is one that (a) lasts a long time, (b) can be seen, (c) can be heard, (d) gives off steam.

20

(*b*) 23. That which is *omnipresent* is (a) nowhere, (b) everywhere, (c) a welcome gift, (d) invisible.

(*b*) 24. The Latin root for *head* is used in which word?—(a) aquatint, (b) caption, (c) deception, (d) amour.

(*a*) 25. The Latin root for *year* is used in which word?—(a) perennial, (b) banana, (c) birthday, (d) decade.

Key to Review Test

Check your test answers by the following key. Deduct 4% per error from a possible 100%.

1. True	6. True	11. brother	16. love	21. (d)
2. True	7. False	12. bad	17. death	22. (c)
3. False	8. True	13. water	18. flock	23. (b)
4. False	9. False	14. believe	19. hand	24. (b)
5. True	10. False	15. hundred	20. place	25. (a)

Score: _____100_____ %

2

Latin Derivatives

ROOTS

1. *port, portat*
2. *prim*
3. *reg*
4. *rupt*
5. *sanct*
6. *scrib, script*
7. *seg, sect*
8. *sequ, secut*
9. *sign*

10. *sol*
11. *son*
12. *spec, spect*
13. *spir, spirat*
14. *tempor*
15. *terra*
16. *tort*
17. *tract*
18. *turb*

19. *urb*
20. *vac*
21. *vers, vert*
22. *vid, vis*
23. *vinc, vict*
24. *vit, viv*
25. *voc, vocat*

Chapter 2 continues our study of Latin roots and their derivatives. Follow the same procedure as in Chapter 1.

EXERCISES

COVER THIS STRIP

Roots

---

1. **port, portat:** carry.
   Derivatives: *comport, deport, disport, export, import, portable, portage, portfolio, porter, portmanteau, purport, rapport, report, support, transport.*

port
carry

■ The words *porter*, *export*, and *purport* all have the root ____*port*____ , which means c____*arry*____ .

transport
portable
portfolio
portmanteau

■ One can easily *trans*____*ports*____ a ____*port*____*able* typewriter, a ____*portfol*____*io* (brief case), or a ____*portman*____*teau* (leather suitcase that opens into two compartments like a book).

(a)

■ To make a *portage* between lakes means (a) to carry gear, (b) to stop for lunch. (*a*)

deportment

■ Your ____*deport*____*ment* is your behavior or way of *carrying* yourself.

---

2. **prim:** first.
   Derivatives: *prima donna, primal, primarily, primary, primate, prime, prime minister, primer, primeval, primitive, primitivism, primogeniture, primordial, primrose, primula.*

prime

■ The *first* or top statesman in England is the ____*prime*____ minister.

prima

■ The *first* female singer in opera is the ____*prima*____*a* donna.

primula
primrose
prim

■ We can assume that the *first* flowers of spring include the ____*prim*____*ula*—also called ____*prim*____*rose*—because the Latin root ____*prim*____ means "first."

23

primary
primer

■ We *first* went to a _____prima_____ry school, and our *first* book was a _____prim_____er.

primate
primitive

■ Man, known as a _____prim_____te, has progressed from _____primiti_____ve cave to fancy condominium.

■ The system of *primogeniture* provided that one's estate and title went to the son who was born _____first_____ [first / last].

first

primarily

■ Breathing through your nose is wise, _____primari_____ly (mainly) because it keeps your mouth shut.

---

3. **reg**: rule.
   Derivatives: *interregnum, irregular, regal, regalia, regency, regent, regicide, regime, regiment, Regina, region, regular, regulate, regulation.*

regulation
(a)

■ A soldier must obey an army _____regula_____tion because the *reg* in *regulation* means (a) "rule," (b) "fool around." (a)

regiment
regalia

■ If you join our _____regi_____ment, you must wear our _____regal_____ia (official decorations).

Regina
region, regal

■ Elizabeth _____Regi_____na (Queen) *ruled* the entire _____regi_____on in a _____reg_____al (royal) manner.

regicide
irregular

■ In 1649 King Charles I was beheaded, an act of _____regic_____ide as ir_____regular_____ as it was barbaric.

regimen

■ My doctor ordered me to follow a _____regi_____men (health system) of tasteless food and hard exercise.

interregnum

■ The period between two successive reigns or *rulers* is known as an *inte*_____rregnum_____ .

reg

■ The *regents* evidently run a university, because the three-letter Latin root _____reg_____ means "rule."

4. **rupt:** break.
   Derivatives: *corrupt, disrupt, erupt, interrupt, rupture.*

interrupt

■ You're *breaking* into our conversation. Please don't *inter̲r̲u̲p̲t̲* us.

corrupt

■ Bribed? Then "Honest Abe" Jones is *co̲r̲r̲u̲p̲t̲* !

rupt

■ The Latin root for *break* is r̲u̲p̲t̲ .

erupt

■ Soon this rumbling volcano will e̲r̲u̲p̲t̲ (break out).

rupture

■ Uncle Rudy dug deep and managed to _____ r̲u̲p̲t̲u̲*re* (break) a gas main. For good measure, the heavy lifting gave

rupture

Rudy an abdominal _____ r̲u̲p̲t̲u̲*re*.

disrupt

■ Hecklers may *dis* r̲u̲p̲t̲ the political rally.

5. **sanct:** holy.
   Derivatives: *sanctified, sanctify, sanctimonious, sanctimony, sanction, sanctitude, sanctity, sanctuary, sanctum, sanctum sanctorum.*

sanctified

■ The Normandy beach is *holy* ground, s̲a̲n̲c̲t̲i̲f̲ *ied* by the blood of American soldiers.

sanctitude

■ The priest had an air of _____ s̲a̲n̲c̲t̲i̲t̲*ude* (holiness).

holy
sanctum
sanctorum

■ Since *sanct* means _____ h̲o̲l̲y̲ [drowned / holy], we refer to the *holy* of *holies* as the _____ s̲a̲n̲c̲t̲*um* _____ s̲a̲n̲c̲t̲o̲r̲*um.*

sanctuary

■ A church is a true _____ s̲a̲n̲c̲t̲u̲a̲*ry* (holy refuge).

sanction

■ Slavery? How can any nation _____ s̲a̲n̲c̲t̲i̲o̲*n* (approve) it?

25

sanctimonious
sanctimony
sanctity

■ Tartuffe speaks _*santimoni*ous_ (pretending to be holy) words, but what a difference between the hypocrite's _*sanctimo*ny_ and genuine _*sancti*ty!_

Quiz

Write the meaning of each boldface Latin root.

1. **reg**ulation   r_*ule*_
2. **prim**itive   f_*irst*_
3. **sanct**uary   h_*oly*_
4. inter**rupt**   b_*reak*_
5. **port**able   c_*arry*_

1. rule
2. first
3. holy
4. break
5. carry

6. **scrib, script:** write.
   Derivatives: *ascribe, circumscribe, conscription, describe, inscribe, manuscript, nondescript, postscript, prescribe, proscribe, scribble, scribe, scripture, subscribe, transcribe, typescript.*

scrib
write

■ The five-letter root of *subscribe, proscribe,* and *inscribe* is _*scrib*_ , and it means w_*rite*_ .

postscript

■ An afterthought *written* at the end of a letter is a p_*ostscript*_ .

conscription

■ The army draft, or enrollment, is known as con_*scription*_ .

written
transcribed
manuscripts
scribes

■ The Scriptures were so named because they were _____ [sung / _written_], possibly _____ [transfused / _transcribed_] into beautiful *manu*_*script*_ by industrious _____ [porters / _scribes_].

prescription

■ My doctor peered at my tongue, then hastily wrote a *pre*_*scription*_ .

(b)

■ A *nondescript* dog is (a) a very individual type, (b) <u>hardly individual enough to be written about</u>. (b)

---

7. seg, sect: cut.
Derivatives: *antivivisection, bisect, dissect, intersect, sect, sectarian, section, sector, segment, trisect, vivisection.*

intersect

■ Our streets *cut* across one another, so let's meet where they *int_ersect_____* .

bisect
trisect

■ *Cut* angle A into two equal parts and angle B into three equal parts; in other words, *bis_ect_____* angle A and *tr_isect_____* angle B.

segment
dissect

■ The butcher *cut* off a ___*segm*ent of salami, then began to *di_ssect_____* my chicken.

sect
section

■ Members of a strange religious *sect_____* (cult) live in my _____*secti*___on (part) of town.

sectarian

■ Splitting away from the main church are several small _____*sectar*_ian groups.

vivisection
antivivisection

■ *Cutting* into a live animal for medical research is known as *viv_isection_____* ; opposition to such experiments is *ant_ivivisection_* .

---

8. sequ, secut: follow.
Derivatives: *consecutive, consequently, execution, executive, obsequies, obsequious, persecute, prosecute, sequel, sequence, subsequently.*

subsequently
sequel

■ *Tom Sawyer* was a success, and *sub_sequently_____* (at a following time) Mark Twain wrote a _____*sequ*_el (follow-up) about Huck Finn.

consecutive

■ If this baseball team loses three *con_secutive_____* (in a row) games, these fans will hang the coach and won't even

obsequies

attend the *ob_sequies_____* (funeral rites).

27

(a)
■ The roots *sequ*, *secut* mean (a) follow; (b) sexy. (*a*)

executive
execution
■ The one *following* up company plans is the *executive* ___ , responsible for *execution* ___ of the board's decisions.

obsequious
■ Lord Bigmouth had a *following* of *obsequious* ___ (submissive) servants.

sequence
■ Shakespeare describes the seven ages of man in *sequence* ___ (order), from infancy to feeble old age.

Consequently
■ Gravitation works day and night. *Consequently* ___ (as a result), my lawn is covered with oak leaves.

prosecute
persecute
■ In America we may *prosecute* ___ (put on trial) a person in court; but we do not *persecute* ___ (cruelly harass) our citizens.

_____

9. **sign:** sign.
   Derivatives: *assign, consign, countersign, design, designate, ensign, insignia, resign, signal, signalize, signatory, signature, signet, significant, signify.*

sign
sign
■ In the words *signalize, countersign,* and *designate* the root is ___ *sign* ___ , and—who'd guess it?—it means *sign* ___ .

signature
■ *Sign* the check with your own ___ *signa*ture.

significant
signifies
■ One's *signature* on a document is very *significant* ___ [sagacious / significant] since it *signifies* ___ [beclouds / signifies] one's intentions.

signet
■ An initial or other special *sign* is carried on a *signet* ___ [signet / garnet] ring.

an ensign
■ A military banner or other *sign* of authority is known as ___ *an ensign* ___ [lasagne / an ensign].

signatory

■ Countries that have *signed* a treaty are _signatory_ [secessionist / signatory] nations.

sign
assignment

■ Remember that the Latin root *sign* means _sign_ . If necessary, repeat it ten times—what an _assign_ ment!

---

10. **sol**: alone.
     Derivatives: *desolation, isolate, sole, soliloquy, solitaire, solitary, solitude, solo.*

solitaire

■ Boomer sat *alone*, playing _solitai_ re.

solitary

■ The vicious prisoner was put in _solitar_ y confinement.

solo
solitude

■ I warbled my _sol_ o, "In my _solitu_ de I dream of you"—and my canary threw seeds at me.

isolate

■ Smallpox? Then we must *is* _olate_ you!

desolation

■ The fire left behind it a scene of utter *de* _solation_ (loneliness and ruin).

sole
soliloquy

■ Macbeth was now the _sole_ character on stage. As though thinking aloud, he began his _soliloqu_ y.

Quiz

Write the meaning of each boldface Latin root.

1. **bisect**   c _ut_

2. **sanctuary**   h _oly_

3. **isolate**   a _lone_

4. **insignia**   s _ign_

5. **consecutive** f _ollow_

1. cut
2. holy
3. alone
4. sign
5. follow

11. son: sound.
Derivatives: *assonance, consonance, resonance, sonar, sonata, sonatina, sonic, sonics, sonnet, sonorous, supersonic.*

sonic
supersonic

■ The plane burst through the *sound* barrier, letting out a _____*sonic*_____ boom, and accelerated to *sup__ersonic_____* (faster than sound) speeds.

dissonance

■ Such discordant *sounds*! Such *dis__sonance____* !

sonata
sonatina
resonance

■ Yasha pounded out a four-movement Mozart _____*sona*_ta and a short _____*sonati*_____na, then told us our piano had fine *re__sonance_____* (vibrant sound).

sound

■ The Latin root *son* means __*sound*___ [boy / sound].

sonar

■ We located the sunken ship by means of *sound*-wave apparatus called _____*sona*_r.

sonnet
sonorous

■ The poet read his _____*sonne*_____t in a rich _____*sonor*__ous (deep and vibrant) voice.

assonance

■ Imperfect rhyme involving identical vowel sounds (e.g., fame–lake, hope–boat) is known as *as__sonance____* ; imperfect rhyme involving identical consonant sounds (e.g., dog–dig, live–love)

consonance

is known as *con__sonance____* .

12. spec, spect: look.
Derivatives: *aspect, circumspect, inspect, introspection, perspective, prospect, respect, retrospect, spectacle, specter, spectroscope, spectrum.*

spect
look

■ The root in *inspect, aspect,* and *prospect* is __*spect*_____ , and it means *l__ook_____* .

circumspect

■ To be cautious and *look* around before acting is to be _____*circumspect*_____ [circumspect / circumscript].

introspection

■ Marcel Proust had a habit of *looking* into his mind and memories—he was given to <u>introspection</u> [introspection / interdiction].

retrospect

■ *Looking* back he saw things in ret<u>rospect</u> .

perspective

■ Another viewpoint would have given him a different *per<u>spective</u>* .

(d)

■ One word that did *not* develop from the root for *look* is (a) specter, (b) spectrum, (c) spectacles, (d) spaghetti. (d)

---

13. **spir, spirat:** breathe.
    Derivatives: *aspirate, aspire, conspire, expire, inspire, perspire, respiration, spiracle, spirit, spirometer.*

breathe

■ *Spirat* means <u>breathe</u> [spin / breathe].

respiration
perspiration

■ To *breathe* through the lungs is called *resp<u>iration</u>* ; to *breathe* through the skin is *per<u>spiration</u>* .

spiracle

■ The zoological term for a whale's breathing hole is <u>spiracle</u> [spiracle / oracle].

spirit
expired

■ In the sea battle Captain Ahab yielded up his <u>spir</u> *it* and *ex<u>pired</u>* .

spirometer

■ A machine which measures one's lung capacity, or *breath*, is called a <u>spectroscope</u> [spectroscope / spirometer].

(a)

■ Poetic *inspiration* was originally thought to be (a) a breathing in of a divine influence, (b) the product of indigestion. (a)

---

14. **tempor:** time.
    Derivatives: *contemporary, contretemps, extemporaneous, extempore, extemporize, pro tem, tempo, temporal, temporary, temporize.*

contemporary

■ Emerson and Thoreau lived at the same *time*—they were <u>contemporary</u> [congruent / contemporary] writers.

tempor

■ The root ___tempor___ means *time*.

time
temporarily

■ To be chairman *pro tem* means "for the ___time___ being," or ___temporarily___.

extem-
  poraneous

■ Talks or remarks made at the *time* without preparation are said to be ___extemporaneous___ [extenuating / extemporaneous].

temporize

■ To delay, or consume *time*, by needless discussions is to ___temporize___ [temporize / expedite].

contretemps

■ An inopportune or embarrassing occurrence is known as a ___contretemps___ [nondescript / contretemps].

tempo

■ Parade music has a brisk ___temp___o.

15. **terra:** earth.
    Derivatives: *disinter, inter, terrace, terra cotta, terra firma, terramycin, terraqueous, terrazzo, terrestrial, terrier, territory.*

terramycin

■ One antibiotic derived from an *earth* is called ___terra___*mycin.*

terra

■ The Latin root for *earth* is t___erra___ .

earth

■ *Terra firma* refers to firm ___earth___ [water / earth].

terra

■ Unglazed, brown-red *earthenware* is known as ___terra___ cotta.

(a)

■ *Terrain* has to do with (a) land surfaces, (b) ammunition. (a)

terrestrial

■ The *earth's land* as distinct from water is ___terrestrial___ [global / terrestrial].

terrier

■ A small hunting dog which burrowed into the *earth* for small game was called a _____terr_____ier.

(b)

■ A body that is *interred* has been (a) cremated, (b) buried. (*b*)

Quiz

Write the meaning of each boldface Latin root.

1. earth
2. sound
3. look
4. time
5. breathe

1. **terri**tory   *earth*

2. super**son**ic   *sound*

3. per**spect**ive   *look*

4. con**tempora**ry   *time*

5. in**spire**   *breath*

---

16. **tort**: twist.
    Derivatives: *contortion, distort, retort, tort, tortoise, tortuous, torture.*

distort

■ Scowls will d*istort* _____ your face, so smile.

contortion

■ The acrobat *twisted* into an odd con*tortion* _____ .

retort

■ Groucho was quick with a ret*ort* _____ (witty reply).

torture

■ *Twisting* the limbs to encourage confessions or religious conversion was a type of medieval _____*tortu*_re.

tort

■ The Latin root t*ort* _____ means "twist."

twist

■ Tabloids are guilty of *distortions*. This means that they _____*twist*_____ [verify / twist] the facts.

tort

■ In law, an injury for which you can sue is a _____*tort*_ [tort / sanct].

33

tortuous
tortoise

■ The road was so steep and _____ _tortu_ous (twisted) that a _____ _tortoi_se passed us twice.

---

17. **tract:** draw, pull.
   Derivatives: *attract, attractive, contract, detract, distract, extract, protract, retract, subtract, tract, tractable, tractate, traction, tractor.*

tractor
traction

■ The farmer's _tracto_r, which was *pulling* a plow, got stuck in mud and lost _tratio_n (drawing power).

tractable

■ The bronco was tamed and is now quite _tracta_ble (easily handled).

distract
extract

■ The dentist tried to *dis_tract_* (draw attention away) me with questions about politics, while trying to e_xtract_ my molar.

draw
attractive

■ *Tract* means _draw_ [draw / repel], and boys find Lisa very _attracti_ve.

protract
contract

■ If you *pr_otract_* (draw out) this strike, you'll be breaking your c_ontract_ (agreement).

detract

■ Nothing you say can d_etract_ (take away) from Amy's splendid reputation.

retract

■ Better *re_tract_* (take back) that statement, or he'll punch your nose.

tractate
tract

■ The minister referred to his essay as a _tract_ate, or religious _tract_ .

---

18. **turb:** agitate, whirl.
   Derivatives: *disturb, disturbance, imperturbable, perturbation, perturbed, turbid, turbine, turbojet, turbulent.*

disturb

■ Even earthquakes don't *dis_turb_* Joe's slumber.

34

perturbed turbulent	■ Much *per__turbed___* by the accusations, Ignatz leaped into the ___*turbule*nt* waters.
(b)	■ The Latin root *turb* refers to (a) gutter edging, (b) agitation. (*b*)
turbid	■ The Missouri is muddied by its current; so the water is ___*turb*id* (cloudy and agitated).
disturbance	■ A hive of bees caused a *dis__turbance___* at our picnic.
imperturbable	■ With bases loaded, the *imp__er turb able___* (calm) Casey swung his bat—and struck out.
turbine	■ A motor driven to rotation by the thrust of fluids or gases is called a ___*turbi*ne.*
turbojet	■ A jet engine using a turbine to drive an air compressor is a ___*turbo*jet.*

19. **urb:** city.
    Derivatives: *interurban, suburban, suburbanite, suburbs, urban, urbane, urbanism, urbanite, urbanity, urbanize.*

city	■ To *urbanize* a district is to make it become like a ___*city*___ [city / farm].
urb	■ The three-letter Latin root that means *city* is *u__rb.___* .
interurban	■ Buses that travel between *cities* are *inter__urban___* .
suburbs	■ On the outskirts of the *cities* lie the ___*suburbs*___ [subways / suburbs].
(a) urbanities	■ An *urbane* fellow is (a) polished and suave, (b) countrified and crude. (*a*) He is accustomed to those *citified* refinements of manners known as the ___*urbanities*[gaucheries / urbanities].

20. **vac:** empty.
Derivatives: *evacuate, vacancy, vacant, vacate, vacation, vacuity, vacuous, vacuum.*

evacuate

■ Floods made us _evacuate_ our homes.

vacation

■ It rained during our ___vacati___on abroad, and in the hotels we got soaked in more ways than one.

vacate

■ "Pay for your room or ___vaca___te," growled the manager.

vac
vacuum

■ The three-letter root ___vac___ means *empty*, and nothing is *emptier* than a ___vacu___um.

vacancy
vacant

■ As soon as the landlord has a ___vacanc___y, he'll rent us the ___vacan___t apartment.

vacuous

■ Look alert. The professor will throw questions at you if you wear a ___vacuou___s expression.

(b)

■ A reference to your "mental *vacuity*" should be taken as (a) a compliment, (b) criticism. (b)

Quiz

Write the meaning of each boldface Latin root.

1. inter**urb**an   _city_

2. **turb**ulent   _agitate_

1. city
2. agitate
3. twist
4. draw
5. empty

☆3. **tort**uous   _twist_

✶4. pro**tract**   _draw_

5. **vac**uity   _empty_

---

21. **vers, vert:** turn.
Derivatives: *conversation, convert, diversion, extrovert, introvert, inverted, perversion, reverse, revert, subvert, versatile, verse, version, versus, vertebra, vertebrate, vertex, vertical, vertigo.*

introvert
extrovert

■ Shy Sherlock, who *turns* to his inner thoughts and feelings, is an *introvert*____ . Sociable Sophie, who *turns* to outer activities, is an *extrovert*____ .

versatile

■ Diane *turns* to art, to music, and to sports. In fact, she's very ____*versati*le.

vertebra

■ Helping you to *turn* your spine is your ____*vertab*ra.

vertebrate

■ You have a spinal column, so you're a ____*vertebra*te.

revert

■ Some drug addicts are "cured," then *re*vert____ (turn back) to their old habits.

vertex
vertigo

■ When I reached the ____*verte*x (top) of the mountain, things seemed to *turn* dizzily. I had ____*verti*go.

subvert

■ Traitors may *su*bvert____ (overturn) the government.

vertical

■ A line that *turns* at right angles to a horizontal line is ____*vertica*l.

convert

■ Killer Kane *turned* to the church and became a *c*onvert____ .

perversion

■ *Turning* to abnormal sexual behavior is called *per*version____ .

22. **vid, vis:** see.
Derivatives: *advise, envision, evidence, improvisator, invidious, providence, revise, supervise, visible, visionary, visit, vista, visualize.*

vis
see

■ The words *visible, visit,* and *supervise* have the same three-letter root *vis*____ , which means s*ee*____ .

view

■ A *vista* is a ____*view* [view / southern mansion].

37

vid see	■ The words *evidence* and *providence* have the same three-letter root ___vid___ , which also means ___see___ .
foresee	■ To the Puritans *divine providence* meant that God would ___foresee___ [ignore them / foresee].
invidious	■ Comparisons which are unfair and offensive are said to be ___invidious___ [invaluable / invidious].

23. **vinc, vict:** conquer.
    Derivatives: *convict, conviction, convince, evince, invincible, victim, victimize, victor, Victorian, victorious, victory.*

victory invincible	■ The Nazis expected to win a ___victo___ry, but the Allies were *in___vincible___* (unconquerable).
convict	■ Defeated by the evidence, Bugsy became a prison c___onvict___ .
victor victim	■ Jungle beasts fight to the death. The ___victo___r (conqueror) does not spare the ___victi___m.
convince victimize	■ Old Ned was easy to *con___vince___* (conquer by argument), and any swindler who peddled gold bricks could ___victim___ize him.
conquer (b)	■ *Vict* means ___conquer___ , and to *evict* tenants is to (a) reward them, (b) remove them. (b)
conviction victorious	■ I have a *con___viction___* (strong belief) that our soccer team will be ___victori___ous.
Victorian	■ Flourishing during the reign of Queen Victoria were the somewhat prudish *V___ictorian___* writers such as Charles Dickens.
evince	■ Lefty held four aces, but his face did not *e___vince___* (reveal) any emotion.

24. vit, viv: life.
Derivatives: *convivial, devitalized, revive, vital, vitality, vitals, vitamin, vivace, vivacious, vivid, vivify, viviparous, vivisection.*

vital
vitals

■ Desdemona was ___*vit*al (essential) to his happiness, and because she was dead, Othello stabbed himself in the *vitals* (heart, lungs, etc.).

devitalized
vitamin

■ If you eat de*vitalized* (energy-deprived) foods, you'd better take ___*vitam*in pills.

vitality

■ Buster is a bundle of ___*vitali*ty (energy).

convivial

■ Flo and Moe love food, friends, and *life*. In other words, they're con*vival* people.

vit
viv

■ Two Latin roots, only three letters long, that are full of *life* are ___*vit* and ___*viv* .

vivid
vivacious
vivace

■ I have a ___*vivi*d (lifelike) memory of my ___*vivaci*ous (lively) grandmother tootling the ___*viva*ce (lively) movement of a Sousa march on her piccolo.

viviparous

■ Most mammals bring forth *living* young rather than eggs; in other words, they are ___*vivipar*ous.

vivisection
revive

■ My pet was a laboratory victim of ___*vivisecti*on (cutting a live animal). We were unable to re*vive* my beloved cat.

---

25. voc, vocat: call.
Derivatives: *advocate, avocation, convocation, equivocal, evoke, invoke, irrevocable, provoke, revoke, vocable, vocabulary, vocal, vocation, vociferous.*

convocation

■ A *calling* together of students to assembly is a ___*convocation* [convocation / convection].

spoken
call

■ *Vocal* promises are _spoken_ [written / spoken]; after all, the root *voc* means c_all_ .

vocation

■ Your career job, or *calling*, is your ___ *vocation*.

avocation

■ Your hobby is your *av_ovocation_*.

advocate

■ I *ad_vocate_____* (recommend) that you choose your field of specialization wisely because by commencement day that decision will be practically _irrevocable_ [irrepressible / irrevocable].

irrevocable

invokes

■ At the beginning of his epic, the poet Homer _invokes_ [invokes / inspires] the gods.

invocation

■ Today a minister usually gives the *in_vocation_____* .

equivocal

■ A sentence which seems to say two opposite things is said to be _equivocal_ [omniscient / equivocal].

Quiz

Write the meaning of each boldface Latin root.

1. conquer
2. life
3. see
4. turn
5. call

1. **invinc**ible — _conquer_
2. **viv**acious — _life_
3. super**vise** — _see_
4. extro**vert** — _turn_
5. **voc**ation — _call_

REVIEW TEST

Write *True* or *False*.

True	1. A *sanctuary* is a fairly safe place.
False	2. The *primrose* is a late bloomer.
True	3. *Nondescript* houses are quite undistinguished.
true	4. *Tractable* animals are rather tame.
False	5. A *circumspect* fellow is reckless.
false	6. An *obsequious* person has a regal manner.
true	7. *Imperturbable* people are calm and cool.
true	8. To *temporize* is to delay.
true	9. *Vertigo* involves a dizzy feeling.
false	10. An *equivocal* remark is clear and vivid.

Write the meaning of each boldface Latin root. The first letter of each answer is given.

11. con**vinc**e the jury   c _onquer_
12. a **rupt**ured lung   b _reak_
13. di**stort**ed features   t _wisted_
14. a game of **sol**itaire   a _lone_
15. good re**son**ance   s _ound_
16. **urb**an problems   c _ity_
17. a Republican **reg**ime   r _ule_
18. super**vis**e the class   s _ee_
19. to e**vac**uate the city   e _mpty_
20. inter**sect**ing highways   c _ut_

Write the letter that indicates the best completion.

(_d_) 21. *Respiration* refers to (a) the heart, (b) sweat, (c) first aid, (d) breathing.
(_b_) 22. An example of a *viviparous* creature is (a) an eagle, (b) a rabbit, (c) a chicken, (d) a butterfly.

41

(*b*) 23. To *disinter* a body is to take it out of (a) the water, (b) the earth, (c) a hospital, (d) wreckage.

(*c*) 24. *Portable* television sets are, by definition, (a) in color, (b) solid state, (c) able to be carried, (d) manufactured abroad.

(*a*) 25. A *signet* ring has on it (a) a sign, (b) an emerald, (c) a diamond, (d) a curse.

Key to Review Test

Check your test answers by the following key. Deduct 4% per error from a possible 100%.

1. True	6. False	11. conquer	16. city	21. (d)
2. False	7. True	12. break	17. rule	22. (b)
3. True	8. True	13. twist	18. see	23. (b)
4. True	9. True	14. alone	19. empty	24. (c)
5. False	10. False	15. sound	20. cut	25. (a)

Score: _____%

3

Latin Derivatives

PREFIXES

---

1. *ad*
2. *ante*
3. *bi*
4. *circum*
5. *co*
6. *contra, contro, counter*
7. *de*
8. *inter*
9. *intra, intro*

10. *mis*
11. *multi*
12. *post*
13. *pre*
14. *pro*
15. *quadr*
16. *quasi*
17. *quint*
18. *retro*

19. *semi*
20. *sub*
21. *super*
22. *trans*
23. *tri*
24. *ultra*
25. *uni*

A knowledge of Latin prefixes is indispensable to a mastery of English vocabulary. Prefixes multiply the use we make of roots.

For example, we have seen that *scrib, script* means "write," and that with prefixes we get combinations like *circumscribe, conscription, describe, inscribe, nondescript, postscript, prescribe, proscribe, subscribe,* and *transcribe.* These prefixes are a key to the meaning of such combinations.

Sometimes the spelling of a prefix is modified for the sake of pronunciation. For instance, the prefix *sub,* meaning "under," changes to *suc* in *succinct* and to *sup* in *supplant;* the prefix *ad,* meaning "to," changes to *af* in *affiliate* and to *an* in *annul.* The process is called assimilation.

Time has a way of changing the spelling, meaning, and application of words; so we should be ready to supplement our analysis of word parts by consulting a dictionary.

In this chapter we will focus on twenty-five basic prefixes and their most common meanings.

EXERCISES

COVER THIS STRIP

Prefixes

1. **ad:** to; toward.
   Examples: *adhesive, admissible, advocate.*

adhesive

■ A substance such as tape that sticks *to* other things is _____ *adhesive.*

advocate

■ To speak in favor of a measure is to ___*advocate*___ [advocate / deprecate] it.

may

■ *Admissible* evidence ___*may*___ [may / may not] be brought into a court case.

■ The prefix *ad* is slippery and often changes to an "assimilated" form. It appears, for example, as *ac* in *accord* (because *adcord* would be hard to pronounce). Other assimilated forms of *ad* include *ag* in *aggressive*, ___*al*___ in *allude*, ___*an*___ in *annex*, and ___*as*___ in *assign*.

al
an
as

2. **ante:** before.
   Examples: *antebellum, antedate, anterior.*

before

■ *Antebellum* days came ___*before*___ [before / after] the Civil War.

antedated

■ The Civil War ___*antedated*___ [antedated / succeeded] the first World War.

anterior

■ That which is toward the front or which comes *before* is ___*anterior*___ [anterior / posterior].

3. **bi:** two.
   Examples: *bicameral, bifocal, bipartisan.*

two

■ A *bicameral* legislature has ___two___ [one / two] chambers.

bifocals

■ Glasses with *two* different focal lengths are called ___bifocals___ [monocles / bifocals].

bipartisan

■ A committee which represents *two* parties is ___bipartisan___ [bipartisan / partisan].

---

4. **circum:** around.
   Examples: *circa, circumference, circumvent.*

circumference

■ The line *around* a circle is the ___circumference___ [circumference / diameter].

(a)

■ To *circumvent* the villain is (a) to get around him and outwit him, (b) to fall into his trap. (a)

about

■ Dante's *Divine Comedy* was written *circa* 1320, that is, ___about___ [after / about] 1320.

---

5. **co:** together.
   Examples: *coagulate, coeducation, coexistence, coincidence.*

(a)

■ When blood or any other fluid *coagulates*, it (a) clumps together, (b) gets thinner. (a)

together

■ *Coeducation* refers to the teaching of male and female students ___together___ [together / separately].

coexistence

■ People of different religions and ideologies should strive for peaceful ___coexisten___ce (living together).

coincidence

■ My birthday and my bypass operation on the same day? What a co___incidence___ !

con
cor

■ The prefix *co* is assimilated as *com* in *compassion*, as *col* in *collate*, as _con_ in *congenital*, and as _cor_ in *correlate*.

Quiz

Write the meaning of each boldface Latin prefix.

1. **bi**nomial _two_

2. **ad**vantage _to, toward_

3. **co**operation _together_

4. **circum**navigate _around_

5. **ante**cedent _before_

1. two
2. to
3. together
4. around
5. before

6. **contra, contro, counter:** against.
   Examples: *contraband, controvert, countercharge.*

■ A *countercharge* is (a) an admission of guilt, (b) a charge by the accused against his accuser. (_b_)

(b)

■ To argue *against* a certain idea is to _controvert_ [corroborate / controvert] it.

controvert

■ *Contraband* is _illegal_ [legal / illegal] merchandise.

illegal

7. **de:** away; down.
   Examples: *degradation, delusion, derision.*

■ Those who live in *degradation* are usually far _down_ [up / down] on the socio-economic ladder.

down

■ The lunatic was lured *away* from reality by _delusions_ [delusions / allusions] of grandeur.

delusions

■ An object of *derision*, Fulton was greeted by (a) jeers and ridicule, (b) warm applause. (_a_)

(a)

8. **inter:** between.
   Examples: *intercultural, interlinear, interregnum.*

between

■ An *interlinear* translation has the meaning inserted _____*between*_____ [opposite / between] the lines.

between

■ The *interregnum* is the period _____*between*_____ [during / between] the rule of kings.

intercultural

■ Relations *between* cultural groups are said to be _____*intercultural*_____ [intercultural / subcultural].

9. **intra, intro:** within.
   Examples: *intramuscular, intrastate, intravenous.*

within

■ *Intramuscular* pains are _____*within*_____ [between / within] the muscles.

intravenous

■ That which is *within* the veins is _____*intravenous*_____ [invidious / intravenous].

Albany

■ *Intrastate* commerce goes on between New York City and _____*Albany*_____ [Chicago / Albany].

10. **mis:** wrong, bad.
   Examples: *misadventure, misdemeanor, misnomer.*

misadventure

■ We enjoyed our picnic, except for the _____*misadvent*_____ure (accident) involving the rattlesnake.

(a)

■ Overtime parking is *wrong* behavior of a minor sort. It is therefore classed as a (a) misdemeanor, (b) felony. (*a*)

(b)

■ Our plumber is called Speedy, but that's a *misnomer* (wrong name). He is very (a) fast, (b) slow. (*b*)

Write the meaning of each boldface Latin prefix.

1. **inter**linear _between_

2. **mis**represent _wrong_

3. **contra**dict _against_

4. **de**tour _away_

5. **intra**mural _within_

1. between
2. wrong
3. against
4. away
5. within

---

11. **multi:** many.
    Examples: *multimillionaire, multiped, multitude.*

many

■ A *multiped* insect has _many_ [many / two] feet.

are not

■ If your possessions are worth $3,469.12, you _are not_ [are / are not] a *multimillionaire.*

multitude

■ The ninety thousand frantic spectators at a soccer game are quite a _multitude_ [multitude / solitude].

---

12. **post:** after.
    Examples: *posterior, posterity, posthumous.*

after

■ Mark Twain's *The Mysterious Stranger* was published *post-humously,* that is, _after_ [before / after] his death.

posterity

■ Those generations which come *after* us are our _posterity_ [ancestors / posterity].

posterior

■ That part of us which comes *after* us is our _poster_ior.

---

13. **pre:** before.
    Examples: *preamble, precedence, prejudice.*

before

■ That which has *precedence* comes _before_ [before / after] the rest.

48

before

■ The word *prejudice* implies that a judgment is made _before_ [before / after] the facts are studied.

preamble

■ The beginning of a constitution is a good place for the _preamble_ [amendments / preamble].

---

14. **pro:** forward; favoring.
    Examples: *progeny, prognosis, prolabor.*

prognosis

■ The doctor noted gloomily that I had contracted leprosy and gave me his _prognos_is (medical forecast).

progeny
(a)

■ Those interested in their _proge_ny (offspring) tend to look (a) forward, (b) backward. (_a_)

prolabor

■ Gary and Mary argue constantly because he is promanagement and she is _prolab_or (favorable to workers).

---

15. **quadr:** four.
    Examples: *quadrangle, quadrant, quadruplets.*

quadrants

■ The pie graph was equally divided into four _quadrant_s.

quadruplets

■ After taking a fertility drug the woman gave birth to _quadruple_ts.

four
four

■ A *quadrangle*, as on a college campus, is an area with _4_ sides and _4_ angles.

Quiz

Write the meaning of each boldface Latin prefix.

1. **post**pone   _after_

2. **multi**tude   _many_

3. **quadr**illion   _four_

4. **pro**pulsion   _forward_

5. **pre**natal   _before_

1. after
2. many
3. four
4. forward
5. before

49

16. **quasi** (kwā′sī): seemingly but not actually.
     Examples: *quasi-antique, quasi-poetry, quasi-scientific.*

■ A writer who refers to "the *quasi-scientific* mumbo-jumbo of astrology" _does not_ [does / does not] believe that astrology is a true science.

does not

■ At Gettysburg, Lincoln's words—noble and rhythmical—were ___ *quasi* ___-*poetry.*

quasi-poetry

■ Sandstorms battered our new desert home, quickly turning it into (a) a genuine antique, (b) a quasi-antique. (*b*)

(b)

17. **quint:** five.
     Examples: *quintessence, quintet, quintuplets.*

■ Our woodwind ___ *quintet* ___t (five musicians) played Mozart, and I think Mozart lost.

quintet

■ Their first kiss was the *quintessence*—that is, the ultimate or ___ *fifth* ___ [third / fifth] essence—of happiness.

fifth

■ "I'm pooped," said the stork. "I just brought Mrs. Shlep a set of ___ *quintuple* ts" (five offspring).

quintuplets

18. **retro:** back.
     Examples: *retroactive, retrogress, retrorocket.*

■ If civilization is *retrogressing*, it is (a) improving, (b) going back to a worse condition. (*b*)

(b)

■ A *retrorocket* tends to ___ *retard* ___ [speed up / retard] a space ship.

retard

■ A law or ruling which affects an earlier period is *retroactive* [retroactive / radioactive].

retroactive

19. **semi:** half.
  Examples: *semicentennial, semidiameter, semilunar.*

half

■ A *semilunar* shape is like that of the _half_ [full / half] moon.

fifty

■ *Semicentennials* celebrate a period of _50_ years.

radius

■ The *semidiameter* of a circle is equal to its _radius_ [radius / circumference].

20. **sub:** under.
  Examples: *subconscious, subcutaneous, subtrahend.*

under

■ The *subconscious* operates _under_ [within / under] the conscious mind.

under

■ A *subcutaneous* infection is _under_ [on / under] the skin.

subtrahend

■ In subtraction the number written *under* the other number is called the _subtrahend_ [subtrahend / minuend].

Quiz

Write the meaning of each boldface Latin prefix.

1. **semi**tone _half_

2. **retro**spect _back_

3. **sub**marginal _under_

4. **quint**ile _five_

5. **quasi**-bargain _not actually_

1. half
2. back
3. under
4. five or fifth
5. not actually

21. **super:** above; beyond.
  Examples: *supersensory, supersonic, superstructure.*

beyond

■ *Supersensory* impressions are _beyond_ [within / beyond] the normal limits of the senses.

above

■ The *superstructure* of a warship is __*above*__ [above / below] the main deck.

supersonic

■ Speeds *beyond* the speed of sound are ____*super*_sonic.

---

22. **trans:** across.
    Examples: *transgress, transpolar, transversal.*

across

■ A *transpolar* flight goes ____*across*____ [around / across] the pole.

transversal

■ In geometry a line that cuts *across* two other lines is called a __*transversal*__ [tangent / transversal].

(b)

■ To *transgress* is (a) to respect the rules, (b) to step across the rules or violate them. (*b*)

---

23. **tri:** three.
    Examples: *tricuspid, trilingual, triplicate.*

triplicate

■ Two copies weren't enough for my boss. No, everything had to be in ____*triplica*_te (three copies).

tricuspid

■ Dr. Pullem, my dentist, triumphantly held up a bloody, *three-*pointed tooth known as a ____*tricusp*____id.

trilingual

■ My Swiss friend speaks French, German, and English. He's ____*trilingu*____al.

---

24. **ultra:** very; beyond.
    Examples: *ultraconservative, ultramodern, ultraviolet.*

beyond

■ *Ultraviolet* rays are invisible because they lie *beyond* [beyond / inside] the violet end of the visible spectrum.

ultra-conservative

■ Mr. Skraggs bitterly fought equal pay for women, social security, "and all them other radical notions." Skraggs was an *ultra-conserva*tive.

ultramodern

■ The Gelts had a dream kitchen—the latest in _____ultra_modern equipment—but they always ate out.

---

25. **uni:** one.
Examples: *unicameral, unicorn, unicycle.*

unicameral

■ A legislature with *one* chamber is _____unicameral_____
[unicameral /bicameral].

one

■ The horns on a *unicorn* reach the grand total of __one__ .

unicycle

■ A tricycle has three wheels; a bicycle has two wheels; a _____unicycle_____ has *one* wheel.

Quiz

Write the meaning of each boldface Latin prefix.

1. **trans**fusion _____across_____

2. **tri**pod _____three_____

3. **super**saturated _____above_____

4. **uni**son _____one_____

5. **ultra**fastidious _____very_____

1. across
2. three
3. above
4. one
5. very

REVIEW TEST

Write *True* or *False*.

False	1. To *advocate* a policy is to speak against it.
True	2. The Revolutionary War *antedated* the War of 1812.
True	3. A *semimonthly* magazine comes out twice a month.
True	4. To *retrogress* is to go back to an earlier condition.
False	5. Opera stars strive to win the audience's *derision*.
True	6. *Binoculars* are used by two eyes at the same time.
True	7. *Profeminists* usually favor women's rights.
False	8. Phone calls from Boston to Seattle are *intercontinental*.
False	9. *Quasi-Chinese* music is the native music of China.
True	10. The killer's nickname, "Gentle John," is a *misnomer*.

Write the meaning of each boldface Latin prefix. The first letter of each answer is given.

11. an unusual **circum**stance   *around*

12. **com**passion for the blind   *together*

13. a **contro**versial issue   *against*

14. problems in **tri**gonometry   *three*

15. a **multi**tude of unpaid bills   *many*

16. **quint**essence of greed   *five*

17. Chapman's **trans**lation   *across*

18. to run **inter**ference   *between*

19. **sub**zero weather   *under*

20. the campus **quadr**angle   *four*

Write the letter that indicates the best completion.

(*b*) 21. A *post-mortem* is held on a person who is (a) old, (b) dead, (c) diseased, (d) dying.

(*a*) 22. The *preamble* to a document comes (a) at the beginning, (b) in the middle, (c) at the end, (d) in the amendments.

54

(*b*) 23. The Latin prefix for *above* is used in which word?—(a) anteroom, (b) supernatural, (c) retrorocket, (d) submerge.

(*c*) 24. The prefix in *united* and in *unification* means (a) nation, (b) states, (c) one, (d) peace.

(*d*) 25. The Latin prefix for *beyond* is used in what word?—(a) navigate, (b) submit, (c) infrared, (d) ultraviolet.

Key to Review Test

Check your test answers by the following key. Deduct 4% per error from a possible 100%.

1. False	6. True	11. around	16. five, fifth	21. (b)
2. True	7. True	12. together	17. across	22. (a)
3. True	8. False	13. against	18. between	23. (b)
4. True	9. False	14. three	19. under	24. (c)
5. False	10. True	15. many	20. four	25. (d)

Score: _____%

NOTE: For supplementary exercises on additional Latin roots and their derivatives, see APPENDIX B, page 315.

4

Greek Derivatives

1. *anthrop*
2. *astr*
3. *auto*
4. *bibli*
5. *bio*
6. *chrom*
7. *chron*
8. *crypt*
9. *cycl*
10. *dec*
11. *dem*
12. *derm*
13. *dyn*
14. *gram, graph*
15. *hetero*
16. *homo*
17. *hydr*
18. *log*
19. *metr, meter*
20. *morph*
21. *neur*
22. *orth*
23. *paleo*
24. *pan*
25. *path*

Socrates never heard of a *telephone* or an *astronaut* or *psychiatry*—and yet these words are derived from Greek roots. As more scientific discoveries are made year after year, the chances are good that new names will continue to be built on the old Greek stems and prefixes. Knowing the meaning of these Greek forms can throw a high-wattage light on many English words.

Historically, Greek and Latin came flooding into our language in three waves: (1) religious terms at about the beginning of the Christian era; (2) literary and cultural terms during the Renaissance, the revival of learning of the fifteenth and sixteenth centuries; and (3) scientific terms in recent centuries.

Chapters 4 and 5 focus on fifty important Greek terms and their clusters of derivatives. First, memorize the Greek term and its definition, given at the beginning of each frame. Next, note carefully the example derivatives that follow. Try to understand the connection between each of these derivatives and its Greek root. Then fill in the blanks.

Roots

COVER THIS STRIP

1. **anthrop:** man.
   Derivatives: *anthropocentric, anthropogenesis, anthropogeography, anthropoid, anthropology, anthropometry, anthropophagy, misanthropy, philanthropy.*

anthropoids

■ The *man*-like apes are called _____ *anthro* poids.

anthrop

■ The Greek root for *man* is a *nthrop* ___ .

anthropology

■ The study of *man* is ___ *anthropology* ___ [philology / anthropology].

anthropophagy

■ Cannibalism, or the eating of man's flesh, is known as ___ *anthropophagy* ___ [anthropophagy / herbivorousness].

man

■ *Anthrop* means ___ *man* ___ .

anthropocentric

■ A *man*-centered universe is obviously *anthropocentr* ic.

misanthrope

■ One who hates *mankind* is a ___ *misanthrope* [misanthrope / metronymic].

philanthropist
anthrop
man

■ A charitable fellow is a ___ *philanthrop* ist (from *phil*, meaning loving, and a *nthrop* ___ , meaning *man* ___).

2. **astr:** star.
   Derivatives: *aster, asterisk, asteroid, astral, astrobiology, astrodome, astrogate, astrolabe, astrology, astrometry, astronaut, astronomy, astrophysics, disaster.*

stars

■ *Asteroids* are tiny planets that look like ___ *stars* ___ [apes / stars].

astr	■ The Greek root for *star* is a<u>ster</u> .
astronomy astrology	■ The scientific study of the *stars* is ____<u>astrono</u>my, and fortune-telling by the *stars* is ____<u>astrolo</u> gy.
astrogate astronauts	■ Those who fly toward the *stars* are said not to navigate but to ____<u>astro</u>gate, and the fliers themselves are called <u>astronauts</u> [dreadnaughts / astronauts].
asterisks	■ Printer's *stars* (as in H*Y*M*A*N K*A*P*L*A*N) are called ____<u>asteris</u>ks.
disaster	■ The word *dis*<u>aster</u> hints that the *stars* were contrary.

3. **auto:** self.
Derivatives: *autobiography, autocrat, autogenesis, autograph, autohypnosis, autoinfection, automat, automation, automaton, automobile, autopsy, autosuggestion.*

self	■ An *autobiography* is written by one's <u>self</u> [critic / self].
self	■ *Autosuggestion* is given by one's <u>self</u> [doctor / self].
auto	■ The Greek root for *self* is a<u>uto</u> .
automation	■ A system of *self*-operating machinery is called ____<u>automat</u>ion.
automat	■ A *self*-operating restaurant service is an ____<u>autom</u>at.
autocrat automobile autograph	■ I can't admire any ____<u>auto</u>crat (dictator, having *self*-power) riding in his bullet-proof <u>automobile</u> , but I might ask him for his <u>autograph</u> (*self*-written name).

4. **bibli:** book.
Derivatives: *Bible, Biblicist, bibliofilm, bibliography, bibliolatry, bibliomania, bibliophile, bibliopole, bibliotheca.*

bibli ■ The Greek root for *book* is b*ibli* .

bibliography ■ A list of *book* sources is called a _____ bibliogra _phy.

a bibliotheca ■ A library or *book* collection is sometimes called _bibliotheca_____ [volumetrics / a bibliotheca].

bibliomania ■ A craze for collecting *books* is _____ bibliomania _____ [numismatics / bibliomania].

bibliophile
bibliopole ■ The _____ biblio _phile (book-lover) gets *books* from a _____ biblio _ pole (book-dealer).

bibliofilm ■ Scholars record rare *books* on special microfilm known as _____ bibliofilm [movifilm / bibliofilm].

book ■ The root *bibli* means _book_____ .

5. **bio:** life.
   Derivatives: *biochemist, biodynamics, biogenesis, biography, biology, biolysis, biometrics, biophysics, biopsy.*

life ■ *Biology* deals with plant and animal _life_____ [life / fiction].

bio ■ The three-letter Greek root for *life* is _bio_____ .

biography ■ The written account of a *life* is a _____ biogra _phy.

biopsy ■ The diagnostic examination by microscope of a piece of *living* tissue is a _____ bio _psy.

biometrics ■ The calculation of the probable span of human *life* is called _____ biometrics _[kinematics / biometrics].

biophysics ■ The branch of physics that deals with *living* matter is _____ biophysi _cs.

biochemistry

■ The branch of chemistry that deals with *life* processes is _____ *biochemistry*.

(a)

■ *Biogenesis* is the theory that living things can come from (a) living things only, (b) lifeless matter. (*a*)

Write the meaning of each boldface Greek root.

1. **bibli**omania _____ *book*

2. **auto**infection _____ *self*

3. **anthrop**ocentric _____ *man*

4. **astr**al _____ *star*

5. anti**bio**tics _____ *life*

1. book
2. self
3. man
4. star
5. life

6. **chrom:** color.
   Derivatives: *chromatic, chromatology, chrome, chromium, chromosome, chromosphere, panchromatic, polychrome.*

polychromatic

■ A many-colored print is _____ *polychromatic* _____ [polyglot / polychromatic].

color

■ A lens with *chromatic* aberration distorts _____ *color* [sound / color].

chrom

■ The Greek root for *color* is *chrom* _____ .

chromosphere

■ The *colorful* gases seen around the sun during a total eclipse are called the _____ *chromosphere* [biolysis / chromosphere].

color

■ *Chrom* means _____ *color* .

chromosomes

■ Our hereditary markings depend on tiny _____ *chromo*somes.

7. **chron:** time.
   Derivatives: *chronic, chronicle, chronograph, chronological, chronology, chronometer, chronometry, chronoscope, synchronize.*

time

■ *Chronological* order is ___time___ [time / place] order.

time

■ *Chron* means *time* ___.

synchronized

■ A motion picture film and its sound effects should be *timed* together, or *syn*chronized___.

chronometer
chronometry

■ A watch or clock is sometimes called a ___chrono___meter, and the scientific measurement of *time* is ___chronome___try.

chron

■ The Greek root for *time* is ___chron___.

chronic

■ If your back aches for a long *time* you have a ___chronic___ backache.

___

8. **crypt:** secret.
   Derivatives: *crypt, cryptic, cryptogram, cryptographer, cryptography, cryptology, cryptonym.*

secret

■ A *cryptic* remark has a ___secret___ [clear / secret] meaning.

crypt

■ The Greek root for *secret* is *cr*___ypt___.

cryptogram
cryptographer

■ A *secret*, coded message is a ___crypto___gram, and the fellow who decodes it is a ___cryptograph___er.

cryptonym

■ A *secret* name is a ___cryptonym___ [cognomen / cryptonym].

crypt

■ Bodies were often hidden away in a ___crypt___ [chromosphere / crypt].

___

9. **cycl:** circle; wheel.
   Derivatives: *cycle, cyclograph, cycloid, cyclometer, cyclone, cyclorama, cyclotron, encyclical, encyclopedia.*

■ An *encyclopedia* gives instruction in (a) science only, (b) the *circle* of arts and sciences. (*b*)

(b)

cycl

■ The Greek root for *circle* or *wheel* is c*ycl*_____ .

cyclone

■ A storm that has *circling* winds is called a __*cyclone*____ .

cyclorama

■ A *circular* room with large pictures is a _____*cyclor*ama.

cyclotron

■ An apparatus that accelerates atomic particles in *circles* is a ____*cyclotr*____on.

wheel
motorcycle

■ A *cyclometer* measures ___*wheel*____ [wheel / Russian] revolutions and might be useful on a ___*motorcycle*___ [foot / motorcycle].

10. **dec:** ten.
    Derivatives: *decade, decagon, decaliter, Decalogue, Decameron, decameter, decasyllable, decathlon, decennial, decimal, decimate.*

decade
decaliter
decameter

■ *Ten* years equal a _____*deca*___de; *ten* liters equal a ___*decaliter*; *ten* meters equal a ____*decamet*er.

dec

■ The Greek root for *ten* is d*ec*_____ .

ten

■ A *decathlon* consists of ___*ten*____ [five / ten] athletic events.

ten

■ A *decennial* celebrates ____*10*____ years.

Decalogue

■ The *Ten* Commandments are called the ____*Decalogue*____ [Heptateuch / Decalogue].

■ Boccaccio's tales were supposedly told during a plague by *ten* people on *ten* days—hence, they are entitled the _Decameron_ [Pentateuch / *Decameron*].

Quiz

Write the meaning of each boldface Greek root.

1. **crypt**ogram   s*ecret*
2. bi**cycle**   w*heel*
3. **dec**imal   t*en*
4. **chrom**atism   c*olor*
5. **chron**ology   t*ime*

1. secret
2. wheel
3. ten
4. color
5. time

11. **dem**: people.
Derivatives: *demagogue, demiurge, democracy, democrat, demography, endemic, epidemic, pandemic.*

democracy

■ Government by the *people* is called _democra_cy.

demagogue

■ One who uses false claims and emotional appeals to stir up the common *people* is a _demago_gue.

people

■ The Greek root *dem* means _people_ .

endemic

■ A disease restricted to *people* in one locality is _endemic_ [endemic / cycloid].

epidemic
pandemic

■ A disease that spreads among *people* is epi_demic_, and if it hits *people* over a very wide area it is _pandemic_ [panoramic / pandemic].

people

■ *Demography* is a study of how _people_ [people / cattle] are distributed.

dem

■ The Greek root for *people* is _dem_ .

12. **derm:** skin.
    Derivatives: *dermatitis, dermatoid, dermatologist, derma-*
    tophyte, epidermis, hypodermic, pachyderm.

skin

■ *Dermatitis* is an inflammation of the ___Skin___ [joints /
skin].

dermatologist

■ A *skin* infection should be treated by a ___dermatolog___ist.

derm

■ The Greek root for *skin* is d___erm___ .

pachyderms

■ Thick-*skinned* animals, like elephants and rhinoceroses, are
___pachyderms___ [anthropoids / pachyderms].

epidermis

■ Our outermost layer of *skin* is the epi___dermis___ .

hypodermic

■ An under-the-*skin* injection is a hypo___dermic___ .

13. **dyn:** power.
    Derivatives: *dynamic, dynamism, dynamite, dynamo, dy-*
    namometer, dynasty, dyne, electrodynamics, hydrodynam-
    ics, thermodynamics.

(b)

■ A *dyne* is a unit of (a) time, (b) force or power. (b)

dynamometer

■ Mechanical *power* can be measured by a ___dynamo___meter.

dyn

■ The Greek root for *power* is d___yn___ .

dynamic

■ An energetic person is said to be ___dynam___ic.

dynasty

■ A *powerful* family which has ruled for some generations is
a ___dynasty___ .

power

■ *Dyn* means ___power___ .

power

■ The *dynamos* at Niagara produce electrical ___power___ .

dynamite

■ One *powerful* explosive is ___dynamite___ .

---

14. **gram, graph:** write.
Derivatives: *autograph, biography, calligraphy, crypto-gram, diagram, epigram, geography, graffiti, gramophone, grammar, graphic, graphite, graphology, holograph, lithograph, mimeograph, photograph, seismograph, telegram, typography.*

writing

■ A *mimeograph* makes duplicates of ___Writing___ [secrets / writing].

writing

■ *Graphite* is used in pencils for ___Writing___ [erasing / writing].

write

■ The Greek roots *gram* and *graph* mean ___write___ [heavy / write].

calligraphy

■ One's penmanship, or *handwriting*, is called ___Calligraphy___ [calliope / calligraphy].

seismograph

■ Seismic disturbances, or earthquakes, are *recorded* on the *seis___mograph___* .

(b)

■ *Graphology* tries to analyze character by means of (a) head bumps, (b) handwriting. (*b*)

(b)

■ The *graffiti* found on walls are (a) insects, (b) rude sketches and writing. (*b*)

grandma

■ Which word wandered into the wrong line-up?—*epigram, telegram, grammar, grandma, lithograph.* ___grandma___

---

15. **hetero:** other.
Derivatives: *heterodox, heterodyne, heterogeneous, heterograft, heteromorphic, heteronym, heteroplasty, heterosexual.*

other

(a)

■ *Hetero* means ___other___ . Members of a *heterogeneous* group are (a) of various types, (b) all alike. (*a*) other

■ A *heterosexual* person is attracted to the _Other_____ [same / other] sex.

heterodox

■ Religious or political beliefs that are *other* than the usual kind are _____*hetero*___*dox.*

heteroplasty
heterograft

■ Surgery in which the grafted tissue comes from *another* person is called _____*hetero*___*plasty* or _____*hetero*___*graft.*

Quiz

Write the meaning of each boldface Greek root.

1. **dem**ocrat   _people_____
2. litho**graph**   w_rite_____
3. **dyn**amism   p_ower_____
4. **hetero**geneity   o_ther_____
5. pachy**derm**   s_kin_____

1. people
2. write
3. power
4. other
5. skin

---

16. **homo:** same.
    Derivatives: *homeopathy, homochromatic, homogamy, homogeneous, homogenize, homograft, homologous, homonym, homosexual.*

homogeneous

■ If those in a group are the *same*, that group is _____*homogeneous*_____ [homogeneous / heterogeneous].

homonyms

■ Words that have the *same* sound, like "bare" and "bear," are called _____*homonyms*_____ [antonyms / homonyms].

homo

■ The Greek root for *same* is h_omo_____ .

color
homochro-
   matic

■ *Chrom* means _____*color*_____ , and flowers which are all the *same* color are _____*homochromatic*_____ [homochromatic / heterochromatic].

homogenized

■ Milk which is uniformly of the *same* texture has been ___*homogeniz*___ ed.

homosexual

■ One who has sexual desire for those of the *same* sex is ___*homosexual*___ [homosexual / heterosexual].

---

17. **hydr**: water.
    Derivatives: *hydraulics, hydrocarbon, hydrocephaly, hydrogen, hydrography, hydrokinetics, hydrometer, hydropathy, hydrophobia, hydroponics, hydrotherapy.*

water

■ *Hydraulics* deals with the mechanical properties of *water* and other liquids.

water

■ *Hydropathy* and *hydrotherapy* involve treatment of disease by use of *water* .

hydr

■ The Greek root for *water* is *hydr* .

hydrophobia

■ Because rabies brings on a fear of *water*, the disease is also known as ___*hydropho*___ bia.

hydrocephaly

■ Excessive fluid in the skull is called ___*hydrocephaly*___ [hydrocephaly / heteroplasty].

fluids

■ *Hydroponics* is the science of growing plants in ___*fluids*___ [sand / fluids].

---

18. **log**: word; study.
    Derivatives: *apology, biology, decalogue, dialogue, doxology, embryology, eulogy, geology, hydrology, logic, logorrhea, mineralogy, monologue, philology, prologue, tautology, theology.*

study

■ *Biology* is the ___*study*___ [breeding / study] of plant and animal life.

study

■ *Mineralogy* is the s___*tudy*___ of minerals.

log

■ The Greek root for *study* is l*og* _____ .

hydrology

■ The *study* of water and its distribution is *hydrology* _____ [hydrolysis / hydrology].

embryology

■ The *study* of embryo development is _____ *embryology* [embryology / embryectomy].

word

■ The root *log*, as in *monologue*, *dialogue* and *eulogy*, means _____ *word* _____ [word / log].

words

■ A *tautology*—as in "small little midget"—uses too many w*ords* _____ .

words

■ A person with *logorrhea* pours out too many w*ords* _____ .

19. **metr, meter:** measure.
Derivatives: *ammeter, barometer, centimeter, chronometer, geometry, hexameter, hydrometer, metrology, metronome, micrometer, pentameter, seismometer, speedometer, thermometer, trigonometry.*

measure

■ A *barometer* is used to _____ *measure* _____ [measure / lower] air pressure.

measure

■ A *chronometer* is used to m*easure* _____ time.

micrometer

■ One instrument which *measures* tiny distances is the _____ *micrometer* _____ [micrometer / microcosm].

geometry
trigonometry
metr

■ Mathematics courses that deal with *measurement* include geo*metry* _____ and trig*onometry* _____ . In these two words the root that means *measure* is *metr* _____ .

(b)

■ *Metrology* is the science of (a) metals, (b) weights and measures. (*b*)

20. **morph**: form.
    Derivatives: *amorphous, anthropomorphic, isomorph, metamorphosis, Morpheus, morphine, morphology.*

(b)

■ Ovid's *Metamorphoses* tells how the gods caused people to change their (a) financial condition, (b) form or shape. (*b*)

form

■ *Morph* means f*orm*_____ .

morphology

■ In linguistics the study of the internal structure and *form* of words is called _____*morph*_____ *ology.*

amorphous

■ *Formless* sulphur is _____*amorphous*_____ [amorphous / crystalline].

forms

■ *Morpheus* was the god of dreams, named after the _____*forms*_____ [colors / forms] seen in dreams.

form
man

■ An *anthropomorphic* god is in the _____*form*_____ (*morph*) of a _____*man*_____ (*anthrop*).

Quiz

Write the meaning of each boldface Greek root.

1. hydro**meter**   *measure*_____
2. **hydro**phobia   w*ater*_____

1. measure
2. water
3. study
4. form
5. same

3. geo**logy**   s*tudy*_____
4. iso**morph**   f*orm*_____
5. **homo**logous   s*ame*_____

21. **neur**: nerve.
    Derivatives: *neural, neuralgia, neurasthenia, neurocirculatory, neurogenic, neurologist, neuromotor, neuromuscular, neuron, neurosis, neurotic.*

nervous

■ A *neurotic* suffers from a _____*nervous*_____ [speech / nervous] disorder.

nerves

■ *Neuritis* is a painful inflammation of the ___nerves___ [skin / nerves].

neur

■ The Greek root for *nerve* is n___eur___ .

neurosis

■ The *neurotic* has what is called a ___neurosis___ [neurosis / psychosis].

neurasthenia

■ If you develop fatigue, worries, and pains without apparent cause, your condition is called ___neurasthe___nia.

neurologist

■ If you need a *nerve* specialist, go to a ___neurolog___ist.

22. **orth:** right; true.
   Derivatives: *orthochromatic, orthodontics, orthodox, orthogenesis, orthography, orthopedics, orthopsychiatry, orthoscope.*

(a)

■ The *orthodox* religion is (a) the established "true" faith, (b) a modern variation of religious faith. (a)

orth

■ The Greek root for *right* or *true* is o___rth___ .

orthopedist

■ To *right* or correct skeletal deformities is the job of the ___orthopedist___ [orthopedist / cyclopedist].

orthodontist

■ The straightening and *trueing* of teeth is done by the ___orthodontist___ [neurologist / orthodontist].

right

■ *Orthography* deals with ___right___ [right / foreign] spelling.

true

■ *Orthochromatic* film should produce ___true___ [altered / true] colors.

23. **paleo:** ancient.
   Derivatives: *paleobotany, Paleocene, paleography, paleolithic, paleontology, Paleozoic, paleozoology.*

ancient	■ The *Paleozoic, Paleocene,* and *paleolithic* periods belong to an ___*ancient*___ [ancient / recent] era.
paleo	■ The Greek root for *ancient* is p*aleo* ___.
paleontology	■ The study of *ancient* forms of plant and animal life is called ___*paleont*___ ology.
paleolith	■ An *ancient* stone tool is a ___*paleo*___ lith.
ancient writing	■ The word *paleography* has two Greek roots, meaning ___*ancient*___ and ___*writing*___ .

24. **pan:** all.
    Derivatives: *panacea, Pan-American, Pan-Asiatic, panchromatic, pancreas, pandemic, pandemonium, panegyric, Panhellenic, panorama, pantheism, pantheon, pantomime.*

all	■ *Panchromatic* film is sensitive to ___*all*___ [no / all] colors.
all	■ A *panacea* is a supposed cure for ___*all*___ [one / all] disease or trouble.
pan	■ The Greek root for *all* is p*an* ___ .
panorama	■ A picture with a view in *all* directions is a ___*panorama*.
pandemic	■ A disease that is very widespread is ___*pandem*ic.
Panhellenic	■ A league of *all* the campus Greek-letter (Hellenic) fraternities and sororities is ___*Panhellen*___ ic.
Pantheon	■ A temple for *all* the gods was the ___*Pantheon*___ [Colosseum / Pantheon].
all	■ *Pan* means ___*all*___ .

25. **path**: disease; feeling.
    Derivatives: *antipathy, apathy, empathy, neuropathy, osteopathy, pathetic, pathologist, pathos, psychopath, sympathy, telepathy.*

path

■ The Greek root *p*<u>ath</u> means *feeling*.

pathetic

■ A *feeling* of pity is aroused by *pathos* or that which is <u>*path et*</u> *ic*.

sympathy

■ Your compassion for another person is *sym<u>pathy</u>* , and your complete projection of yourself into the *feelings* of

empathy

another person is *em<u>pathy</u>* .

diseases

■ The root *path* means *feeling*, but it can also mean *disease*; thus, a *pathologist* is a specialist in <u>*diseases*</u> [paths and trails / diseases].

psychopath

■ A serious mental disorder would be found in a <u>*psychopath*</u> [psychopath / bibliopole].

Quiz

Write the meaning of each boldface Greek root.

1. **orth**ography   <u>right</u>

2. **neur**on   <u>nerve</u>

3. **paleo**botany   <u>ancient</u>

4. **apath**etic   <u>feelings</u>

5. **pan**acea   <u>all</u>

1. right
2. nerve
3. ancient
4. feeling
5. all

REVIEW TEST

Write *True* or *False*.

_____True_____ 1. *Cryptography* deals with secret writing.

_____False_____ 2. *Bibliomania* refers to excessive use of alcohol.

_____True_____ 3. *Graphite* can be used to write with.

_____True_____ 4. *Paleontologists* are interested in fossils.

_____False_____ 5. *Autosuggestion* requires two or more people.

_____False_____ 6. *Orthodox* beliefs are new and daring.

_____False_____ 7. *Homogenized* milk has its cream floating at the top.

_____True_____ 8. *Dermatology* deals with the skin.

_____False_____ 9. *Neurasthenia* refers to a hardening of the arteries.

_____True_____ 10. A wristwatch is a type of *chronometer*.

Write the meaning of each boldface Greek root. The first letter of each answer is given.

11. an **anthrop**omorphic god   *man*

12. **pan**hellenic organizations   *all*

13. suffering from de**hydr**ation   *water*

14. the Dewey **dec**imal system   *ten*

15. the **chrom**osome number   *color*

16. a sudden meta**morph**osis   *form*

17. overuse of anti**bio**tics   *life*

18. faith in **dem**ocracy   *people*

19. the **hetero**doxies of Berkeley   *other*

20. a sensitive volt**meter**   *measure*

Write the letter that indicates the best completion.

(*b*) 21. An *asterisk* is a printing symbol that looks like (a) a number, (b) a star, (c) a slanted line, (d) a question mark.

(*a*) 22. *Pathogenesis* has to do with the origin of (a) a disease, (b) a path, (c) God, (d) sin.

73

(c) 23. A *dynamometer* measures (a) speed of rotation, (b) spark, (c) power, (d) sound.

(c) 24. The Greek root for *circle* is used in which word?—(a) cryptic, (b) cardiac, (c) encyclical, (d) eclipse.

(b) 25. The Greek root which is common to both *geology* and *proctology* means (a) *earth*, (b) *study*, (c) *tunnel*, (d) *the end*.

Key to Review Test

Check your test answers by the following key. Deduct 4% per error from a possible 100%.

1. True	6. False	11. man	16. form	21. (b)
2. False	7. False	12. all	17. life	22. (a)
3. True	8. True	13. water	18. people	23. (c)
4. True	9. False	14. ten	19. other	24. (c)
5. False	10. True	15. color	20. measure	25. (b)

Score: _____%

5

Greek Derivatives

ROOTS		PREFIXES
1. *phil*	11. *amphi*	18. *hypo*
2. *phon*	12. *anti*	19. *kilo*
3. *physi*	13. *arch*	20. *meta*
4. *pseudo*	14. *dia*	21. *mono*
5. *psych*	15. *epi*	22. *neo*
6. *pyr*	16. *eu*	23. *peri*
7. *soph*	17. *hyper*	24. *poly*
8. *tele*		25. *syn, sym*
9. *the*		
10. *therm*		

Chapter 5 continues our study of Greek derivatives. Follow the same procedure as in Chapter 4.

EXERCISES

Roots

1. **phil:** loving.
   Derivatives: *Anglophile, bibliophile, Francophile, philander, philanthropy, philatelist, philharmonic, philodendron, philogynist, philology, philoprogenitive, philosophy, philter.*

phil

■ The Greek root for *loving* is p*hil* _____ .

bibliophile

■ One who *loves* books (*bibli*) is a *bibliophile* _____ ile.

philanthropist

■ One with *love*, or charity, for man (*anthrop*) is a _____ *philanthrop* _____ ist.

philosopher

■ One who *loves* wisdom (*soph*) is a _____ *philosph* _____ er.

philogynist
philanderer

■ One who *loves* women (*gyn*) is a _____ *philogyn* _____ ist; but if he trifles with their *love* he may be called a _____ *philanderer* _____ [demagogue / philanderer].

philharmonic

■ If you *love* musical harmony, you might join a _____ *philharmon* ic orchestra.

Francophile

■ If you *love* or admire the French, you are a *Francophile* _____ [Francophobe / Francophile].

philatelist

■ If you *love* stamps and collect them, you are a *philatelist* _____ [psychopath / philatelist].

2. **phon:** sound.
   Derivatives: *phoneme, phonetic, phonics, phonograph, phonology, phonometer, phonoscope, telephone.*

phon

■ The word *telephone* deals with *sound*, as is suggested by its Greek root p*hon* _____ .

sound	■ *Phonetic* spelling is based on the ___sound___ [sound / general appearance] of words.
phoneme	■ In linguistics, a specific speech *sound* is called a ___phon___eme.
phonometer	■ An instrument which measures (*meter*) the intensity and the frequency of *sound* vibrations is a ___phonometer___ [chronometer / phonometer].
(b)	■ *Phonics* deals with (a) picture transmission, (b) speech sound, especially as related to the teaching of reading and pronunciation. (*b*)
sound	■ *Phon* means ___sound___ .

3. **physi:** nature.
   Derivatives: *physical, physician, physicist, physiocrat, physiognomy, physiography, physiology, physiotherapy.*

nature	■ A *physicist* studies the laws of ___nature___ [poetry / nature].
physi	■ The Greek root for *nature* is ph___ysi___ .
physiography	■ The description of *nature* and natural phenomena is sometimes called ___physiology___ [empathy / physiography].
(a)	■ A *physiocrat* believes that the only true source of wealth is (a) the land and its products, (b) gambling. (*a*)
nature	■ *Physi* means ___nature___ .
physiology	■ The branch of biology that deals with the parts and the functions of the body is ___physiolo___gy.
physiognomy	■ Your face is your ___physiog___nomy.

4. **pseudo:** false.
   Derivatives: *pseudoaquatic, pseudoclassic, pseudomorph, pseudonym, pseudopod, pseudoscience.*

■ An author's fictitious or *false* name, such as *Mark Twain* or *George Eliot* or *Lewis Carroll*, is a ___pseudonym___ [surname / pseudonym].

pseudonym

■ *Pseudo* means f___alse___ .

false

■ When a critic refers to a novel as "a pseudoclassic," he means that it is (a) a genuine classic, (b) not a genuine classic. (*b*)

(b)

■ Unreliable studies such as phrenology and astrology are actually ___pseudosciences___ [social sciences / pseudosciences].

pseudo-
sciences

■ A *pseudoaquatic* plant ___is not___ [is / is not] genuinely aquatic.

is not

■ A *pseudomorph* is a mineral which looks like another one, and the word literally means ___false___ ___form___ .

false form

5. **psych:** mind; spirit.
   Derivatives: *psyche, psychedelic, psychic, psychiatrist, psychoanalysis, psychodrama, psychograph, psychology, psychometry, psychoneurosis, psychopath, psychosis, psychosomatic, psychotherapy.*

■ *Psychiatry* treats disorders of the ___mind___ [eye / mind].

mind

■ Freudian analysis, which aims to cure the *mind*, is ___psychanaly___ *sis*.

psycho-
analysis

■ The Greek root for *mind* is *ps___ych___* .

psych

■ A chart of one's personality traits is a ___psychograph___ [psychograph / pseudomorph].

psychograph

■ A *psychic* shock or trauma has a permanent effect on the
_____*mind*_____ [heart / mind].

mind

■ Drugs like LSD which affect the *mind* are ___*psychedelic*.

psychedelic

Quiz

Write the meaning of each boldface Greek root.

1. **pseudo**pod   *false*_____

2. **physi**cian   *nature*_____

3. **phon**ograph   *sound*_____

4. **psych**osis   *mind*_____

5. **phil**harmonic   *love*_____

1. false
2. nature
3. sound
4. mind
5. loving

---

6. **pyr**: fire.
   Derivatives: *pyre, pyretic, Pyrex, pyrexia, pyrites, pyritology, pyrochemical, pyrogenic, pyrolysis, pyromancy, pyromaniac, pyrometry, pyrophobia, pyrosis, pyrostat, pyrotechnics.*

■ A *pyromaniac* has a compulsion to *start fires*_____
[steal things / start fires].

start fires

■ *Pyrotechnics* is the art of making and displaying
_____*fireworks*_____ [advertisements / fireworks].

fireworks

■ The Greek root for *fire* is *pyr*_____ .

pyr

■ Hindu widows used to be cremated on their husband's funeral
___*pyr*_e.

pyre

■ American women use heat-resistant glassware called
___*Pyre*_x.

Pyrex

■ A child with *pyrexia* is suffering from *fever*_____ [chills /
fever].

fever

79

fire

■ A *pyrostat* is an alarm device protecting against _fire_ [burglar / fire].

pyrophobia

■ An irrational fear of *fire* is called ___pyropho___bia.

unhappy

■ A *pyromaniac* and a *pyrophobe* would probably be ___unhappy___ [happy / unhappy] together.

---

7. **soph:** wisdom.
   Derivatives: *gymnosophist, philosophy, Sophia, sophism, sophisticated, sophistry, Sophocles, sophomore, sophomoric, theosophy.*

wise

■ The word *sophomore* has two Greek roots: *soph*, which means ___wise___ [wise / strong], and *mor* (as in *moron*), which means *foolish*. Therefore an immature person who acts like a

sophomoric

know-it-all is said to be ___sophomoric___ [sophomoric / heterogeneous].

sophistry

■ Since the *sophists* were notorious for their clever but deceptive logic, a misleading argument is sometimes called a ___sophist___ry.

sophisticated

■ People who are *worldly-wise*, rather than simple, are ___sophisticat___ed.

sophisticated

■ A rocket or electronic device that is very subtle and complicated in design is also said to be ___sophisticat___ed.

wisdom

■ According to its Greek roots, the word *philosophy* means *the love of w*___isdom___ .

---

8. **tele:** far.
   Derivatives: *telecast, telegenic, telegraph, telekinesis, telemechanics, telemeter, telepathy, telephone, telephoto, telescope, telethermometer, telethon, teletype, television.*

far

writing

■ The word *telephone* literally means *far + sound*. Similarly, *telegraph* means *f*___ar___ *+ w*___riting___ .

far seeing	■ *Television* means ____far____ + ____seeing____ [advertising / seeing].
tele	■ The Greek root for *far* is *tele* ____ .
tele- thermometer	■ A thermometer that measures temperature from *afar* is a ____telethermomet____ er.
telephoto	■ Photos can be taken from *afar* by ____telepho____ to.
telemechanics	■ Mechanisms can be radio-operated from *afar* by techniques of ____tele____ mechanics.
telepathy	■ Transmitting thoughts without use of the five senses is called ____tele____ pathy.

9. **the:** god.
   Derivatives: *atheism, monotheism, pantheism, pantheon, polytheism, theanthropic, theism, theocentric, theocracy, theology, theosophy.*

God	■ *Theism* and *monotheism* generally refer to a belief in G_od_ ____ .
polytheism	■ Belief in many *gods* is *poly* _theism_ ____ .
atheism	■ Belief in no *god* is a _theist_ ____ .
the	■ The Greek root for *god* is *the* ____ .
theocracy	■ Puritan New England, ruled by *God* and the church, was a ____theocracy____ [democracy / theocracy].
theology	■ The study of *God* and religious doctrines is called ____theolo____ gy.
god	■ *The* means _God_ ____ .

theocentric

■ A cultural pattern in which *God* is the center of interest is _____*theocentric*_____ [anthropocentric / theocentric].

10. **therm:** heat.
Derivatives: *diathermy, hydrothermal, isotherm, thermal, thermesthesia, thermocouple, thermodynamics, thermograph, thermolysis, thermometer, thermonuclear, thermopile, thermos, thermostat.*

heat

■ In a *thermonuclear* blast the nuclear fission releases _____*heat*_____ [psychic waves / heat].

(a)

■ A *thermostat* controls (a) heat, (b) water. (*a*)

(b)

■ The word *hydrothermal* literally means (a) electric power, (b) hot water. (*b*)

thermograph

■ A record of temperature is made by the _____*thermograph*.

isotherm

■ A line on the weather map between points of equal temperature is an _____*isotherm*_____ [isotherm / isobar].

thermo-
dynamics

■ The relations between *heat* and other forms of energy are dealt with in _____*thermodynam*_____ics.

thermos

■ Coffee keeps its *heat* in a _____*thermo*s jug.

Quiz

Write the meaning of each boldface Greek root.

1. god
2. fire
3. far
4. wisdom
5. heat

1. **the**osophy   *god*_____
2. **pyr**ometry   *fire*_____
3. **tele**scope   *far*_____
4. **soph**omore   *wisdom*_____
5. dia**therm**y   *heat*_____

Prefixes

11. amphi: around; on both sides.
   Examples: *amphibians, amphibolous, amphitheater.*

■ Since frogs live *both* on land and in water they are
_____*amphibians*_____ [bisexuals / amphibians].

amphibians

■ An arena with the spectators seated *around* it is an
_____*amphithea*_____ter.

amphitheater

■ A statement with two possible meanings—such as "The Duke
yet lives that Henry shall depose"—is _____*amphibolous*_____
[amphibolous / anthropomorphic].

amphibolous

---

12. anti: against.
   Examples: *antibiotic, antipathy, antithesis.*

■ An *antipathy* is a feeling _____*against*_____ [for / against]
something.

against

■ In *antithesis* the two parts of a sentence present a
_____*contrast*_____ [similarity / contrast].

contrast

■ A substance such as penicillin or streptomycin which works
against certain germs and viruses is known as (a) insulin, (b) an
antibiotic. (*b*)

(b)

---

13. arch: chief.
   Examples: *archangel, archfiend, architect.*

■ An *archangel* is a _____*chief*_____ [common / chief] angel.

chief

■ In Milton's *Paradise Lost* the *archfiend* is (a) a run-of-the-
mill devil, (b) Satan himself. (*b*)

(b)

■ The *chief* worker in charge of designing a building is the
_____*architect*_____ [stonemason / architect].

architect

---

14. **dia:** through.
    Examples: *diabetes, diameter, diathermy.*

through

■ *Diathermy* sends heat _through_ [through / around] one's body.

diameter

■ The distance *through* a circle is called the _diameter_ .

(b)

■ A disease associated with excess sugar passing *through* the body is (a) carditis, (b) diabetes. (b)

---

15. **epi:** upon; beside.
    Examples: *epicenter, epidermis, epitaph.*

upon

■ The *epidermis* is the outer, nonsensitive layer that lies _upon_ [upon / below] the true skin.

epicenter

■ The point above and *upon* the center of an earthquake is the _epicenter_ [seismograph / epicenter].

epitaph

■ The inscription *upon* a tomb is an _epitaph_ [anagram / epitaph].

---

16. **eu:** good; well.
    Examples: *eulogy, eupepsia, euphoria, euthanasia.*

well-being

■ *Euphoria* is a feeling of _well-being_ [pain / well-being].

good

■ *Eupepsia* means _good_ [good / bad] digestion.

praises

■ A *eulogy* _praises_ [praises / condemns].

euthanasia

■ Mercy killing is known as _euthanasia_ [asphyxia / euthanasia].

17. **hyper:** excessive.
Examples: *hypercritical, hyperopia, hyperthyroidism.*

hypercritical

■ One who finds fault with an *excessive* number of details is ___*hypercritical*___ [hypocritical / hypercritical].

hyperopia

■ A person whose eyes can see an *excessive* distance probably has ___*hyperopia*___ [myopia / hyperopia].

excessive

■ *Hyperthyroidism*, marked by rapid pulse and sleeplessness, may be caused by ___*excessive*___ [insufficient / excessive] activity of the thyroid gland.

18. **hypo:** under.
Examples: *hypocrite, hypothermia, hypothesis.*

below

■ A patient with *hypothermia* has a temperature ___*below*___ [above / below] normal.

hypothesis

■ An assumption which *underlies* an investigation is called a ___*hypothesis*___ [hypothesis / prosthesis].

hypocrite

■ A person who pretends to be sincere, honest, or good but *under* it all is insincere, dishonest, or evil is a ___*hypocri*te___.

19. **kilo:** thousand.
Examples: *kilocycle, kilometer, kilowatt.*

thousand

■ A *kilocycle* equals one ___*thousand*___ [hundred / thousand] cycles per second.

kilometer

■ One *thousand* meters equal one ___*kilometer*___ .

one

■ Problem: One *thousand* watts of electrical energy used for sixty minutes equal ___*one*___ [one / 60,000] kilowatt-hour[s].

20. **meta:** change; after.
    Examples: *metabolism, metamorphic, metempsychosis.*

metamorphic
■ Rocks such as marble which have *changed* their form under pressure are ____metamorphic____ [anthropomorphic / metamorphic].

metabolism
■ The body's chemical and physical *changes*, with release of energy, are aspects of ____metabolism____ [morphology / metabolism].

(b)
■ *Metempsychosis* assumes that at one's death his soul (a) also dies, (b) makes a change, passing into another body. (*b*)

21. **mono:** one.
    Examples: *monodrama, monolith, monomania.*

one
■ A *monolith* consists of ____one____ [one / more than one] stone.

monodrama
■ A play with *one* performer is a ____monodrama____ [mono-drama / melodrama].

monomania
■ Captain Ahab's irrational interest in *one* subject, Moby Dick, amounts to ____monomania____ [bipolarity / monomania].

22. **neo:** new.
    Examples: *neoclassicism, neologism, neophyte.*

new
■ A *neophyte* in a religious order is a ____new____ [new / elderly] member.

neologism
■ A *new* word, freshly coined, is a ____neologism____ [neologism / hyperbole].

neoclassicism
■ A period of a *new* version, or revival, of classical literary style is known as ____neoclassicism____ [romanticism / neo-classicism].

23. **peri:** around.
Examples: *perimeter, periphrasis, periscope.*

around

■ The *perimeter* of a ranch is the distance ___around___ [across / around] it.

(b)

■ An optical instrument used in submarines for looking *around* an obstruction is known as a (a) stereoscope, (b) periscope. (*b*)

(a)

■ *Periphrasis* is a *roundabout* way of phrasing, as illustrated in (a) "I did dance and Joe did shout," (b) "I danced and Joe hollered." (*a*)

24. **poly:** many.
Examples: *polygon, polysyllable, polytechnic.*

many

■ A *polytechnic* institution offers courses in ___many___ [one or two / many] technical fields.

polygon

■ A plane figure with *many* sides is a ___polygon___ [polygon / mastodon].

(b)

■ A *polysyllable* has *many* (at least four) syllables, like the word (a) "logic," (b) "transcendentalism." (*b*)

25. **syn, sym:** together.
Examples: *synchronize, syndrome, synthesis.*

(a)

■ *Synthesis* involves (a) bringing things together, (b) taking things apart. (*a*)

synchronized

■ Actions that are timed *together* are ___synchronized___ [acclimated / synchronized].

syndrome

■ Symptoms which occur *together* and indicate a specific disease are called a ___syndrome___ [syndrome / eupepsia].

REVIEW TEST

Write *True* or *False*.

True   1. The *archdeacon* has a higher rank than the deacon.

False   2. *Hyperacidity* refers to a lack of enough stomach acid.

True   3. *Metamorphic* rocks have undergone a change of form.

False   4. A *polytheist* believes in the oneness of God.

False   5. The feminine name *Sophia* originally meant "stupid."

True   6. An *amphibian* plane can take off from land or sea.

False   7. *Antipathy* is warm affection.

True   8. A *phonoscope* enables one to see certain characteristics of sounds.

True   9. *Synchronized* movements are timed together.

False   10. A *kilogram* weighs one thousand pounds.

Write the meaning of each boldface Greek root or prefix. The first letter of each answer is given.

11. a **pseudo**medieval ballad   *false*

12. a jutting **peri**scope   *around*

13. the doctor's **dia**gnosis   *through*

14. cooking with **Pyr**ex   *fire*

15. the actor's **mono**cle   *one*

16. **neo**-impressionism in art   *new*

17. the gentle **phil**osopher   *love*

18. suffering from **hypo**glycemia   *under*

19. a sensitive **therm**ocouple   *heat*

20. cutting the **epi**cardium   *upon*

Write the letter that indicates the best completion.

(*a*)   21. *Euphoria* refers to a feeling of (a) well-being, (b) weariness, (c) drowsiness, (d) hunger.

(*c*)   22. *Physics* is the study of (a) diseases, (b) chemicals, (c) nature, (d) beauty.

(d) 23. *Psychosurgery* involves cutting into (a) the lungs, (b) the face, (c) the muscles, (d) the brain.

(c) 24. *Tele* means (a) *sound,* (b) *star,* (c) *far,* (d) *sight.*

(b) 25. The Greek root which is common to both *pantheism* and *theology* means (a) *all,* (b) *god,* (c) *study,* (d) *nature.*

Key to Review Test

Check your test answers by the following key. Deduct 4% per error from a possible 100%.

1. True	6. True	11. false	16. new	21. (a)
2. False	7. False	12. around	17. loving	22. (c)
3. True	8. True	13. through	18. under	23. (d)
4. False	9. True	14. fire	19. heat	24. (c)
5. False	10. False	15. one	20. upon	25. (b)

Score: _____%

NOTE: For supplementary exercises on additional Greek roots, see APPENDIX B, page 318.

6

Words Often Misused

1. a
2. an
3. accept
4. except
5. affect
6. effect
7. amount
8. complexioned
9. conscience
10. conscious

11. consensus
12. enthusiastic
13. etc.
14. feature
15. funny
16. hanged
17. hung
18. have
19. imply
20. infer

21. its
22. it's
23. leave
24. let
25. less
26. liable
27. likely
28. loose
29. lose
30. lots of

Common, trivial words—these are a disaster area for many college students. If English professors earned a nickel every time they red-penciled *it's, too,* and *their,* they could retire at forty. Are you anxious to learn *ambivalence, denouement,* and *existentialism*? Be patient. You will master them later. First be sure that you are not misusing *affect, than,* and *whose.* Your thoughts may be profound, yet your composition will look amateurish if it is speckled with flaws. Your ploy should be to keep your teachers happy and in a generous mood, and so your aim number one must be to use basic words correctly. Demonstrate in themes that you understand the difference in meaning between *its* and *it's* and your teacher will want to embrace you.

To write *loose* when one means *lose* is usually classed as an error in spelling rather than in vocabulary, but actually it is both kinds of error. Look at it this way: Students can easily write *loose* and *lose;* they just aren't always sure which word means what. So spelling fault or vocabulary fault, the quibble is pointless. Words are being misused. And whatever one calls the disease, it has to be cured.

Most words in Chapters 6 and 7 look deceptively easy. But don't be overconfident. These words are demons. Be sure to write the correct answers in full—either in the blanks provided or on a separate sheet of paper—before you check the answer column. Your fingers are an extension of your brain; they must learn to do the right thing automatically. Thus, the act of writing and rewriting these demons correctly is vital.

COVER THIS STRIP

1. **a:** one (used before a consonant sound: "*a* girl, *a* historian, *a* mark, *a* fat ox").
2. **an:** one (used before a vowel sound: "*an* itch, *an* honor, *an* easy mark, *an* ox").

consonant
a

■ The words *city, year,* and *pretty* begin with a _consonant_ [vowel / consonant] sound, so we use the word _a_ [a / an] immediately in front of each of them.

vowel
an

■ The words *apple, ear,* and *idiotic* begin with a _vowel_ [vowel / consonant] sound, so we use the word _an_ [a / an] immediately in front of each of them.

an
a
a

■ Write *a* or *an*:
Jenks is _an_ absent-minded man. He dictated _a_ letter to his dog and tried to give his secretary _a_ bath.

an
a
an

■ Such magic! The guest flicks _an_ ancient cigar and turns _a_ Persian rug into _an_ ashtray.

an
an
a

■ I remember _an_ evening when my roommate typed thirty words _an_ hour and erased twenty words _a_ minute.

3. **accept** (ak-sept'): to take or receive. "*Accept* the lemons of life, and make lemonade."
4. **except** (ik-sept'): all but; excluding. "This singer has everything *except* talent." *Except* has to do with an *exception*.

accept
except

■ The church will ac_cept_ all your paintings ex_cept_ the nude.

except
accept

■ Every teacher _except_ Smedley will _accept_ the two percent raise.

accept
except

■ The opera singer was glad to ___accept___ the gift package, which was quite ordinary ___except___ for its ticking sound.

except
accept
except

■ Flem had no coins ___except___ a wooden nickel, yet he would never ___accept___ a free drink— ___except___ when he was awake.

---

5. **affect** (ə-fect′): *Verb*—to produce a change; to influence. "The damp air may *affect* Joe's lungs."
6. **effect** (i-fect′): *Noun*—result. "Physicists study cause and *effect*." *Verb*—to cause or bring about. "Dad tried to *effect* a change in my study habits."

affect

■ Marriage will ___affect___ Tony's career. [Verb: means "to influence."]

effect

■ Marriage will have an excellent ___effect___ on Tony. [Noun: means "result."]

effect

■ Marriage will ___effect___ an improvement in Tony's habits. [Verb: means "to bring about."]

affect

effect

■ The concussion did not ___affect___ my academic grades, which were low anyhow, and seemed to have no lasting ___effect___ .

effect
effect

■ Baseball representatives can probably ___effect___ a compromise, but they must consider the ___effect___ on the box office.

effect
affect

■ Drugs had a tragic ___effect___ ; his hallucinations still ___affect___ him day and night.

---

7. **amount:** quantity; mass (not to be confused with *number*, which refers to countable objects). "Joe ate a huge *amount* of ice cream and a small *number* [not *amount*] of doughnuts."

Write *amount* or *number:*

number

■ Sheila collected an unusual __*number*__ of mosquito bites.

number
amount

■ The mugger separated me from a large __*number*__ of credit cards and a small __*amount*__ of cash.

number

■ The sink had no drainpipe, so I washed a great __*number*__ of dishes and my feet at the same time.

number

amount

■ St. Patrick chased a vast __*number*__ of snakes out of Ireland, but they return to those who drink a certain __*amount*__ of whiskey.

---

8. **complexioned** (kəm-plek′shənd): having a specified skin color. (Avoid the colloquial *complected.*)

(a)

■ The Rose Bowl queen was fair- (a) complexioned, (b) complected. (*a*)

complexioned

■ After a day in the coal mine, the miners were sooty-__*complexioned*__ .

complexioned
complexioned

■ Phineas claimed that his skin ointment was as good for light-__*complexioned*__ people as for dark-__*complexioned*__ people, and it probably was.

complexioned

■ The word *complected* is considered colloquial or dialectal, and most good writers prefer to use __*complexioned*__ .

---

9. **conscience** (kon′shəns): a moral sense steering toward right action.
10. **conscious** (kon′shəs): aware; able to feel and think.

conscience

■ *Science* means "knowledge," and your so-called knowledge of right and wrong is your c__*onscience*__ .

conscious

■ At age twelve Manuel became _conscious_ of girls as being different from boys.

conscience
conscious

■ The big employers must develop their _conscience_ as well as their investments; they must become _conscious_ of the needs of employees.

conscious
conscience

■ The infant was found, scarcely _conscious_ , by the side of the road. Who could have abandoned it? Had they no _conscience_ ?

Quiz

Write the letter that indicates the best definition.

1. (i)	(i) 1. a	a. result
2. (e)	(e) 2. an	b. aware
3. (g)	(g) 3. accept	c. all but
4. (c)	(c) 4. except	d. quantity
5. (h)	(h) 5. affect	e. one (used before vowels)
6. (a)	(a) 6. effect	f. sense of right and wrong
7. (d)	(d) 7. amount	g. to take
8. (j)	(j) 8. complexioned	h. to influence
9. (f)	(p) 9. conscience	i. one (used before consonants)
10. (b)	(b) 10. conscious	j. having a certain skin tone

11. **consensus** (kən-sen′səs): a general opinion.

wordiness
avoid

■ Since _consensus_ means "a general opinion," the phrase "consensus of opinion" is an example of the _wordiness_ [crispness / wordiness] that careful writers usually _avoid_ [avoid / favor].

consensus

■ We are due for an earthquake soon, according to a _consensus_ [consensus / consensus of opinion] of experts.

consensus

■ More women should enter politics, according to a _consensus_ of congressional leaders.

of opinion

■ News item: "The consensus of opinion of fashion designers is that dresses will be shorter next summer." What must be cut in that sentence (not counting dresses)? __of opinion__

---

12. **enthusiastic:** eager; ardent. (Avoid using the colloquial *enthused*.)

enthusiastic

■ The strip teaser performed before an __enthusiastic__ [enthused / enthusiastic] crowd.

was enthusiastic

■ The Englishman __was enthusiastic__ [enthused / was enthusiastic] about the house with two bathrooms.

enthusiastic

■ We were all __enthusiastic__ [enthused / enthusiastic] when Tom Mix untied his girl from the railroad tracks.

(b)

■ In formal writing the use of *enthused* is generally (a) acceptable, (b) undesirable. (*b*)

---

13. **etc.:** et cetera (et set′rə); and others; and so forth. (The abbreviation *etc.* is usually avoided in formal writing. Use its English equivalent.)

(b)

■ Poe later wrote "The Tell-Tale Heart," "The Black Cat," (a) etc., (b) and other horror stories. (*b*)

(b)

■ If accepted at Harvard, I will take courses in physics, chemistry, (a) etc., (b) and mathematics. (*b*)

etc.

■ To pronounce and spell *etc.* correctly, you should think of the first three letters of *et cetera*—they give us the abbreviation __etc.__ .

(a)

■ *Etc.* means "and so forth"—thus to write "and etc.," with its additional "and," is (a) incorrect, (b) correct. (*a*)

---

14. **feature** (fē′chər): *Noun*—a distinct quality; part of the face; a motion picture. *Verb*—to make prominent; to make a specialty of. (Avoid the informal use of *feature* to mean "imagine" or "to conceive of.")

imagine

■ I cannot _____ [feature / imagine] a world without music.

comprehend

■ The average, well-fed American can hardly _____ [feature / comprehend] the utter poverty of Calcutta.

feature

■ The Hilton dining room will *f*_____ lobster thermidor this evening.

imagine
feature

■ Can you _____ [imagine / feature] what Aunt Fanny would think of that shocking double _____ at the Pussycat Theater?

---

15. **funny:** comical; laughable; humorous. (Avoid *funny* in formal writing when you mean "strange, peculiar, odd.")

strange

■ We thought it was _____ [funny / strange] that our low-salaried sheriff could buy a yacht.

unusual

■ When Hilda found the letters from John's three other wives, she realized that something _____ [funny / unusual] was going on.

funny

■ Mark Twain's lectures were extremely *f*_____ .

mournful

■ The widow sat near the casket with a _____ [mournful / funny] look on her face.

---

16. **hanged:** suspended by the neck until dead.
17. **hung:** fastened or supported from above (not referring to death by hanging).

hung

■ We *h*_____ our clothes on a hickory limb.

hanged hung	■ The posse h_____ Wee Willie, and the rest of us h_____ our heads in shame.
hung	■ Nancy h_____ the mistletoe above her typewriter.
hanged	■ The prisoner had a choice: he could be shot or _____ .
hanged hung	■ Nathan Hale was _____ , but we have _____ his picture in our hall of fame.

18. **have:** to possess. (Use *have* as an auxiliary verb in phrases like "should *have*," "could *have*," "might *have*," and AVOID the nonstandard "should of," "could of," . . . .)

Write *have* or *of* in the sentences that follow:

have	■ The lost aviator should _____ stayed in bed.
have of	■ The material might _____ cost ten dollars a yard, but none _____ the bathers wore twenty cents worth.
have of of	■ Junior must _____ reached for the hammer instead _____ the swatter when he saw the fly on the top _____ the baby's head.
have have	■ You should _____ warned me that Ambrose would sing here, so that I could _____ gone to the ball game instead.
of have	■ Olaf washed the top windows _____ the building and must _____ stepped back to admire his work.

19. **imply** (im-plī′): to hint at; to suggest without stating; to signify.
20. **infer** (in-fûr′): to draw a conclusion.

imply infer	■ These bloodstains *im*_____ that the victim may have been knifed. What do you *in*_____ ?

97

imply

■ Her high grades i_____ unusual intelligence.

infer

imply

■ From various evidence I i_____ that the baseball fans no longer admire Lefty Smeeby. Their jeers i_____ that they have lost confidence in him.

imply

infer

■ Melvin's smiles _____ success. We can _____ that Betty has accepted his marriage proposal.

inferred

■ Hot tar was spilled at the intersection, from which the police _____ed that there was dirty work at the crossroads.

Quiz

Write the letter that indicates the best definition.

1. (d)	(d)	1. consensus	a. and so forth
2. (g)	(g)	2. enthusiastic	b. strangled on a gallows
3. (a)	(a)	3. etc.	c. humorous
4. (i)	(i)	4. feature	d. the general opinion
5. (c)	(c)	5. funny	e. to conclude
6. (b)	(b)	6. hanged	f. to suggest
7. (j)	(j)	7. hung	g. eager
8. (h)	(h)	8. have	h. to own (auxiliary verb)
9. (f)	(f)	9. imply	i. to make prominent
10. (e)	(e)	10. infer	j. supported from above, as on a hook

21. **its** (possessive): "The basset hound stepped on *its* ear."
22. **it's** (contraction): it is. "Frankly, *it's* a hot dog."

it's

its

■ Surely _____ no fun for a rabbit to be held by _____ ears. (Hint: Write *it's* only if "it is" can be substituted for it.)

it's

its

■ As for this camel, _____ a poor specimen; it has bumps on _____ back.

its

its

■ I wanted to be a lion tamer, but when the circus lion bared _____ fangs and _____ claws, I decided to become a clown.

its its	■ This lake is perfect, except that _____ fish are tiny and _____ mosquitoes are big as eagles.
it's it's	■ Truly _____ lucky to own a shiny penny—if _____ wrapped in fifty-dollar bills.
it's its	■ "If _____ true that the cow jumped over the moon," Junior asked teacher, "how did it get _____ thrust?"

23. **leave:** to depart. "We will *leave* at dawn."
24. **let:** to allow. "Please *let* us help."

let	■ Society must l_____ women develop to their full potential.
leave let	■ Before we l_____ , l_____ us come to an understanding.
let leave	■ The hostess will _____ you kiss her when you _____ .
let leave	■ The pacifist would not _____ his son _____ for the front.

25. **less:** a smaller quantity (but use *fewer* when referring to a smaller number). "We used *less* fertilizer and harvested *fewer* tomatoes."

Write *less* or *fewer*:

less fewer	■ Now that Oswald does _____ speeding, he gets _____ traffic tickets.
fewer less	■ Eat _____ hot fudge sundaes, and you will weigh _____ .
fewer fewer	■ As their romance cooled, they exchanged _____ letters and made _____ telephone calls.

fewer less less fewer	■ This year I have _____ bees, and that means _____ honey, _____ money, and _____ stings.

---

26. **liable** (li′-ə-bəl): legally responsible; exposed to a risk or danger. "Parents will be held *liable*." "The professor identified a new disease to which infants are *liable*." (Do not use *liable* to mean "probable.")
27. **likely:** probable; to be expected. "It is *likely* to rain."

likely	■ Edith is *li*_____ to be valedictorian.
likely liable	■ A crash is *li*_____ to occur on this one-lane country road, and one of us will be *li*_____ .
likely	■ Take a bath, and the telephone is _____ to ring.
likely liable	■ The patient who fell off the stretcher is _____ to hold the hospital _____ for negligence.
liable likely	■ If I am _____ for that million-dollar loss, you are _____ to collect about four dollars.

---

28. **loose** (rhymes with *goose*): not tight; unfastened.
29. **lose:** to suffer a loss.

loose lose	■ The goose is *l*_____ ! We must not *l*_____ it.
loose lose	■ In time of war a *l*_____ tongue can cause us to *l*_____ a troopship.
lose loose	■ When I _____ weight, my pants hang _____ .
lose lose loose	■ Not only did I _____ the fight, but I may also _____ this _____ tooth.

loose

■ The word *goose* rhymes with the word *l*_____ .

---

30. **lots of; a lot of:** many; a great deal. (The informal phrases "lots of" and "a lot of" are acceptable but tend to be used far too frequently; they should be avoided in formal writing. Incidentally, "a lot" is two words, not one.)

numerous

■ Shakespeare wrote _____ [a lot of / numerous] sonnets.

Many
considerable

■ _____ [Lots of / Many] farms were struck by the hailstorm and _____ [lots of / considerable] damage was done.

many

■ Grandpa bought a few lots near the garbage dump and made _____ [lots of / many] other bad investments.

informal
sparingly

■ The phrases "lots of" and "a lot of" are considered _____ [formal / informal] and should therefore be used _____ [sparingly / lots of times] in student research papers.

Quiz

Write the letter that indicates the best definition.

1. (c)
2. (h)
3. (e)
4. (a)
5. (f)
6. (b)
7. (i)
8. (j)
9. (d)
10. (g)

(c) 1. its   a. to permit
(h) 2. it's   b. legally responsible
(e) 3. leave   c. possessive form of *it*
(a) 4. let   d. to suffer a loss
(f) 5. less   e. to depart; to go
(b) 6. liable   f. a smaller amount
(i) 7. likely   g. many; a great deal
(j) 8. loose   h. contraction for "it is"
(d) 9. lose   i. probable
(g) 10. lots of   j. unfastened; not tight

REVIEW TEST

Write *Correct*, if the italicized word is used correctly. Otherwise, write the word that should be used.

an   1. Brutus is *a* honorable man.

correct   2. We have *an* orange cat that watches mice—just watches them.

accept   3. The grateful native offered me his pet boa constrictor, but I did not *except* it.

correct   4. Would sudden wealth *affect* me? I'll never find out.

number   5. Sunshine will bring out a greater *amount* of voters.

conscience   6. Throwing your parakeet to the cat! Have you no *conscious*?

correct   7. Some comedians can be *funny* without a script.

enthusiastic   8. Even Gloomy Gus, our coach, was *enthused* about our prospects.

hung   9. On Christmas Eve we *hanged* our stockings on the mantel.

correct   10. His high fever may *imply* serious illness.

correct   11. Try not to *lose* that fat wallet.

likely   12. It's *liable* to snow tomorrow.

complexioned   13. The funeral director, like the corpse, was dark-*complected*.

correct   14. Giving the waiter a big tip had a marvelous *effect*.

correct   15. Life is an elevator. It has *its* ups and downs.

Write the better choice.

16. What will be the ___*effect*___ [affect / effect] of another tax raise?

17. Surprisingly, our teacher does have a ___*conscience*___ [conscious / conscience].

18. The cattle thief was ___*hanged*___ [hanged / hung] from the apple tree.

19. Scarface won't talk, and we must ___*infer*___ [imply / infer] that he is protecting someone.

20. During the classical period Beethoven composed ___*a number of*___ [lots of / a number of] symphonies.

21. Better highway signs will result in ___*fewer*___ [fewer / less] accidents.

22. Please ___*let*___ [leave / let] Tina plant the watermelon seeds.

23. Cooper wrote *The Leatherstocking Tales* _____ [and other novels / etc.].

24. Dorothea Fry should __*have*__ [have / of] been our college president.

25. Like the Whiffenpoofs, many of us __*lose*__ [lose / loose] our way.

Key to Review Test

Check your test answers by the following key. Deduct 4% per error from a possible 100%.

1. an	10. Correct	19. infer
2. Correct	11. Correct	20. a number of
3. accept	12. likely	21. fewer
4. Correct	13. complexioned	22. let
5. number	14. Correct	23. and other novels
6. conscience	15. Correct	24. have
7. Correct	16. effect	25. lose
8. enthusiastic	17. conscience	
9. hung	18. hanged	

Score: _____%

7

Words Often Misused

1. majority
2. nice
3. passed
4. past
5. principal
6. principle
7. prejudiced
8. supposed to
9. used to
10. really

11. reason
12. regardless
13. so
14. suspicion
15. than
16. then
17. themselves
18. their
19. there
20. they're

21. this
22. to
23. too
24. try
25. unique
26. which
27. who's
28. whose
29. your
30. you're

Follow the same procedure as in Chapter 6.

1. **majority:** more than half of the total number; the excess over all the rest of the votes. (A *plurality*, however, refers to the excess of votes received by the leading candidate over the second of three or more candidates. Do not use *majority* to refer to most of a single thing. WRONG: "Bill ate the majority of the watermelon.")

most

■ The elderly couple were sick during _____ [most / the majority] of the trip on the pleasure cruiser.

most

■ Myrtle did _____ [most / the majority] of the engine design.

did
10

■ Anna had 80 votes; Ben, 40 votes; Clarence, 30 votes. Anna _____ [did / did not] receive a majority of the votes. She won the election by a majority of _____ [10 / 40 / 80].

did not
6

■ In another election, Alice had 95 votes; Bill, 89 votes; Chester, 72 votes. Alice _____ [did / did not] receive a majority of the votes. She won the election by a plurality of _____ [6 / 13 / 95] votes.

majority
most

■ Mr. Grunt has cut down twelve of his twenty pine trees. He has, therefore, cut a *ma*_____ of his trees. He will spend _____ [most / the majority] of the money he earns on a hernia operation.

2. **nice:** pleasant; agreeable; satisfying; refreshing; comfortable; cordial; amiable; genial; dainty; delicate; delicious; attractive; engaging; fascinating; seductive; enchanting; delightful; charming; gratifying; cheerful. (Avoid overuse of *nice*. Try to use a more precise word in its place.)

vague

■ The phrase "a nice trip" expresses approval in a _____ [vague / precise] way.

(b)

■ Which gives a clearer description? (a) a nice room, (b) a comfortable room. (   )

(b)

■ Which gives a clearer description? (a) a nice clerk, (b) an amiable clerk. (   )

Examples:
expensive
refreshing
smogless

■ Substitute a more precise word for "nice":

nice car	_____	car
nice drink	_____	drink
nice weather	_____	weather

---

3. **passed:** went by (verb, past tense of *pass*). "The gassy truck *passed* the joggers."
4. **past:** beyond; earlier; an earlier period. (*Past* is not a verb.) "During the *past* minute, six gassy trucks have gone *past* the joggers."

Write *passed* or *past*:

passed

■ Tony _____ the tavern. (Here Tony is the subject of a missing verb, and the verb ends in *ed*.)

past

■ Tony walked _____ the tavern. (Here Tony is the subject of the verb *walked*, and the missing word is not a verb.)

past
passed

■ Some years in the _____ Tom wanted to be a barber. He took a licensing test and _____ by a hair.

past
passed
passed

■ The bullet screamed _____ my ear, and I heard it twice; first, when it _____ me, and then when I _____ it.

past
passed

■ At half-_____ ten Mary bid six spades, and I _____ .

---

5. **principal:** main; head of a school; chief actor or doer; a capital sum. " 'Spend the interest and save the *principal*'—that was the *principal* lesson that the school *principal* taught us."

6. **principle:** a rule of action or conduct. (Note that *principle* and *rule* both end in *le*.) "Isaac Newton worked out the *principle* of gravitation."

principle

■ The professor explained a basic *prin*_____ of thermodynamics. (Refers to a *rule*.)

principal

■ The *prin*_____ cause of divorce is marriage.

principal
principal

■ The high school _____ played the _____ role in the faculty play.

principle
principal

■ Jane Pittman was a woman of lofty _____ , and that is a _____ reason we honor her.

principal
principle

■ My _____ objection is to speech courses that stress the questionable _____ , "Say it with sincerity, whether you believe it or not."

Be sure to include the final *d*, as shown, in the following words:

7. **prejudiced:** biased. "Tom was *prejudiced*" (not "was prejudice").

8. **supposed to:** "We are *supposed* to study" (not "suppose to").

9. **used to:** "I *used* to be a dog-sitter" (not "use to").

Write the missing word in full:

used

■ Joe *u*_____ to pass the crematorium and ask, "What's cooking?"

supposed

■ Students are *s*_____ to write compositions weekly, not weakly.

used
prejudiced

■ I *u*_____ to be *pr*_____ against pigeons— but they're delicious.

■ You are not s_____ to loaf. Father u_____ to say that even God put in a six-day week.

■ Smart shoppers are *pre*_____ against chemical preservatives. We are *s*_____ to read food labels carefully.

■ Whenever the Miltown Misfits lost a baseball game, their coach *u*_____ to say the umpires were *p*_____ .

---

10. **really:** actually; genuinely; in fact. (Avoid overuse of *really* in your compositions. The word can usually be deleted without loss.)

■ Cross out every useless *really* in the following passage:

I was really anxious for school to begin this fall. I have always really enjoyed studying and meeting people, and I really believe that the opportunities here at Knockwurst College are really outstanding.

■ In the foregoing passage the word *really* can be cut _____ times without loss; in fact, these deletions have resulted in a more _____ [wordy / mature] style.

Choose the fresher, more effective modifier:

■ Interpretations of Beckett's play (a) differ significantly, (b) really differ. ( ) Yet critics do agree that the play is _____ [really / strangely] provocative.

■ *Really* is _____ [really / perfectly] grammatical, but constant repetition of the word is _____ [really / certainly] inadvisable.

Quiz

Circle the choice that results in the more acceptable sentence.

1. letters
2. sparkling
3. passed
4. past
5. principle
6. principal
7. prejudiced
8. supposed
9. used
10. remarkably generous

1. Fay wrote the majority of the (letters / correspondence).
2. Patrick had a kindly face and (nice / sparkling) eyes.
3. The years (passed / past) like falling leaves.
4. History is a thing of the (passed / past).
5. Live by the (principal / principle) of the golden rule.
6. The (principal / principle) influence on a man is a woman.
7. All human beings are (prejudice / prejudiced) in some way.
8. An actor is (suppose / supposed) to be a jack of all traits.
9. Bread (use / used) to be ten cents a loaf.
10. His sponsor was (remarkably generous / really nice) to him.

---

11. **reason:** cause; purpose. (Avoid "the reason is because," since that phrase says in effect: "the cause is because.")

BAD: The reason Sam shot the dog is because it had rabies.
ACCEPTABLE: The reason Sam shot the dog is that it had rabies.
ACCEPTABLE: Sam shot the dog because it had rabies.

that

■ A possible reason for Shaw's longevity is _____ [that / because] he was a vegetarian.

that

■ The main reason my great-grandfather was late for his tennis match today is _____ [that / because] he ran the marathon this morning.

■ Choose the better sentence:

   a. Sue smiles because she loves her job.
   b. The reason Sue smiles is because she loves her job.

(a)
                                     ( )

   a. The reason Max got a ticket is because he hit a police car.
   b. Max got a ticket because he hit a police car.

(b)
                                     ( )

---

12. **regardless:** heedless; in spite of; anyway. (Do not use the nonstandard term *irregardless*.)

regardless

■ Use correct English _____ [regardless / irregardless] of how it may shock a few illiterate friends.

regardless

■ Americans must have equal opportunities, _____*less* of sex, color, or creed.

(b)

■ In the word *regardless*, the suffix *less* expresses a negative; therefore, the addition of the negative prefix *ir*—creating a double negative—is (a) logical, (b) illogical. ( )

an incorrect
regardless

■ Adding the prefix *ir* to the word *regardless* would create _____ [a correct / an incorrect] expression, _____*less* of who used it.

13. **so:** therefore; as indicated. (Avoid the overuse of *so* to mean "very," in formal writing.)

extremely

■ The view of the sea from Malibu is _____ [so / extremely] beautiful.

very

■ After a hard day of banquets and toasts, the mayor is usually _____ [so / very] tired.

(b)

■ "Americans have admired their war generals; *so* we have elected several to the presidency." Here the word *so* is used in its acceptable formal sense to mean (a) "very," (b) "therefore." ( )

14. **suspicion:** distrust; doubt. (Avoid using the noun *suspicion* when the verb *suspect* is called for.)

suspected

■ When the bank teller saw her customer holding a gun, she _____ [suspected / suspicioned] that he would request instant cash.

suspected	■ The young couple often flung dishes and pounded heads against the wall, and we _____ [suspicioned / suspected] that they were solving some minor marital problems.
(a)	■ In a detective story the butler was usually the first person to be (a) suspected, (b) suspicioned. ( )
(a)	■ *Suspected* is a verb; *suspicion* is (a) a noun, (b) a verb. ( )

15. **than** (used in comparisons). "Fido bites harder *than* Rover."
16. **then:** at that time. "We were younger and thinner *then*."

then	■ Now and _____ Junior loses a tooth.
than	■ The wrestler's nose was flatter _____ a bicycle seat.
then than	■ Our government operated on a smaller budget _____ _____ now.
then than	■ The shepherd saw her sweater and _____ realized that the wool looked better on the girl _____ on the sheep.
than then	■ The word _____ suggests a comparison; the word _____ suggests time.

17. **themselves** (reflexive and emphatic form of *them*). (Do not use nonstandard variations such as *theirselves* or *themselfs*.)

themselves	■ Teachers don't fail students; students fail _____ [themselves / theirselves].
themselves	■ Talented women must move *th*_____ from the kitchen to the public arena.
themselves	■ The salesmen *th*_____ had more crust than a pie factory.

■ The ministers *th*_____ tell us that God helps those that help *th*_____ .

---

18. **their** (possessive). *"Their* dog has fleas."
19. **there:** in that place. "Sit *there* and wait."
20. **they're:** they are. *"They're* sleeping."

■ The dentist will have to straighten _____ teeth, because _____ not going to straighten themselves.

■ Soon the three wise men arrived _____ on _____ camels.

■ The weather was so hot _____ that the boys wanted to take off _____ skin and sit around in _____ bones.

■ The old folks say _____ happy in _____ merry Oldsmobile.

■ The salesmen over _____ are live wires. A widow wants a burial suit for her husband, and _____ selling her _____ best silk suit with two pairs of pants.

Quiz

Circle the choice that results in the more acceptable sentence.

1. The reason Tom speeds is (because / that) he wants attention.
2. Buy the bagels (regardless / irregardless) of price.
3. The leading man was (extremely / so) handsome.
4. The swimmer (suspicioned / suspected) that the sharks were looking for lunch.
5. All my friends were (their / there / they're)—both of them.
6. Writers must learn to criticize (theirselves / themselves).
7. Let us go (than / then), you and I.
8. After a meal my friends picked (their / there / they're) teeth.
9. Linda's diamond looks bigger (than / then) a tennis ball.
10. The parents admit that (their / there / they're) to blame.

21. **this.** (Refers to something nearby or just mentioned. Avoid the vague use of *this*, particularly in reference to something not yet mentioned.)

Write *Right* or *Wrong*, depending on whether the word *this* is used correctly. Assume that each sentence is the opening line of a theme.

Wrong
■ _____ This poem is about this Viking who elopes with this princess.

Right
■ _____ Longfellow's "A Skeleton in Armor" is about a Viking who elopes with a princess; the poem describes the fate of this pair in America.

Wrong
■ _____ I still remember this boy in our schoolyard who threw this big snowball at me.

Right
■ _____ To this day I remember the boy in our schoolyard who threw a big snowball at me.

Wrong
■ _____ This friend of mine has this hobby of collecting Avon bottles.

---

22. **to:** toward; until; also used before a verb, as in "*to* fly." "Gus threatened *to* sing *to* us."
23. **too:** more than enough; also. "He's *too* skinny, *too*."

too
to
■ The bronco was _____ nervous for me _____ ride it.

to
to
■ The guests began _____ stagger _____ the bathroom.

too
to
too
■ Edna was only _____ happy _____ be given tuba lessons, and I was, _____ .

to
too
to
■ Soldiers have _____ get up much _____ early—no wonder they are ready _____ kill.

113

■ Hazel said _____ the salesman: "You are asking _____ much for a car that has been hit by a truck and by lightning, _____ ."

---

24. **try:** to attempt. (Write "try to" instead of the informal "try and.")

■ I will try _____ [to / and] analyze how James Fenimore Cooper portrays women in his novels.

■ The marriage vows should suggest that a couple try _____ [to / and] live within their income.

■ Careful writers prefer the phrase (a) "try and," (b) "try to." ( )

■ Gunther will try _____ [to / and] do the triple somersault, and tomorrow I will try _____ [to / and] visit him in the hospital.

---

25. **unique:** the only one of its kind; peerless. "Poe's 'Ulalume' is *unique*." (Avoid the somewhat illogical "more unique" and "most unique.")

■ The world has only one Taj Mahal; that beautiful building is *u*_____ .

■ Your right thumbprint is unique, the only one of its kind. It is, therefore, _____ [possible / impossible] for any other fingerprint to be more one-of-its-kind than that one.

■ Sandra's Hawaiian muumuu is more _____ [unique / exotic] than her J. C. Penney dress.

■ Only two copies of Franklin's original *Almanack* are known to exist. Each copy is extremely _____ [unique / rare], but it is not _____ [unique / rare].

■ Suppose you had the only 1807 dollar of its kind in the world; that coin would be _____ .

unique

---

26. **which.** (Reference to a thing previously mentioned. But use *who* or *that*, not *which*, when referring to a person.) "A man *who* saw me coming sold me this horse *which* just died."

■ This is the little boy _____ [who / which] hit a home run through our window.

who

■ Our cat is one creature _____ [who / which] never cries over spilt milk.

which

■ The man _____ [who / which] lives in the apartment above us wears shoes _____ [who / which] are made of wood.

who
which

■ Alvin owns a parrot _____ [who / which] doesn't talk but is a good listener.

which

■ Boris is a barber _____ [who / which] will take a big load off your mind.

who

---

27. **who's:** who is. "*Who's* calling, please?"
28. **whose** (possessive). "*Whose* shoes are these?"

■ Find out _____ car was smashed and _____ to blame. (Hint: Write *who's* only if "who is" would be correct in the blank.)

whose
who's

■ The aged alumni, _____ class reunion this is, are getting together to see _____ falling apart.

whose
who's

■ Mr. Bigmouth wants to know _____ marrying _____ daughter.

who's
whose

■ A girl _____ fit as a fiddle should have a beau.

who's

115

who's
whose

■ "I'd like to catch the actor _____ careless," said Hamlet, "and _____ spear keeps jabbing me in the third act."

whose
who's

■ The word _____ is possessive; the word _____ means "who is."

29. **your** (possessive). "Put on *your* gas mask."
30. **you're**: you are. "*You're* beautiful."

your
you're

■ Hold _____ horses—_____ traveling too fast.

you're

■ Until April 15 _____ deep in the heart of taxes.

your
you're

■ Wilhelm, _____ poems are so sweet that _____ giving us diabetes.

you're
your

■ When _____ famous, the public takes an interest in _____ sins.

You're
your

■ Y_____ old only if you feel that _____ future is behind you.

you're
your
your

■ "Listen," said Barnum to Tom Thumb, "_____ so little that you have to stand on _____ chair to brush _____ teeth."

Quiz

Circle the choice that results in the more acceptable sentence.

1. your
2. rare
3. Whose
4. too
5. to
6. who's
7. to
8. an
9. you're
10. which

1. This is (your / you're) life.
2. A snowstorm in Pasadena is extremely (rare / unique).
3. (Whose / Who's) cat has been eating my tropical fish?
4. Mr. Brunk jumped when the fire became (to / too) hot.
5. Try (to / and) impress your teacher by reading extra books.
6. Joe sang, "I wonder (whose / who's) kissing her now."
7. The batter swung like a fence and fell (to / too) the ground.
8. Ten years ago I had (an / this) unforgettable accident.
9. Read constantly, or (your / you're) wasting time in college.
10. The donkey is a small beast (who / which) carries a big load.

REVIEW TEST

Write *Correct*, if the italicized word is used correctly. Otherwise, write the word that should be used.

_____ 1. My motto is, never hit a fellow *which* is down.

_____ 2. Kate's companion was harder to get rid of *than* malaria.

_____ 3. The reason our coach succeeds is *that* he pays high salaries.

_____ 4. Smedley believes in the *principle*, "Love thy neighbor."

_____ 5. Officials should keep *their* campaign promises.

_____ 6. David started at the bottom and stayed *there*.

_____ 7. Stay out until midnight and your mother *suspicions* the worst.

_____ 8. The doctor advised Ned to try *and* give up spicy foods.

_____ 9. My cousin grunted and *passed* the turnips to his sister.

_____ 10. People on juries should not be *prejudice*.

_____ 11. Frank *use* to have a million-dollar figure, but inflation set in.

_____ 12. The traffic officers found *too* much alcohol in Jim's blood.

_____ 13. If *they're* your friends, they will respect your privacy.

_____ 14. Do what is right, *irregardless* of public opinion.

_____ 15. Find out *whose* toupee fell from the balcony.

Write the better choice.

16. Take off _____ [your / you're] shoes at the temple door.

17. Malone delivered _____ [a nice / an impressive] speech.

18. The undercover agents disguised _____ [themselves / theirselves] as truckers.

19. Lack of money is the _____ [principle / principal] root of evil.

20. In those days a farmer's wife was _____ [supposed / suppose] to slave in the kitchen.

21. You are happiest when _____ [your / you're] in love.

22. Rossini spent _____ [most / a majority] of the winter in an asylum.

23. My job is perfect for someone _____ [who's / whose] able to work thirty hours a day.

24. Betty practiced law for the _____ [past / passed] few years.

25. The trained seal was _____ [highly / so] intelligent.

Key to Review Test

Check your test answers by the following key. Deduct 4% per error from a possible 100%.

1. who (that)	6. Correct	11. used	16. your	21. you're
2. Correct	7. suspects	12. Correct	17. an impressive	22. most
3. Correct	8. to	13. Correct	18. themselves	23. who's
4. Correct	9. Correct	14. regardless	19. principal	24. past
5. Correct	10. prejudiced	15. Correct	20. supposed	25. highly

Score: _____%

8

Words Often Confused

1. adapt
2. adopt
3. advice
4. advise
5. allusion
6. illusion
7. assistance
8. assistants
9. brake
10. break
11. breath
12. breathe
13. capital
14. capitol
15. choose
16. chose
17. close
18. clothes
19. cloths
20. complement
21. compliment
22. decent
23. descent
24. desert
25. dessert
26. dual
27. duel
28. eminent
29. imminent
30. foreword
31. forward
32. instance
33. instants
34. later
35. latter
36. lead
37. led
38. marital
39. martial

To use a medicine because it looks "something like" the one you need can lead to trouble. To use a word because it sounds "something like" the one you need also leads to trouble.

We paid special attention in Chapters 6 and 7 to the more treacherous sound alikes (homonyms), such as *its/it's, whose/who's,* and *your/you're.* We will now take up other word pairs that have a shady reputation for tripping up the unwary student.

These common words look as harmless as old luggage, yet each should be handled as if it held a little bomb. "A sandy *desert*" is hardly the same as "a sandy *dessert,*" and "*marital* music" is hardly the same as "*martial* music"; so be sure you know your homonyms.

Most of the word pairs in this chapter sound alike or are very similar in sound. You should train both your ear and your eye to notice the slight difference in sound or spelling in each pair, so that you will choose the correct word.

Study carefully the words at the top of each frame. Then fill each blank with the correct word. As always, keep a dictionary near you. A dictionary is bound to be useful, and that's not just a pun.

Enough *foreword*—now go *forward*!

EXERCISES

COVER THIS STRIP

1. **adapt:** to fit for a new use; to adjust to a new situation. "Can man *adapt* to life on the moon?" "This play is an *adaptation* of a novel."
2. **adopt:** to take into one's family; to pick up and use as one's own. "They found me in a trash barrel and *adopted* me."

adapt

■ I could ad＿＿＿＿ to army life if they'd let me sleep till noon.

adopt
adapt

■ If we ＿＿＿＿＿ a bright chimpanzee, it would probably ＿＿＿＿＿ quickly to California life.

adapt
adopt

■ Hollywood wants to ＿＿＿＿＿ your life story to film. Better ＿＿＿＿＿ a pseudonym because this movie may be X-rated.

adopt

■ Who deserves little Ignatz—his natural mother or the couple who happened to ＿＿＿＿＿ and raise him?

3. **advice** (ad-vīs'): *Noun*—counsel. "Dad gives me *advice*, not money."
4. **advise** (ad-vīz'): *Verb*—to counsel; to recommend. "Please *advise* me."

advice
advise

■ As a young singer I asked a vocal critic for ad＿＿＿＿ . He said: "I ＿＿＿＿＿ you to sell fish."

advice

■ Joe's ＿＿＿＿＿ costs nothing, and it's worth it.

advise
advice

■ I ＿＿＿＿＿ you to take teacher's ＿＿＿＿＿ .

advise
advise
advice

■ My friends ＿＿＿＿＿ me to forget my lost sweetheart. Believe me, it's easier to ＿＿＿＿＿ than to take ＿＿＿＿＿ .

120

Advice
advise

■ _____ rhymes with "ice"; _____ rhymes with "eyes."

---

5. **allusion:** a casual reference. "Flaky resented my *allusion* to his driving record."
6. **illusion:** a misleading image; a misconception; delusion. "The hundred-dollar bill was an optical *illusion*."

illusion

■ I crawled across the hot sand, and horrors! The lake was an _____ .

allusion

illusion

■ When I made an _____ to a ghost I had seen, Tom turned pale. "I've seen it, too," he said. "Then it's not an _____ . That's the spirit!"

illusion
allusion

■ Louie had the _____ that he'd get better grades if he dropped a casual _____ now and then to Bill Shakespeare or Hank Longfellow.

allusion
illusion

■ The bully made a nasty _____ to my maternal ancestry, and I, unfortunately, was under the _____ that I could knock him down.

Quiz

Write the letter that indicates the best definition.

1. (e)
2. (c)
3. (a)
4. (b)
5. (f)
6. (d)

( ) 1. adapt	a. opinion as to what to do
( ) 2. adopt	b. to recommend; to give opinion
( ) 3. advice	c. to take to one's self or family
( ) 4. advise	d. a mistaken impression
( ) 5. allusion	e. to adjust to new circumstances
( ) 6. illusion	f. a passing reference

---

7. **assistance:** the help or aid that is given. "Give *assistance*."
8. **assistants:** helpers. "Snow White had seven *assistants*."

assistants

■ The paramedic and several *as*_____ removed Junior from the wreckage.

assistance

■ My truck needed a push, and two Brownies came to my _____ .

assistance

■ Can I be of any _____ , madam?

assistants
assistance

■ One of our mayor's _____ went to Alcoholics Anonymous for _____ , mainly because of his wife and kidneys.

assistance
assistants

■ Muggles stole the cow without a bit of _____ , but he needed four _____ to write the ransom note.

9. **brake:** a device for stopping a vehicle. "Step on the *brake*."
10. **break:** to shatter. "*Break* the glass."

brake

■ All my car needs is *br*_____ pads and a new motor.

brake
break

■ Hit the _____ , or we'll _____ our necks!

break

■ "Waiter," I asked, "did this chicken _____ its leg?"—"You wanna eat it, mister, or dance with it?"

brake
break

■ The emergency _____ stopped us in time. Now let's drive so that we don't _____ the law.

break

■ The drug addict couldn't _____ his dangerous habit.

11. **breath:** air that is inhaled or exhaled.
12. **breathe:** to inhale or exhale air.

breath
breathe

■ The village gossip was out of *br*_____ . "Don't _____ a word of this to anybody," he panted.

breath

■ Gaston loved garlic, and his _____ was like a flame thrower.

breathe
breath

■ Near the finish line Ben began to _____ like
an overworked steam engine, and I felt his hot _____
on my shoulder.

breathe

■ Whenever I _____ the foul smoky gases of that
tannery, I get homesick for Los Angeles.

Quiz

Write the letter that indicates the best definition.

1. (b)
2. (d)
3. (f)
4. (a)
5. (c)
6. (e)

( ) 1. assistance   a. to crack into pieces
( ) 2. assistants   b. help that is given
( ) 3. brake   c. air from the mouth
( ) 4. break   d. those who help
( ) 5. breath   e. to inhale and exhale
( ) 6. breathe   f. a car-stopper

13. **capital:** *Adjective*—excellent; written with large letters; involving execution. "She is against *capital* punishment."
Noun—accumulated assets; a city which is the seat of government. "The *capital* of Alabama is Montgomery."
14. **capitol:** the statehouse; the building where legislators meet.
"The governor stood on the steps of the *capitol*."

capital
capital

■ A backer of *cap*_____ punishment says he has a
_____ idea: "Suspend the criminal instead of the sentence."

capitol

■ Rain leaked through the roof of the _____
and soaked a senator making a dry speech.

capitol
capital

■ "We can repair the dome of this _____ ,"
said the senator, "but that will take _____ ."

capital
capitol

■ Printed in _____ letters above the main entrance
to the _____ was the word LEGISLATURE.

15. **choose** (present tense): to select. "Don't *choose* booze."
16. **chose** (past tense): selected. "Yesterday Mose *chose* a rose."

choose

■ Henry Ford said, "You can *ch*_____ any color of Ford you want, as long as it is black."

chose
choose

■ Dad handed Uncle Kruse a few coins and _____ his words carefully: "Don't _____ booze, Kruse; it's bad news."

chose
choose

■ The actress _____ her seventh husband at least as carefully as we would _____ a pair of jogging shoes.

Choose
chose

■ _____ rhymes with "booze"; _____ rhymes with "rose."

chose

choose

■ When Mary was young she _____ to study word processing, and now she has six job offers from which to _____ .

---

17. **close:** to shut. "*Close* your mouth."
18. **clothes:** garments. "Al wore his Sunday *clothes* on Tuesday."
19. **cloths:** pieces of fabric. "Linen *cloths* covered the tables."

clothes
close

■ I stuffed my *cl*_____ into my suitcase and then couldn't _____ the cover.

cloths
close
clothes

■ Here are a towel and some wash _____ , but please _____ the bathroom door when you change your _____ .

cloths
clothes

■ Our factory buys huge bolts of cloth, and the trick is to turn these _____ into _____ .

clothes
close
cloths

■ At the car wash I wore my old _____ . My job was to _____ the car doors and to wipe the left fenders with dry _____ .

Write the letter that indicates the best definition.

1. (f)
2. (b)
3. (a)
4. (c)
5. (d)
6. (g)
7. (e)

(   )   1.   capital   a.   to select
(   )   2.   capitol   b.   the statehouse
(   )   3.   choose   c.   selected
(   )   4.   chose   d.   to shut
(   )   5.   close   e.   pieces of woven fabric
(   )   6.   clothes   f.   money; assets
(   )   7.   cloths   g.   articles of dress

---

20. **complement:** *Noun*—that which completes a thing; the counterpart. "Her white shoes serve as a *complement* to her black dress." *Verb*—to complete. "Her shoes *complement* her dress."

21. **compliment:** *Noun*—words of praise. "Thanks for the *compliment*." *Verb*—to praise. "Such a dessert! Let me *compliment* the chef."

complement

■ Gardens *comp*_____ the tidy English cottages.

compliment

complement

■ "You have brains, Gwendolyn, and that's not an idle _____ ," said Mother. "You'll be the perfect _____ to Sir Percy, who is a shmoe."

complement

compliment

complement

■ "Here's a rosy apple, teacher, to _____ your cheeks."—"What a sweet _____ , Archy! I hope you can earn an *A* today to _____ that *F* you got yesterday."

compliment

■ Like perfume, a _____ should be inhaled, not swallowed.

---

22. **decent:** proper and fitting. "Joe had a *decent* burial."

23. **descent:** a coming down; ancestry. "A man of Irish *descent* made a *descent* into the cellar."

descent

■ The elevator's rapid *de*_____ made my stomach hit my tonsils.

decent

■ Mary thinks I'm not making a _____ salary as a custodian, but I'm cleaning up.

descent
decent

■ The parachute slowed Edna's _____ , and she made a fairly _____ landing in an elm tree.

descent
decent

■ Hugo is of Austrian _____ , and he bakes a very _____ apple strudel.

---

24. **desert:** *Noun* (dez'ərt)—a dry wasteland. *Verb* (di zērt')—to abandon one's post or duty. "She's rich. He won't *desert* her."

25. **dessert:** a delicacy served at the end of a meal.

desert
dessert

■ "Only a rat would *des*_____ ," said our sergeant, as he cut a slab of apple pie for _____ . "Pass me the cheese."

desert
dessert

■ Crossing the sandy _____ , we had dates for _____ .

desert

■ "I'll never _____ my ship," said the brave captain, "glub . . . glub . . . ."

dessert

■ What has a double portion of *s*'s and calories? _____ .

Quiz

Write the letter that indicates the best definition.

1. (a)
2. (d)
3. (b)
4. (c)
5. (e)
6. (f)

( ) 1. complement   a. the counterpart
( ) 2. compliment   b. good; respectable
( ) 3. decent   c. a downward slope
( ) 4. descent   d. flattering words
( ) 5. desert   e. a dry, sandy region
( ) 6. dessert   f. pie, ice cream, etc.

---

26. **dual:** *Adjective*—double; twofold.

27. **duel:** *Noun*—a combat between two antagonists.

duel

■ Macbeth and Macduff have a *du*_____ to the death.

dual
duel

■ In a warplane with _____ wings, the Red Baron won many a fiery _____ .

dual
duel

■ Dmitri has a _____ personality. You never know whether he's going to embrace you or _____ with you.

duel
duel

■ When challenged to a _____ , Mark Twain told the gunslinger, "How about a _____ with water pistols at sixty paces?"

dual

■ With _____ exhaust pipes you can pollute the air twice as fast.

---

28. **eminent:** outstanding; famous. "She's an *eminent* author."
29. **imminent:** about to happen; threatening. "Disaster was *imminent*."

eminent
imminent

■ One _____ statesman predicts that a nuclear war is _____ .

eminent

■ When slick ads refer to "_____ medical authorities," they mean three underpaid drug clerks.

eminent
imminent

■ The _____ scientist who denied that a volcanic eruption was _____ now lies under three feet of lava.

imminent

■ People who are fearless when danger is _____ probably don't know what's going on.

---

30. **foreword:** a preface; introductory note.
31. **forward:** onward; toward what lies ahead.

forward
foreword

■ Our nation will go *for*_____ , according to this author in his _____ .

127

forward

■ Volunteers, please step _____ .

foreword
forward

■ Read the _____ of a technical book before plunging _____ into the chapters ahead.

forward

■ My mule is backward about going _____ .

forward

■ All _____ motion isn't progress, if your brakes don't work.

foreword

■ The introduction or "before" word of a book is known as the _____ .

Quiz

Write the letter that indicates the best definition.

1. (e)
2. (c)
3. (b)
4. (f)
5. (a)
6. (d)

( ) 1. dual   a. prefatory statement
( ) 2. duel   b. lofty; outstanding
( ) 3. eminent   c. a fight between two parties
( ) 4. imminent   d. toward what is ahead
( ) 5. foreword   e. double
( ) 6. forward   f. about to happen

---

32. **instance:** an example. "She recalled an *instance* of wife-beating in the bridal suite."
33. **instants:** moments. "Tragedy struck within *instants*."

instance

■ The playboy cited an *inst*_____ of a New Year's party that broke up in March.

instants

■ The three sprinters hit the tape within _____ of each other.

instance
instants

■ I was worried, for _____ , when the old plane shook for several _____ and a voice said: "This is your pilot, Orville Wright."

instance

■ Using my toothbrush to clean his typewriter keys was another _____ of poor manners.

instants

■ The lights turned green, and _____ later the horns were honking up a storm.

---

34. **later:** afterwards; more late. "He returned *later*."
35. **latter:** the last mentioned. "Stephen Douglas or Abe Lincoln? She married the *latter*."

later

■ It's *lat*_____ than you think.

latter
later

■ We're out of dates and figs, but we'll have the _____ a little _____ .

latter

■ When Jim and Josephine eloped, I held the ladder for the _____ .

later
latter

■ So it's chili and coffee? I'll have the former now, and _____ I'll have the _____ .

---

36. **lead:** *Noun* (led)—a heavy metal. *Verb, present tense* (lēd)—"A bee can *lead* us to honey."
37. **led:** *Verb, past tense*—"He was *led* to the gallows."

lead

■ You have to face the music if you want to *le*_____ the band.

led
lead

■ Last month a traitor _____ us into a trap, and his gunners filled us with hot _____ .

lead
lead

■ A poet with only a _____ pencil can _____ us to a nobler way of life.

led
lead

■ Our nation was _____ by statesmen with visions, not illusions, statesmen with wings on their shoes, not _____ in their pants.

---

38. **marital:** pertaining to marriage.

39. **martial:** pertaining to war.

marital

■ "Thanks to my husband for three years of *mar*_____ bliss," said Mrs. Roe on her golden anniversary.

martial
martial

■ Will nations abolish _____ conflict or will _____ conflict abolish nations?

marital

■ Love one another, if you want _____ happiness.

marital
martial

■ Wagner's "Wedding March" is _____ music; "Marine's Hymn" is _____ music.

Quiz

Write the letter that indicates the best definition.

1. (f)
2. (d)
3. (b)
4. (h)
5. (c)
6. (g)
7. (e)
8. (a)

( ) 1. instance   a. concerning war

( ) 2. instants   b. after that

( ) 3. later   c. to show the way

( ) 4. latter   d. fleeting moments

( ) 5. lead   e. concerning marriage

( ) 6. led   f. an example

( ) 7. marital   g. guided

( ) 8. martial   h. the last one mentioned

REVIEW TEST

Write in full the word that is indicated in brackets.

_____ 1. I'll [ch-se] sweet tea and take my lumps.

_____ 2. Free [adv-e] is worth what you pay for it.

_____ 3. Senator Oldy panted on the steps of the [capit-l].

_____ 4. Bill doesn't order [des-rt], but he tastes ours.

_____ 5. Smog is bad only for people who [bre-th-].

_____ 6. Don't wear new [clo-s] when you paint the ceiling.

_____ 7. Bobby Fischer was our most [-minent] chess player.

_____ 8. I read the book from [for-rd] to index.

_____ 9. My dog [l-d] me to the flea market.

_____ 10. The dinner bell rang, and we sat down in a matter of [instan-].

_____ 11. The violin was fighting a [du-l] with the piano.

_____ 12. The yodeler was of Swiss [d-c-nt].

_____ 13. A [compl-m-nt] a day keeps divorce away.

_____ 14. "Pay up," snarled Flem, "or we [br-k] your fingers."

_____ 15. Could you [ad-pt] to the life of the wealthy?

_____ 16. The "liberating" general declared [mar-l] law.

_____ 17. I'm in quicksand! Come to my [assistan-]!

_____ 18. The gambler's dream of wealth was an [-lusion].

Matching. Write the letter that indicates the best definition.

( ) 19. complement
( ) 20. imminent
( ) 21. cloths
( ) 22. marital
( ) 23. adapt
( ) 24. decent
( ) 25. latter

a. garments
b. pertaining to war
c. words of praise
d. respectable
e. threatening
f. the last one mentioned
g. that which completes
h. of marriage
i. pieces of fabric
j. to adjust to circumstances

Key to Review Test

Check your test answers by the following key. Deduct 4% per error from a possible 100%.

1. choose	10. instants	19. (g)
2. advice	11. duel	20. (e)
3. capitol	12. descent	21. (i)
4. dessert	13. compliment	22. (h)
5. breathe	14. break	23. (j)
6. clothes	15. adapt	24. (d)
7. eminent	16. martial	25. (f)
8. foreword	17. assistance	
9. led	18. illusion	

Score: _____%

9

Words Often Confused

1. medal	14. personal	27. shown
2. metal	15. personnel	28. stake
3. miner	16. plain	29. steak
4. minor	17. plane	30. stationary
5. moral	18. presence	31. stationery
6. morale	19. presents	32. vain
7. naval	20. quiet	33. vein
8. navel	21. quite	34. waist
9. peak	22. road	35. waste
10. peek	23. rode	36. weak
11. pedal	24. role	37. week
12. peddle	25. roll	38. weather
13. petal	26. shone	39. whether

Continue as in the previous chapter. Study the definitions at the top of each frame; then fill the blanks with the correct words.

Again, be sure to cover those answers in the left-hand column until you have completed the frame. (If you *peek* before you write, you won't reach the *peak* of your potential.)

COVER THIS STRIP

1. **medal:** a decorative award for a distinguished act.
2. **metal:** a substance such as silver, tin, or steel.

medal

■ Goering wore many a *me*_____ on his uniform and probably on his pajamas.

metal
medal
medal

■ Gold is a precious _____ , and Olympic winners are awarded a gold _____ . Those in second place are awarded a silver _____ .

metal

■ Ben's mouth, with its _____ fillings, looks like mother lode country.

medal
metal

■ I was to receive a _____ for being Most Careful Driver, but on the way I hit a _____ post.

3. **miner:** somebody who works in a mine.
4. **minor:** somebody who is below legal age; of lesser importance.

miner

■ "Gold! I found gold!" whispered the dying *min*_____ .

miner
minor

■ The old _____ sang in a _____ key about a goat.

minor
minor

■ A draftee complains, "As a _____ I can die for my country, yet as a _____ I cannot vote."

miner
minor

■ At the end of a hard day a coal _____ does not look like Snow White. However, that to him is of _____ importance.

5. **moral** (mor′əl): *Adjective*—virtuous; of good character, as in "a *moral*, law-abiding family"; virtual—"a *moral* victory." *Noun*—the lesson in a story.
6. **morale** (mər al′): *Noun*—state of mind as to confidence and enthusiasm.

morale
moral

■ After ten losses our team was low in *mor*_____ , and this tie was like a _____ victory.

moral

■ Some people are _____ only because they've never been tempted.

moral

■ A pox on any film of violence whose only _____ is "Shoot first!"

morale

■ Malaria can damage one's _____ .

morale
moral

■ High _____ is desirable, but to succeed you also need talent, skills, and _____ character.

Quiz

Write the letter that indicates the best definition.

1. (d)
2. (f)
3. (b)
4. (e)
5. (a)
6. (c)

(   ) 1. medal   a. the point of a story
(   ) 2. metal   b. one who digs for minerals
(   ) 3. miner   c. self-confidence; spirit
(   ) 4. minor   d. an award for heroism
(   ) 5. moral   e. a youth
(   ) 6. morale   f. material such as copper

---

7. **naval:** pertaining to a navy.
8. **navel:** umbilicus; "belly button."

naval

■ In 1588 England won a great *nav*_____ victory.

naval
navel

■ One sailor on the _____ vessel was stripped to the waist and scratching his _____ .

navel
navel

■ An orange that has a scar on it like a human _____ is called a _____ orange.

naval
navel

■ After a lengthy parade honoring our _____ fleet, one flagbearer complained of an enlarged _____ .

---

9. **peak:** the top of a mountain; the highest point.
10. **peek:** *Noun*—a brief glance. *Verb*—to look slyly.

peak
peek

■ Marcia climbed to the *pe*_____ and got a _____ at distant Catalina.

peek
peak

■ To _____ into Dora's mind—that was the _____ of Joe's ambition.

peek

■ When people _____ at your faults, they have 20-20 vision.

peak
peek

■ When Ingrid reached the _____ of her career, the media began to _____ into her private life.

11. **pedal:** *Noun*—a foot-operated lever. *Verb*—to work the pedals, as on a bicycle.
12. **peddle:** to go from place to place selling goods.
13. **petal:** a flower leaf.

peddle

■ Foxy Frank used to *pe* _____ phony oil stock.

petal
peddle

■ From her little mouth, which was like a rose _____ , came her reply: "Go _____ your papers!"

pedal
petal

■ "Heavy Foot" loved that gas _____ , and today I drop a flower _____ and a tear on his coffin.

pedal
peddle

■ The immigrant would _____ his bike through the Bronx and _____ fish.

peddle
pedal

■ "Don't _____ your radical ideas around here," said the sheriff; "step on the _____ and vamoose."

petal

■ Her corsage was perfect to the last _____ .

136

Quiz

Write the letter that indicates the best definition.

1. (a)
2. (e)
3. (d)
4. (g)
5. (c)
6. (f)
7. (b)

( ) 1. naval   a. concerning a navy
( ) 2. navel   b. a flower leaf
( ) 3. peak   c. a foot-operated lever
( ) 4. peek   d. highest point
( ) 5. pedal   e. "belly button"
( ) 6. peddle   f. to sell items
( ) 7. petal   g. sneak a look

---

14. **personal:** *Adjective*—private. "It's a *personal* problem."
15. **personnel** (accent on *nel*): the people employed in a business. "Miss Boe is in charge of *personnel*."

personnel
personal

■ Any business can succeed if the *per*_____ take a _____ interest in their work.

personal
personnel

■ I made a _____ application for a job at the mortuary, but the _____ manager said business was dead.

personal
personnel
personal

■ My _____ opinion is that when the head of _____ calls me a nerd, he's getting too _____ .

personnel

■ Our office _____ have gear trouble: They talk in high and think in low.

---

16. **plain:** *Adjective*—clear; common looking. *Noun*—a prairie.
17. **plane:** *Noun*—an airplane; a flat, two-dimensional surface.

plain
plane

■ We need *pla*_____ talk between nations, not a _____ loaded with bombs.

plain

■ The rain in Spain fell on the grassy _____ .

plane
plain

■ Our baby, born on a speeding _____ , looks rather _____ , but we'll keep it.

plane
plain

■ Gus studied _____ geometry, and the _____ fact is that he didn't like it.

plain
plain

■ Abraham Lincoln was a _____ man and he used _____ words.

18. **presence:** being present; personal appearance. "We are honored by your *presence*."
19. **presents:** gifts. "Kay exchanged her wedding *presents*."

presence

■ Sherlock was shy in the *pre*_____ of girls.

presents

■ Rosa was buried under a pile of birthday _____ .

presence

■ Office workers noted the _____ of the boss's sons. He was putting on heirs.

presents

■ Christmas cards now cost what Christmas _____ used to cost.

presence
presents

■ I will cherish your _____ at my party more than all birthday _____ .

Quiz

Write the letter that indicates the best definition.

1. (f)
2. (d)
3. (b)
4. (c)
5. (e)
6. (a)

( ) 1. personal   a. gifts
( ) 2. personnel   b. ordinary in looks; a prairie
( ) 3. plain   c. an airship
( ) 4. plane   d. staff of employees
( ) 5. presence   e. being there
( ) 6. presents   f. private

20. **quiet** (kwī′ət): silent; silence.
21. **quite** (kwīt): really; entirely.

quiet
quite

■ To be *qui*_____ is often _____ as important as to talk.

138

quite
quiet

■ Since Albert broke his stereo, our house is _____

_____ .

quiet

■ The baby is _____ . Go see what's the matter.

quite
quiet

■ Slim told _____ a few jokes, but we stifled our smiles and remained _____ .

---

22. **road:** a highway. "This is the *road* to Dublin."
23. **rode** (past tense of *ride*): "She *rode* a pony."

road

■ Why does a chicken cross a *ro*_____ ?

rode
road

■ The horse I _____ along the dusty _____ was a fugitive from a glue factory.

rode

■ My late Uncle Benny _____ a bronco.

road

■ If you must drive a tank down this _____ , I won't stand in your way.

road
rode

■ Down the _____ _____ Lady Godiva wearing a smile.

---

24. **role:** a part taken by an actor. (Otherwise write *roll*.)
25. **roll:** *Noun*—a small cake of bread, etc. *Verb*—to turn over and over.

roll

■ Merrily we *rol*_____ along.

role
roll

■ When Nancy played the _____ of Lady Macbeth, she ate lightly—just coffee and a _____ .

role
roll

■ Both actors wanted the _____ of Hamlet, so they decided to _____ dice for it.

role
roll

■ In this comic _____ , Mr. Ritz would _____ his eyes.

Quiz

Write the letter that indicates the best definition.

1. (c)
2. (e)
3. (a)
4. (f)
5. (d)
6. (b)

( ) 1. quiet   a. a highway
( ) 2. quite   b. to move by rotation
( ) 3. road   c. noiseless
( ) 4. rode   d. a part in a play
( ) 5. role   e. really
( ) 6. roll   f. was riding

---

26. **shone** (past tense of *shine*): "The sun *shone*."
27. **shown** is related to *show*. "I was *shown* the fish."

shone

■ The moon *sho*_____ at night, according to Abner, when we needed it most.

shown

■ She smoked too much. I was _____ her newborn baby, and it had yellow fingernails.

shone
shown

■ The pirate's eyes _____ when he was _____ the treasure chest.

shown

■ Such a doctor! Break an ankle and you'll be _____ how to limp.

shown
shone
shown

■ The customer was _____ twelve pairs of shoes, but suddenly his face _____ when he was _____ the yellow oxfords.

shone

■ The candle _____ like a good deed in a naughty world.

---

28. **stake:** a stick or post; something wagered or risked.
29. **steak:** a slice of meat or fish.

stake

■ Joan of Arc was burned at the *st*_____ .

stake

■ We have a _____ in the future of our nation.

steak

■ Grandpa ate a fat, oily _____ , and he doesn't squeak any more.

stake
stake

■ The prospector drove a _____ into the ground to _____ his claim.

steak
steak

■ I used to order a _____ rare. Now I order a _____ rarely.

stake
steak

■ "I'll _____ a dollar," muttered the waitress, "that this health nut orders the halibut _____ ."

---

30. **stationary:** not moving.
31. **stationery:** writing paper.

stationery

■ At Christmas I got six boxes of *sta*_____ .

stationery
stationary

■ Stanley buys _____ ; then he sits _____ in front of his typewriter.

stationery

■ The word "paper" has an *er* in it, and so does the word _____ .

stationary

■ Is that hydrant really _____ , or did it move out and hit my fender?

stationery
stationary

■ On official _____ Clarence confessed: "If an irresistible force hits a _____ object, I'm probably the driver."

Quiz

Write the letter that indicates the best definition.

1. (d)
2. (f)
3. (c)
4. (b)
5. (a)
6. (e)

( ) 1. shone   a. motionless
( ) 2. shown   b. a piece of meat
( ) 3. stake   c. a post or stick
( ) 4. steak   d. was shining
( ) 5. stationary   e. writing paper
( ) 6. stationery   f. exhibited; displayed

---

32. **vain**: conceited; proud; unsuccessful. "He struggled in *vain*."
33. **vein**: a blood vessel.

vain

■ A v_____ fellow should swallow his pride. It's non-fattening.

vein
vain

■ Every tiny v_____ in your hand is a miracle, according to Walt Whitman, and to deny it is _____ .

vain
vein

■ Being rather _____ , Ashley shaved twice before his date with Mary and he cut a _____ .

vain
veins

■ Julia is a colonial blue blood and _____ about it; yet the blood in your _____s is as pure as hers.

___

34. **waist**: the part of the body between the ribs and the hips; the upper part of a woman's dress.
35. **waste**: *Noun*—useless material; refuse. *Verb*—to squander. "We *waste* our opportunities."

waist

■ Sam sang: "Nut-brown maiden, thou hast a slender w_____ ."

waste

■ Hooked on drugs? What a _____ of life!

waste

■ Don't _____ these apples. You think they grow on trees?

waist
waste

■ As Jeff's arms encircled Donna's _____ , he tripped over a _____ basket.

waist

■ The tailor took Mr. Flubb's _____ measurement.

waste

■ Don't smash your watch. It's a _____ of time.

waist

■ Eating peanuts will expand your _____ . Look at elephants.

---

36. **weak:** lacking in strength; feeble.
37. **week:** a seven-day period.

week
weak

■ After a *we*_____ of fasting, I was _____ as a baby.

week

■ "God created man at the end of the _____ ," says Mark Twain, "when God was tired."

weak
week

■ The strong have oppressed the _____ , not just for a day or a _____ but for centuries.

weak

■ "Don't sneer at our coffee," said the waiter. "You, too, will be old and _____ some day."

---

38. **weather:** *Noun*—atmospheric conditions. "Stormy *weather*!" *Verb*—to wear away; to survive.
39. **whether:** if. "He'll decide *whether* to operate."

weather
whether

■ We predict the *w*_____ , but I doubt _____ we can control it.

weather

■ Fred has a thirty percent chance of becoming a _____ forecaster.

whether

■ Worries, worries! Rich people must decide _____ to drive the Rolls or the Cadillac.

weather
whether

■ You'll love Dakota's winter _____ , _____ you prefer twenty below or forty below.

whether
weather
weather

■ I doubt _____ we could _____ the rigors of Klondike _____ .

Quiz

Write the letter that indicates the best definition.

1. (c)
2. (e)
3. (g)
4. (b)
5. (h)
6. (a)
7. (f)
8. (d)

(　　)　1. vain   a. seven consecutive days

(　　)　2. vein   b. useless material

(　　)　3. waist   c. proud; conceited

(　　)　4. waste   d. if (this or that)

(　　)　5. weak   e. a blood vessel

(　　)　6. week   f. heat, rain, wind conditions

(　　)　7. weather   g. the middle of the torso

(　　)　8. whether   h. inferior in strength; infirm

REVIEW TEST

Write in full the correct word that is in the brackets.

_____ 1. The dinner was all [quite / quiet] cold except for the ice water.

_____ 2. A good nurse knows a [vain / vein] from an artery.

_____ 3. The [weather / whether] man has a sense of humidity.

_____ 4. When the [role / roll] is called up yonder, I'll be there.

_____ 5. The headlights [shone / shown] until the battery died.

_____ 6. John Steinbeck described the Oklahoma [plain / plane].

_____ 7. The office [personnel / personal] treated me like a typhoid carrier.

_____ 8. Franklin was at the [peek / peak] of his reputation.

_____ 9. Getting fired didn't help my [moral / morale].

_____ 10. Women are [shone / shown] one fur coat at a time.

_____ 11. Bronze is an alloy of copper and tin [metal / medal].

_____ 12. All day Tony kept smelling the perfumed [stationary / stationery].

_____ 13. This tavern must not sell liquor to a [miner / minor].

_____ 14. John Paul Jones won a [naval / navel] victory.

_____ 15. To eat a [steak / stake], somebody must kill a cow.

_____ 16. At the end of a [weak / week] the sweatsuit stood up by itself.

_____ 17. We hungry children didn't [waist / waste] a prune pit.

_____ 18. In Italy every [road / rode] leads to Rome.

Matching. Write the letter that indicates the best definition.

( ) 19. medal   a. standing still
( ) 20. pedal   b. personal appearance
( ) 21. vain   c. to sell articles here and there
( ) 22. presence   d. a small blood vessel
( ) 23. stationary   e. an award for achievement
( ) 24. stake   f. gifts
( ) 25. peddle   g. without success
     h. to operate a bicycle
     i. a T-bone
     j. a post or stick

Key to Review Test

Check your test answers by the following key. Deduct 4% per error from a possible 100%.

1. quite	10. shown	19. (e)
2. vein	11. metal	20. (h)
3. weather	12. stationery	21. (g)
4. roll	13. minor	22. (b)
5. shone	14. naval	23. (a)
6. plain	15. steak	24. (j)
7. personnel	16. week	25. (c)
8. peak	17. waste	
9. morale	18. road	

Score: _____%

NOTE: For a supplementary exercise on additional word pairs, see APPENDIX B, page 319.

10

Descriptive Words

1. affable	13. cadaverous	25. dubious
2. altruistic	14. candid	26. eccentric
3. ambidextrous	15. craven	27. enigmatic
4. aromatic	16. dastardly	28. erotic
5. asinine	17. deft	29. exorbitant
6. astute	18. defunct	30. feasible
7. bawdy	19. destitute	31. fluent
8. bellicose	20. diabolic	32. frugal
9. berserk	21. discreet	33. furtive
10. bizarre	22. disenchanted	34. gullible
11. buoyant	23. dogmatic	35. impeccable
12. buxom	24. droll	36. impromptu

The right descriptive word can be worth diamonds in a composition. Of course, as Mark Twain said, it must be the right word, not its second cousin. Naturally, if you know thirty ways to describe a man or a voice or a smile instead of only five ways, you have a wider selection and your chances of picking an effective word are much improved.

Chapters 10 and 11 present descriptive words which should be part of the stock in trade of any writer of themes or reader of literature. Additional adjectives appear in supplementary exercises in Appendix B of this textbook for those who wish an additional challenge.

Study carefully the definitions at the beginning of each frame. Then fill in the blanks with words defined in that frame, unless other choices are offered.

COVER THIS STRIP

1. **affable** (af′ə-bəl): easy to talk to; amiable.
2. **altruistic** (al′trōō-is′tik): unselfish; concerned for the welfare of others.

(b)

■ An *affable* professor is (a) hostile, (b) friendly. (   )

■ An *altruistic* woman is one who sacrifices to help (a) others, (b) only herself. (   )

(a)

■ We found Elmer in a friendly, talkative mood, in fact, quite *af*_____ .

affable

■ Devoted to public charities, Straus was certainly *al*_____ .

altruistic

■ In *A Tale of Two Cities*, the executioner stands grim and silent, hardly an *af*_____ fellow. Then Sydney Carton gives his life—loses his head, in fact—to save a friend. What an *al*_____ deed!

affable

altruistic

3. **ambidextrous** (am′bə-dek′strəs): able to use both hands with equal ease.
4. **aromatic** (ar′ə-mat′ik): fragrant; spicy; sweet-smelling.

(b)

■ *Aromatic* plants are (a) odorless, (b) pleasantly scented. (   )

■ A basketball player who shoots baskets with either hand is _____ [ambidextrous / paraplegic].

ambidextrous

■ Wilma bats the baseball equally well from either side of the plate because she is *am*_____ .

ambidextrous

■ Her boudoir was *ar*_____ with subtle perfumes and incense.

aromatic

aromatic
ambidextrous

■ At harvest these orchards are *ar*_____ , and the owner hires a few fast, cheap, *amb*_____ pickers.

---

5. **asinine** (as′ə-nīn′): stupid; silly; ass-like.
6. **astute** (ə-stōōt′): shrewd; keen in judgment; cunning.

■ The baseball fan's *asinine* comments made it clear that he was (a) a knucklehead, (b) a deep thinker. (   )

(a)

astute

■ Our nation needs _____ [astute / asinine] diplomats.

astute

■ Not everyone is shrewd enough to make *as*_____ investments.

asinine

■ Trusting the strange door-to-door salesman with all my savings was an *as*_____ thing to do.

astute
asinine

■ Even the most *ast*_____ student can make a mistake, but to keep repeating the same mistakes is *as*_____ .

Quiz

Write the letter that indicates the best definition.

1. (e)
2. (c)
3. (b)
4. (f)
5. (a)
6. (d)

( ) 1. affable	a. very stupid
( ) 2. altruistic	b. using both hands equally well
( ) 3. ambidextrous	c. completely unselfish
( ) 4. aromatic	d. keenly intelligent
( ) 5. asinine	e. warm and friendly
( ) 6. astute	f. sweet-scented

---

7. **bawdy** (bô′dē): indecent; obscene.
8. **bellicose** (bel′ə-kōs′): hostile; eager to fight; warlike.

■ *Bawdy* shows can be expected at (a) Sunday schools, (b) Las Vegas. (   )

(b)

bellicose

■ World tension is increased when national leaders exchange _____ [affable / bellicose] remarks.

bellicose

■ Bouncing his knuckles off my nose seemed to me a *be*_____ gesture.

bawdy

■ The minister's daughter blushed at the *ba*_____ anecdote.

bawdy
bellicose

■ When I tried to hush the drunken stranger who was singing a vulgar, *ba*_____ song in our church, he became quite *be*_____ .

---

9. **berserk** (bər-sûrk′): crazed; in a destructive frenzy.
10. **bizarre** (bi-zär′): odd in appearance; grotesque; queer. (Don't confuse with *bazaar*—a market or sale.)

bizarre

■ Halloween masks are usually _____ [bazaar / bizarre].

(a)

■ People who go *berserk* belong in (a) asylums, (b) crowded buses. (   )

berserk

■ The brand-new straitjacket looks stylish on the man who went *ber*_____ .

bizarre

■ The green wig gave my aunt a *bi*_____ appearance.

bizarre
berserk

■ The painting was so *bi*_____ that Twain thought it depicted a cat going _____ in a platter of tomatoes.

---

11. **buoyant** (boi′ənt): tending to float; light of spirit; cheerful.
12. **buxom** (buk′səm): healthily plump; full-bosomed; attractive.

(a)

■ When drowning, grab a *buoyant* material, like (a) cork, (b) a lead pipe. (   )

buxom

■ The Flemish women painted by Rubens tend to be fleshy—that is, _____ [buxom / buoyant].

buxom
buoyant

■ After a week at the health spa, Amy lost her _____m figure, and her step became _____nt.

buoyant

■ The balloonist said that hydrogen was lighter and more _____nt than helium, and that he got a bigger bang out of using it.

buxom
buoyant

■ The astronauts looked _____m in their space suits, and they floated about in _____nt weightlessness.

Quiz

Write the letter that indicates the best definition.

1. (b)
2. (d)
3. (f)
4. (e)
5. (a)
6. (c)

( ) 1. bawdy	a. tending to float; cheerful
( ) 2. bellicose	b. off-color; indecent
( ) 3. berserk	c. attractively plump
( ) 4. bizarre	d. warlike; pugnacious
( ) 5. buoyant	e. peculiar in appearance
( ) 6. buxom	f. destructively enraged

---

13. **cadaverous** (kə-dav′ər-əs): gaunt; haggard; corpse-like.
14. **candid:** frank; unprejudiced; outspoken.

(b)

■ A *cadaverous* person should probably (a) reduce, (b) put on weight. (   )

candid

■ I want the unvarnished truth, so give me a _____ [candid / candied] report.

candid

■ The editor said that my poems stank. He was quite _____d.

cadaverous

■ After forty days of fasting, Maximilian looked pale and *cad_____* .

cadaverous
candid

■ The sick hermit was so wasted and _____ that, to be can_____ , the doctor hardly knew whether to feed him or bury him.

---

15. **craven:** cowardly; timid; chicken-hearted.
16. **dastardly:** sneaky and mean; brutal.

(b)

■ It was *dastardly* of Punky Jones to (a) chase the cattle rustlers, (b) trip and rob the blind man. (   )

(a)

■ It was *craven* of me (a) to flee from the dachshund, (b) to challenge the bully. (   )

craven

■ Amid flying bullets one tends to develop a timid, even a *cr*_____ spirit.

dastardly

■ Beating his infants was *das*_____ , even if they did pour syrup on his stamp collection.

dastardly
craven

■ Who painted the captain's horse blue? Private Jubbs did the *d*_____ deed, but he was too *cr*_____ to admit it.

---

17. **deft:** skilled and neat in action; adroit; dexterous.
18. **defunct** (di-fungkt'): dead; deceased; no longer existing.

(a)

■ One must be particularly *deft* to (a) do needlework, (b) ride escalators. (   )

(a)

■ A *defunct* enterprise belongs to (a) the past, (b) the future. (   )

deft

■ I found that to play Chopin's "Minute Waltz" in less than five minutes requires quick, *d*_____ fingers.

defunct

■ Alas, poor Yorick, whose skull I hold—he is _____*ct*.

152

deft
defunct

■ To walk across this boulevard of speeding cars, you must be _____ or soon you'll be _____ .

Quiz

Write the letter that indicates the best definition.

( ) 1. cadaverous   a. dead; functioning no more
( ) 2. candid   b. frank; open and sincere
( ) 3. craven   c. skillful
( ) 4. dastardly   d. cowardly; timid
( ) 5. deft   e. mean; villainous
( ) 6. defunct   f. haggard; like a corpse

---

19. **destitute** (des'ti-tōōt'): extremely poor; lacking the necessities of life.
20. **diabolic** (dī'ə-bol'ik): devilish, fiendish.

(a)

■ His *diabolic* ambition was to destroy (a) mankind, (b) disease. ( )

(b)

■ The *destitute* have more than their share of (a) money, (b) poverty. ( )

destitute

■ Her husband died three days after his insurance lapsed, and she was left *des_____* .

diabolic

■ King Edward IV plotted to have his brother Clarence stabbed and drowned in a barrel of wine. How *dia_____* !

destitute
diabolic

■ The melodrama dealt with a penniless old couple—absolutely *des_____*—the victims of a _____ villain who foreclosed on the mortgage.

---

21. **discreet:** prudent; tactful; careful not to talk or act unwisely.
22. **disenchanted:** set free from one's rosy illusions.

disenchanted

■ Those who expected to find fat gold nuggets lying on the Yukon snowbanks were quickly _____ [vindicated / disenchanted].

(a)

■ A *discreet* roommate (a) keeps a secret, (b) blabs about confidential matters. (   )

discreet

■ This juicy story should not be publicized, fellows, so please be *dis_____* .

disenchanted

■ Those who trusted Stalin's promises were soon *dis_____* .

discreet

■ After marriage William was less *dis_____* in his drinking; and his bride, stumbling among his bottles, was

disenchanted

_____*ed*.

---

23. **dogmatic** (dog-mat′ik): asserting opinions in a dictatorial way; positive; strongly opinionated.
24. **droll** (drōl): comical; quaintly amusing.

(b)

■ A *droll* fellow at the circus is (a) the tiger, (b) the clown. (   )

(b)

■ Highly *dogmatic* conversationalists are usually (a) popular, (b) obnoxious. (   )

droll

■ The audience laughed at Will Rogers' *dr_____* remarks.

dogmatic

■ Military men often become opinionated and *dog_____* .

dogmatic
droll

■ Our landlord kept ordering us in *do_____* fashion to clean our rooms; nor did he smile at Bill's *dr_____* remark that the garbage disposal must have backfired.

Quiz

Write the letter that indicates the best definition.

1. (f)
2. (c)
3. (b)
4. (a)
5. (e)
6. (d)

(   ) 1. destitute   a. losing one's romantic beliefs
(   ) 2. diabolic   b. prudent in speech and conduct
(   ) 3. discreet   c. fiendish; outrageously wicked
(   ) 4. disenchanted   d. comical; whimsically amusing
(   ) 5. dogmatic   e. opinionated; dictatorial
(   ) 6. droll   f. needy; penniless

25. **dubious** (dōō'bi-əs): doubtful; vague; skeptical; questionable.
26. **eccentric** (ik-sen'trik): odd; peculiar; unconventional; off-center.

eccentric

■ The bearded gentleman skating around in the drugstore is thought to be rather _____ [eccentric / conventional].

dubious

■ Although madman Columbus said the world was round, his listeners could see it was flat, and so they were naturally _____ [dubious / delusive].

eccentric

■ Mrs. Doodle often takes her Flemish rabbit for a walk on a leash—another one of her *ec*_____ habits.

dubious

■ The drug addict claimed he could fly from the hotel roof, but his level-headed friends were *dub*_____ .

eccentric
dubious

■ The farmer decided that the nudists were either crazy or highly *ec*_____ ; he was *du*_____ about them.

27. **enigmatic** (en'ig-mat'ik): puzzling; perplexing; mysterious.
28. **erotic** (i-rot'ik): pertaining to sexual love; amatory.

erotic

■ "Adult movies" are usually more _____ [prudish / erotic] than "family movies."

(b)

■ We refer to Mona Lisa's smile as *enigmatic* because it is (a) dazzling, (b) puzzling. (   )

enigmatic

■ I was mystified by the *en*_____ warning.

erotic

■ The sexy passages in *Tropic of Cancer* were so *er*_____ that they gave off blue smoke.

155

erotic

enigmatic

■ If you cut all the *er*＿＿＿＿＿＿＿＿ passages from Noodle's last novel, the book would disappear. When asked why he wrote it, Noodle winked in *en*＿＿＿＿＿＿＿ fashion.

___

29. **exorbitant** (ig-zôr′bə-tənt): extravagant; excessive in price; unreasonable.
30. **feasible** (fē′zə-bəl): capable of being done; practicable; suitable.

exorbitant

■ Five dollars an egg, as paid by those early miners, would ordinarily seem ＿＿＿＿＿＿＿ [cheap / exorbitant].

not feasible

■ To build a bridge across the Pacific is at present ＿＿＿＿＿ [feasible / not feasible].

feasible

■ Your plan to feed the whole world is charitable, but is it *fea*＿＿＿＿＿＿＿ ?

exorbitant

■ "Twenty dollars to clip my dog is an *ex*＿＿＿＿＿＿＿ fee—you've clipped me, too!"

exorbitant
feasible

■ Gasoline prices rose to *ex*＿＿＿＿＿＿＿ levels, and Archy decided that riding a skateboard might be *fe*＿＿＿＿＿＿＿ .

___

Quiz

Write the letter that indicates the best definition.

1. (e)
2. (d)
3. (a)
4. (f)
5. (b)
6. (c)

(   ) 1. dubious   a. mysterious
(   ) 2. eccentric   b. too high-priced
(   ) 3. enigmatic   c. practicable; reasonable
(   ) 4. erotic   d. peculiar; having odd traits
(   ) 5. exorbitant   e. doubtful; skeptical
(   ) 6. feasible   f. having to do with sexual desire

___

31. **fluent** (flōō′ənt): able to speak or write readily; flowing smoothly.
32. **frugal** (frōō′gəl): costing little; spending little; meager; scanty.

156

(b)

■ A tongue-tied immigrant who learned English from a book will probably (a) be fluent, (b) not be fluent. ( )

(a)

■ A *frugal* meal (a) is cheap and plain, (b) contains fruit. ( )

frugal

■ On his tiny pension Mr. Snurd eked out a *fru*_____ existence.

fluent

■ To make the debate squad you should be a *fl*_____ speaker.

frugal
fluent

■ For thirty years the woman saved, suffered, lived a *fr*_____ life, for her dream was to become a lawyer and to deliver *fl*_____ speeches in court.

---

33. **furtive:** stealthy; sly; done in secret; clandestine.
34. **gullible** (gul′ə-bəl): easily cheated or tricked; credulous.

gullible

■ Brooklyn Bridge has often been sold to the _____ [gullible / sophisticated] visitor.

furtive

■ A stealthy gesture is said to be _____ [ambidextrous / furtive].

furtive

■ Mike stole a *fur*_____ glance at the blonde.

gullible

■ The con man got rich selling swampland to *gul*_____ investors.

gullible
furtive

■ Nancy believed the handsome stranger's promises, for she was innocent and *g*_____ ; and she gave his hand a *f*_____ squeeze.

---

35. **impeccable** (im-pek′ə-bəl): faultless; without sin or error.
36. **impromptu** (im-promp′tōō): done on the spur of the moment; offhand.

impeccable

■ Banks should hire employees of _____ [dubious / impeccable] honesty.

(a)

impromptu

impeccable

impromptu

impeccable

■ *Impromptu* remarks are (a) spontaneous, (b) planned in advance. ( )

■ Called on unexpectedly, Daniel Webster delivered a brilliant _____*tu* talk.

■ Our eminent minister was presumably of *imp*_____ moral character.

■ College freshmen must often write an _____*tu* theme in class; and naturally the professor feels insulted if the production is not brilliant and _____*able*.

Quiz

Write the letter that indicates the best definition.

1. (c)
2. (e)
3. (a)
4. (d)
5. (f)
6. (b)

( ) 1. fluent	a. sly; stealthy
( ) 2. frugal	b. improvised; spur of the moment
( ) 3. furtive	c. smooth flowing in speech
( ) 4. gullible	d. easily swindled
( ) 5. impeccable	e. meager and costing little
( ) 6. impromptu	f. flawless

REVIEW TEST

Write the word studied in this chapter that will complete the sentence.

_____ 1. The waiter screamed and threw soup at us. He'd gone [ber-].

_____ 2. My hungry uncle found his false teeth just as the banquet began, and his spirits were now [bu-].

_____ 3. The widow distrusted Mr. Finn because of his [du-] reputation.

_____ 4. Those who expected modern plumbing in Morocco were soon [dis-].

_____ 5. Our lease had expired. It was as [def-] as Benedict Arnold.

_____ 6. Nine dollars for a dish of prunes? Isn't that a bit [ex-]?

_____ 7. The swindler had been talkative and friendly, an [af-] fellow.

_____ 8. Discuss this untidy affair with no one. Try to be [dis-].

_____ 9. Uncle Phil was an oddball; in fact, he was downright [ec-].

_____ 10. He slipped into the vat of cologne and smelled quite [ar-].

_____ 11. Was that an [imp-] speech, or had you rehearsed it for a week?

_____ 12. Please be frank. I want your [ca-] opinion.

_____ 13. The taxi driver swore and raised his fists in [bel-] fashion.

_____ 14. She donated a kidney to save her sister. An [alt-] act!

_____ 15. Don't stammer. With self-confidence you can be smooth and [fl-].

_____ 16. The fire and flood left the old widow [des-].

_____ 17. Tripping and robbing that feeble man was a [das-] act.

_____ 18. Knute likes sexy soap operas, the more [er-] the better.

Matching. Write the letter that indicates the best definition.

( ) 19. asinine   a. capable of being done
( ) 20. deft   b. birdlike
( ) 21. bizarre   c. stupid as a donkey
( ) 22. diabolic   d. pertaining to washing canines
( ) 23. gullible   e. dextrous; skillful in action
( ) 24. dogmatic   f. a church money-raiser sale
( ) 25. feasible   g. easily fooled
                          h. opinionated
                          i. odd in appearance
                          j. devilishly wicked

Key to Review Test

Check your test answers by the following key. Deduct 4% per error from a possible 100%.

1. berserk	10. aromatic	19. (c)
2. buoyant	11. impromptu	20. (e)
3. dubious	12. candid	21. (i)
4. disenchanted	13. bellicose	22. (j)
5. defunct	14. altruistic	23. (g)
6. exorbitant	15. fluent	24. (h)
7. affable	16. destitute	25. (a)
8. discreet	17. dastardly	
9. eccentric	18. erotic	

Score: _____%

NOTE: For a supplementary exercise on descriptive words, see APPENDIX B, page 320.

11

Descriptive Words

1. indomitable
2. inept
3. innate
4. inscrutable
5. insidious
6. intrepid
7. lethal
8. lethargic
9. lucid
10. lunar
11. myopic
12. naive
13. nebulous
14. nostalgic
15. occult
16. ominous
17. opaque
18. ostentatious
19. picayune
20. prolific
21. pusillanimous
22. raucous
23. sagacious
24. sedentary
25. senile
26. sinister
27. stoical
28. succinct
29. taciturn
30. toxic
31. venerable
32. verbose
33. verdant
34. vicarious
35. vindictive
36. zealous

Chapter 11 continues our study of descriptive words. Follow the same procedure as in Chapter 10.

COVER THIS STRIP

1. **indomitable** (in-dom'i-tə-bəl): unconquerable; unyielding.
2. **inept:** clumsy; incompetent; not suitable.

(a)

■ An *indomitable* fighter (a) fights on and on, (b) quits. (   )

inept

■ A pianist wearing mittens would probably be _____
[effective / inept].

indomitable

■ Every nation speaks of its soldiers' *ind*_____
courage.

inept

■ The Dodgers made five errors in the field and were just as
_____*pt* at the plate.

indomitable
inept

■ Wanda climbed to the mountain peak, for her spirit was
_____*ble;* but I slipped off a boulder, for I was
_____*pt.*

3. **innate** (i-nāt'): inborn; natural, not acquired.
4. **inscrutable** (in-skrōō'tə-bəl): mysterious; not able to be
understood.

not innate

■ One's political beliefs are _____ [innate /
not innate].

cannot

■ When we speak of *"inscrutable* fate," we mean that we
_____ [can / cannot] easily foresee the future.

inscrutable

■ At one time no mystery melodrama was complete without
its slinking and *ins*_____ Oriental butler.

innate

■ Ducklings seem to have an *inn*_____ attraction to water.

innate
inscrutable

■ At age five Capablanca had already shown an *inn*_____ talent for chess; and his face over the tournament board was tight-lipped and *ins*_____ .

5. **insidious** (in-sid′ē-əs): treacherous; crafty; more dangerous than is apparent.
6. **intrepid** (in-trep′id): very brave; dauntless; bold.

insidious

■ Traitors who bore from within are _____ [innate / insidious].

intrepid

■ Courageous aviators are said to be _____ [intrepid / craven].

intrepid

■ Only hardy and *int*_____ men could reach the North Pole.

insidious

■ Socrates was accused of corrupting the Athenian youths with *ins*_____ doctrines.

intrepid
insidious

■ Sam danced into the lion's cage to prove how _____*id* he was, but some *ins*_____ fellow had left a banana peel on the floor.

Quiz

Write the letter that indicates the best definition.

1. (f)
2. (d)
3. (b)
4. (c)
5. (a)
6. (e)

( ) 1. indomitable   a. stealthily treacherous
( ) 2. inept   b. inborn
( ) 3. innate   c. mysterious; beyond understanding
( ) 4. inscrutable   d. awkward; clumsy
( ) 5. insidious   e. fearless; brave
( ) 6. intrepid   f. unable to be defeated

7. **lethal** (lē′thəl): causing death; deadly; fatal.
8. **lethargic** (li-thär′jik): sluggish; dull; drowsy.

chlorine

■ A *lethal* gas used in the first World War was _____ [oxygen / chlorine].

163

lethal	■ A gun, a knife, an automobile—any of these may be considered a _____*al* weapon in a court case.
lethargic	■ Basketball coaches don't want _____ [ambidextrous / lethargic] athletes.
lethargic	■ Having swallowed the pig, the snake became *leth*_____ and sleepy.
lethargic lethal	■ This heavy smog has slowed me up, and I feel _____ ; I hope the stuff is not _____*al*.

9. **lucid** (lōō′sid): clear; easily understood; mentally sound.
10. **lunar** (lōō′nər): pertaining to the moon.

(b)	■ A *lunar* eclipse blots out (a) the sun, (b) the moon. ( )
lucid	■ Technical directions ought to be _____ [enigmatic / lucid].
lunar	■ On the moon the astronauts conducted certain _____*ar* experiments.
lucid	■ Velma says her friend is crazy but that he has his _____*id* moments.
lucid lunar	■ The friendly astronomer gave us a _____*d* description of the _____*r* landscape.

11. **myopic** (mī-op′ik): nearsighted.
12. **naive** (na-ēv′): childlike; artless; lacking in worldly wisdom.

myopic	■ Nearsighted people are _____ [myopic / hyperopic].
naive	■ Anyone who thinks that concert artists don't have to practice is pretty _____ [naive / astute].

■ Elmer sat in the front row and strained to see the movie. He was quite *my*_____ .

myopic

■ College freshmen range from the very sophisticated to the very *na*_____ .

naive

■ Without his contact lenses Wilmer is very *my*_____ , and so he dived into the dry swimming pool. He will not make that *n*_____ error again.

myopic

naive

Quiz

Write the letter that indicates the best definition.

( ) 1. lethal	a. nearsighted
( ) 2. lethargic	b. slow-moving; sluggish
( ) 3. lucid	c. easy to understand; clear
( ) 4. lunar	d. childlike; unsophisticated
( ) 5. myopic	e. of the moon
( ) 6. naive	f. deadly

1. (f)
2. (b)
3. (c)
4. (e)
5. (a)
6. (d)

---

13. **nebulous** (neb′yoo-ləs): cloudy; vague; indefinite.
14. **nostalgic** (nos-tal′jik): homesick; yearning for what is past or far away.

■ *Nebulous* plans are (a) clearly detailed, (b) vague. ( )

(b)

■ A *nostalgic* line is (a) "Brevity is the soul of wit," (b) "Gone, gone, are the lovely lasses of yesteryear." ( )

(b)

■ Recalling his three happy years in the fifth grade, Grandpa became *no*_____ .

nostalgic

■ Through the Los Angeles smog we could make out the *neb*_____ outline of the city hall.

nebulous

■ Dad sings "When You and I Were Young, Maggie" and other *no*_____ songs; meanwhile his prospects for finding a job are *ne*_____ .

nostalgic
nebulous

15. **occult** (ə-kult′): beyond human understanding; mysterious.
16. **ominous** (om′ə-nəs): threatening; menacing.

■ *Occult* subjects include (a) geometry, (b) astrology. ( )

(b)

■ Telepathy and reincarnation belong to those puzzling areas known as the *oc_____* .

occult

■ An *ominous* gesture is (a) friendly, (b) threatening. ( )

(b)

■ Over the ball park hung dark and *om_____* clouds.

ominous

■ A spiritualist with *oc_____* powers evoked a baritone ghost—it made *om_____* predictions that curled our hair.

occult
ominous

17. **opaque** (ō-pāk′): not letting light through; obscure; unintelligent.
18. **ostentatious** (os′tən-tā′shəs): showy and pretentious so as to attract attention.

■ *Opaque* glass is sometimes used in (a) bathrooms, (b) automobile windshields. ( )

(a)

■ An *ostentatious* living room seems to say, (a) "I'm simple and comfortable," (b) "Look, look—see how grand and expensive I am!" ( )

(b)

■ It was a bit *ost_____* of Mrs. Schmaltz to go shopping for groceries (a) in her pink Cadillac with chauffeur, (b) on her Schwinn bicycle. ( )

ostentatious

(a)

■ Such a dolt! His mind is absolutely *op_____* .

opaque

■ My dusty glasses were practically *op_____* , yet I saw that Diamond Jim was wearing six or eight sparkling rings. Hm-m, somewhat *ost_____* , I thought.

opaque

ostentatious

Quiz

Write the letter that indicates the best definition.

Answers		
1. (f)	( ) 1. nebulous	a. sentimental about the past
2. (a)	( ) 2. nostalgic	b. supernatural; beyond under-
3. (b)	( ) 3. occult	standing
4. (c)	( ) 4. ominous	c. threatening
5. (d)	( ) 5. opaque	d. not transparent
6. (e)	( ) 6. ostentatious	e. showy to attract attention
		f. vague; misty

---

19. **picayune** (pik′ē-yōōn′): petty; trivial; contemptible.
20. **prolific** (prō-lif′ik): fruitful; fecund; producing many works.

■ Agatha Christie, who wrote mystery novels by the dozen, was obviously very _____ [phlegmatic / prolific].

prolific

■ Charging extra for toothpicks in a restaurant is pretty _____ [picayune / petulant].

picayune

■ Rats multiply fast. They are *pr*_____ .

prolific

■ The holdup netted sixty cents, or some such *pi*_____ amount.

picayune

■ Your fat batch of poems proves that you are *pr*_____ , and my criticism of the spelling in your inspired poetry will seem *p*_____ .

prolific

picayune

---

21. **pusillanimous** (pū′sə-lan′ə-məs): cowardly; fainthearted.
22. **raucous** (rô′kəs): rough-sounding; hoarse; boisterous.

■ The foghorn that awakened me was merely the sergeant's _____ [pusillanimous / raucous] voice.

raucous

■ On the battlefield the braggart Falstaff was actually timid— in fact, (a) pusillanimous, (b) raucous. ( )

(a)

pusillanimous

■ Pancho is shy. He wants to marry Rosa but he is too *pus*_____ to pop the question.

raucous

■ One distrusts car salesmen who are pushy and *ra*_____ .

raucous
pusillanimous

■ A bumblebee chased me out of the park, and I heard *r*_____ laughter from those who thought me *pu*_____ .

---

23. **sagacious** (sə-gā′shəs): shrewd; sound in judgment.
24. **sedentary** (sed′ən-ter′i): involving sitting; physically inactive.

(a)

■ A *sagacious* decision is (a) wise, (b) stupid. (   )

(a)

■ *Sedentary* work is done by (a) bookkeepers, (b) bricklayers. (   )

sagacious

■ Advertising your umbrellas for sale just before the rainy weekend was *sag*_____ .

sedentary

■ The cowboy did not want office work or any other *sed*_____ job.

sagacious
sedentary

■ Old folks are not necessarily *sag*_____ ; some are just *sed*_____ . Some are wise and some otherwise.

Quiz

Write the letter that indicates the best definition.

1. (c)
2. (a)
3. (f)
4. (e)
5. (b)
6. (d)

(   ) 1. picayune   a. producing in abundance
(   ) 2. prolific   b. having sound judgment
(   ) 3. pusillanimous   c. petty; trivial
(   ) 4. raucous   d. involving sitting
(   ) 5. sagacious   e. harsh; rough-sounding
(   ) 6. sedentary   f. timid; cowardly

25. **senile** (sē′nīl): aged and infirm; showing the mental and bodily weaknesses of old age.
26. **sinister** (sin′is-tər): hinting of imminent danger; threatening harm.

■ *Senile* people are often cared for in a home for (a) the aged, (b) wayward girls. (   )

(a)

■ The day our old neighbor wandered away from home in his nightgown we felt he was getting *sen_____* .

senile

■ If you were confronted by *sinister* strangers, you would probably be (a) amused, (b) worried. (   )

(b)

■ The conspirators hatched a *si_____* plot.

sinister

senile
sinister

■ The druggist, who was old and *se_____* , saw nothing *si_____* in Beulah's purchase of a quart of arsenic.

27. **stoical** (stō′i-kəl): indifferent to pain or pleasure.
28. **succinct** (sək-singkt′): concise; terse; brief and meaningful.

succinct

■ Cablegrams at three dollars a word should be _____ [succinct / redundant].

succinct

■ Wordiness is boring, so be *suc_____* .

(a)

■ Even during childbirth she was *stoical:* she was (a) calm and uncomplaining, (b) screaming her head off. (   )

stoical

■ The captured warrior endured the ritual of torture with *st_____* calm.

stoical
succinct

■ Mr. Koltz sat quiet and *st_____* during most of Buster's birthday party, but finally he made a *su_____* announcement: "Shut up!"

29. **taciturn** (tas′i-tûrn′): not inclined to talk; uncommunicative.
30. **toxic** (tok′sik): poisonous.

(a)

■ *Taciturn* people tend to (a) be silent, (b) talk your arm off. (   )

toxic

■ Pesticides are usually _____ [toxic / nutritious].

toxic

■ Wilbur said he wasn't afraid of to_____ fumes. We bury him on Tuesday.

taciturn

■ Chess players are inclined to be reflective and ta_____ .

toxic

■ "I filled my tires with smoggy, to_____ New Jersey air," I explained, "and they died." Replied the

taciturn

ta_____ Vermont mechanic: "Hm-m-mp."

Quiz

Write the letter that indicates the best definition.

1. (e)
2. (d)
3. (f)
4. (a)
5. (c)
6. (b)

(   ) 1. senile   a. concise; brief
(   ) 2. sinister   b. poisonous
(   ) 3. stoical   c. not talkative
(   ) 4. succinct   d. ominous; threatening
(   ) 5. taciturn   e. old and feeble
(   ) 6. toxic   f. showing no emotions

31. **venerable** (ven′ər-ə-bəl): aged and worthy of reverence.
32. **verbose** (vər-bōs′): wordy; long-winded.

venerable

■ Ulysses was a wise and _____ [venerable / venereal] warrior.

(b)

■ *Verbose* statements contain too many (a) ideas, (b) words. (   )

verbose

■ Trim your theme; it is *ver*_____ .

venerable

■ We gazed at the *ven*_____ statue of Abraham Lincoln.

venerable
verbose

■ Every evening my white-haired and *ven*_____ military friend gave me a _____*ose* account of how he won the war.

---

33. **verdant** (vûr′dənt): green; covered with grass; unsophisticated.
34. **vicarious** (vī-kâr′i-əs): participating by imagination in another's experience.

(a)

■ *Verdant* fields are (a) grassy, (b) covered with boulders. (   )

vicarious

■ By identifying yourself with your movie hero you have _____ [venerable / vicarious] pleasure.

verdant

■ William Wordsworth trod these *ver*_____ meadows.

vicarious

■ From the adventures of D'Artagnan, Jane Eyre, and Martin Arrowsmith we derive a *vi*_____ thrill.

verdant
vicarious

■ Novels take us from foamy seas to *ver*_____ hills; they let us live a thousand *vi*_____ lives.

---

35. **vindictive** (vin-dic′tiv): revengeful; spiteful.
36. **zealous** (zel′əs): ardently devoted to a cause; enthusiastic.

vindictive

■ To spite me, Emil bored a hole in my rowboat. It was a _____ [vindictive / venerable] act.

vindictive

■ One who burns your garage in order to get even with you has a *vin*_____ nature.

(b)

■ A *zealous* reader reads with (a) reluctance, (b) enthusiasm. (   )

zealous

■ A town orchestra or museum often exists because of a few *ze*_____ supporters.

zealous

vindictive

■ My roommate, a *ze*———————— musician, played his violin all night until a *vi*———————— neighbor threw a can of beans through our window.

_____

Quiz

Write the letter that indicates the best definition.

1. (e)
2. (d)
3. (b)
4. (f)
5. (a)
6. (c)

(   ) 1. venerable

(   ) 2. verbose

(   ) 3. verdant

(   ) 4. vicarious

(   ) 5. vindictive

(   ) 6. zealous

a. inclined to revenge; spiteful

b. green with vegetation

c. fervent; ardently active

d. wordy; talkative

e. commanding respect because of age

f. sharing the feelings of others

REVIEW TEST

Write the word studied in this chapter that will complete the sentence.

_____ 1. Last night Moe kissed Flo during the [lu-] eclipse.

_____ 2. I buy two-trouser suits because of my [sed-] occupation.

_____ 3. The astronauts reached the moon. What an [int-p-] crew!

_____ 4. The condemned man showed no emotion. He was [sto-].

_____ 5. The coal miner dreamed of trees and [ver-] meadows.

_____ 6. I'm losing my shingles. I'm old, feeble, and [sen-].

_____ 7. Cables are expensive. Keep the message [suc-].

_____ 8. Hold the book closer. I'm [my-].

_____ 9. The storm clouds looked black and [om-].

_____ 10. Thirty errors! Our ball team was incredibly [in-p-].

_____ 11. What a wise choice! You are quite [sag-].

_____ 12. Five pages for a simple message? Joe is too [v-b-s-].

_____ 13. Astrologers are steeped in supernaturalism and the [occ-].

_____ 14. The bloody fight was for a jellybean or other [pic-] item.

_____ 15. Her mink coat and flashy jewelry are a bit [ost-].

_____ 16. Junior thinks babies grow under rocks. How [n-v-]!

_____ 17. Schubert wrote hundreds of songs. He was [pro-].

_____ 18. The old man wallowed in sweet [nost-] memories of college.

Matching. Write the letter that indicates the best definition.

( ) 19. lethal
( ) 20. lucid
( ) 21. pusillanimous
( ) 22. raucous
( ) 23. sinister
( ) 24. venerable
( ) 25. zealous

a. an unmarried woman
b. stony; mountainous
c. deadly
d. harsh-sounding
e. like a smelly animal
f. enthusiastic; dedicated to a cause
g. cowardly
h. easy to understand; clear
i. old and highly respected
j. threatening danger

Key to Review Test

Check your test answers by the following key. Deduct 4% per error from a possible 100%.

1. lunar	10. inept	19. (c)
2. sedentary	11. sagacious	20. (h)
3. intrepid	12. verbose	21. (g)
4. stoical	13. occult	22. (d)
5. verdant	14. picayune	23. (j)
6. senile	15. ostentatious	24. (i)
7. succinct	16. naive	25. (f)
8. myopic	17. prolific	
9. ominous	18. nostalgic	

Score: _____%

NOTE: For a supplementary exercise on descriptive words, see APPENDIX B, page 321.

12

Action Words

1. abscond	13. disconcert	25. orient
2. acquit	14. disparage	26. ostracize
3. adulterate	15. disseminate	27. pander
4. alienate	16. elucidate	28. procrastinate
5. blaspheme	17. expurgate	29. prognosticate
6. bungle	18. extradite	30. rant
7. canonize	19. haggle	31. raze
8. canvass	20. heckle	32. recant
9. cauterize	21. immobilize	33. simulate
10. condone	22. impeach	34. slander
11. decimate	23. intimidate	35. smirk
12. deify	24. laud	36. supersede

The verb is the beating heart of the sentence. A strong, meaningful verb often lets you cut out prepositional phrases that clutter and suffocate a sentence. One student writes, "The temperatures were now at a much lower level than during the previous period." Another writes, "The temperatures plunged." The good writer gets considerable mileage from vigorous, well-selected action words (verbs).

Chapter 12 focuses on action words. Additional action words appear in supplementary exercises in Appendix B of this textbook and in the Instructor's Manual, to be assigned in accordance with your abilities.

The drill technique is the same as in Chapters 10 and 11. Study carefully the words and definitions at the top of each frame, then fill in the blanks without looking back unless necessary.

COVER THIS STRIP

1. **abscond** (ab-skond′): to depart hastily and secretly, especially to escape the law.
2. **acquit** (ə-kwit′): to declare innocent; to absolve.

■ If *acquitted* of a crime you are legally (a) guilty, (b) innocent. (   )

(b)

■ The prisoner was so pretty that the Yukon jury voted unanimously to ac_____ her.

acquit

■ A company clerk known as Honest Jim has _____ [absconded / abdicated] with our money.

absconded

■ Our bank teller, who was five feet tall and ten thousand dollars short, has _____ed.

absconded

■ Although the treasurer did ab_____ one night with the union funds, his lawyer managed later to get him _____ed.

abscond

acquitted

3. **adulterate** (ə-dul′tə-rāt′): to cheapen by adding inferior ingredients; to corrupt.
4. **alienate** (āl′yə-nāt′): to make unfriendly; to estrange.

■ Adding sawdust to sausage meat _____ [fortifies / adulterates] it.

adulterates

■ Insulting your friends in public is usually a good way to _____ [alienate / captivate] them.

alienate

■ If Linus flirts with everybody, he'll soon al_____ his girl friend.

alienate

■ Chemical additives often ad_____ our food.

adulterate

adulterate
alienate

■ Many bakeries add generous amounts of artificial preservative to their bread and thus *ad*_____ it; such practices *al*_____ health-minded customers.

5. **blaspheme** (blas-fēm'): to speak profanely of God or sacred things; to curse.
6. **bungle**: to botch; to perform clumsily.

bungled

■ If her surgeon had been sober, he would not have _____ [bungled / misfired] that operation.

(a)

■ Those who *blaspheme* are (a) cursing, (b) praying. (   )

blaspheme

■ The priest shuddered to hear the atheist *bl*_____ near the cathedral.

bungle

■ If you *bu*_____ your baking, the upside-down cake may come out rightside-up.

bungle
blaspheme

■ Although the clumsy carpenter had to cut only one board, he managed to *b*_____ the job; then he began to *bl*_____ .

Quiz

Write the letter that indicates the best definition.

1. (b)
2. (e)
3. (a)
4. (f)
5. (d)
6. (c)

( ) 1. abscond	a. to add inferior ingredients
( ) 2. acquit	b. to flee from the law
( ) 3. adulterate	c. to do imperfectly
( ) 4. alienate	d. to use profanity
( ) 5. blaspheme	e. to declare not guilty
( ) 6. bungle	f. to make hostile

7. **canonize** (kan'ə-nīz'): to declare a dead person to be a saint.
8. **canvass** (kan'vəs): to go through a district asking for votes, opinions, or orders.

canvass

■ We'll get Dooley elected even if we have to _____ [canvas / canvass] the whole town.

■ The Catholic Church has *canonized* (a) Columbus, (b) Saint Joan of Arc. (   )

canonize

■ Live like a saint and maybe the church will *can_____* you.

canvass

■ "To sell tickets for—pardon the expression—*Gotterdam-merung*," said Silas, "we had to *can_____* the county."

canvass
canonize

■ When Bobo hit that grand slam home run, he became an instant saint; you didn't have to _____*ss* the crowd to know they would practically _____*ze* him.

---

9. **cauterize** (ko'tə-rīz'): to sear with a hot iron, as to cure wounds.
10. **condone** (kən-dōn'): to pardon or overlook a fault.

(a)

■ Infected wounds can be *cauterized* by (a) burning, (b) ice cubes. (   )

condone

■ When a father shrugs off his son's vandalism, he is said to _____ [condone / canonize] it.

cauterize

■ A white-hot needle was used to *cau_____* the ugly scratch.

condone

■ Though Gauguin was an inspired artist, many cannot *con_____* his desertion of his family.

cauterize
condoned

■ The army surgeon's failure to *c_____* Fenwick's bullet wound cannot be _____*ed*.

---

11. **decimate** (des'ə-māt'): to kill many of.
12. **deify** (dē'ə-fī'): to make a god of; to exalt and idealize.

deify

■ We tend to _____ [decimate / deify] our top athletes.

deify

■ A heavyweight champion is not a god, and we should not d_____ him.

decimate

■ With the hydrogen bomb any two nations can _____ [decimate / deify] each other more efficiently.

decimate

■ We gave the South Sea natives the benefits of our modern "syphilization," and managed to dec_____ them.

deify

■ It was the habit of the ancient Greeks to de_____ the sun, the moon, and the winds; it was also their habit to

decimate

dec_____ their enemies.

Quiz

Write the letter that indicates the best definition.

1. (d)
2. (b)
3. (e)
4. (a)
5. (c)
6. (f)

( ) 1. canonize   a. to shrug off a fault
( ) 2. canvass   b. to check opinions of an area
( ) 3. cauterize   c. to slay large numbers
( ) 4. condone   d. to raise to sainthood
( ) 5. decimate   e. to sear a wound
( ) 6. deify   f. to treat as a god

13. **disconcert** (dis′kən-sûrt′): to embarrass; to confuse; to upset.
14. **disparage** (dis-par′ij): to belittle; to speak of with contempt.

disparage

■ To belittle an effort is to _____ [condone / disparage] it.

disconcert

■ Jeering at a speaker tends to _____ [deify / disconcert] him.

disconcert

■ Finding half a worm in my apple was enough to dis_____ me.

disparage

■ Don't dis_____ the restaurant coffee; you, too, may be old and weak some day.

disparage
disconcert

■ The clarinet duet sounded like cats fighting, but let's not _____*ge* it or we may _____*ert* the young artists.

---

15. **disseminate** (di-sem′ə-nāt′): to scatter everywhere; to spread, as if sowing.
16. **elucidate** (i-lōō′si-dāt′): to make clear; to explain.

■ To *elucidate* a literary passage is (a) to disparage it, (b) to clarify its meaning. (   )

(b)

■ To *disseminate* propaganda is (a) to stifle it, (b) to spread it. (   )

(b)

elucidate

■ This poem sounds like jabberwocky. Please *el*_____ it, Sheldon.

disseminate

■ A helicopter was used to drop and *dis*_____ circulars advertising Anti-Litter Week.

disseminate

■ The Internal Revenue Service loved to *dis*_____ among common citizens a tax form that only a genius could

elucidate

*el*_____ .

---

17. **expurgate** (ek′spər-gāt′): to remove obscene or objectionable matter; to purge.
18. **extradite** (ek′strə-dīt′): to return a fugitive to another state or nation.

■ The PTA members *expurgated* our class play. In other words, they (a) cleaned it up, (b) added a few dirty words. (   )

(a)

■ France promised to *extradite* Killer McGee. This means he will be (a) executed there, (b) shipped back to us. (   )

(b)

extradite

■ Argentina was requested by Israel to *ex*_____ a Nazi war criminal.

expurgate

■ Censors used a blue pencil to *ex*_____ the naughty lines.

extradite
expurgate

■ Some countries refuse to *ex*_____ political refugees; some show Hollywood films but will *ex*_____ the kissing scenes.

Quiz

Write the letter that indicates the best definition.

1. (f)
2. (c)
3. (b)
4. (d)
5. (e)
6. (a)

( ) 1. disconcert   a. to return a fugitive across borders
( ) 2. disparage   b. to spread everywhere
( ) 3. disseminate   c. to speak slightingly of
( ) 4. elucidate   d. to clarify
( ) 5. expurgate   e. to eliminate objectionable passages
( ) 6. extradite   f. to embarrass

---

19. **haggle:** to argue in petty fashion about terms and prices.
20. **heckle:** to harass with questions and sarcastic remarks.

(b)

■ Those who *haggle* at a garage sale are probably discussing (a) politics, (b) prices. ( )

(a)

■ To *heckle* the chairman is to shower him with words of (a) sarcasm, (b) praise. ( )

haggle

■ Natives in the marketplace would sometimes *hag*_____ ten minutes over the price of a fish.

heckle

■ Spectators in Hyde Park who disagree with any speakers will mercilessly *hec*_____ them.

heckle
haggle

■ The crowd began to *h*_____ the orator; meanwhile, the peddler and the hippie continued to *h*_____ for the overripe cantaloupe.

181

21. **immobilize** (i-mō′bə-līz′): to make unable to move; to fix in place.
22. **impeach:** to accuse an official of wrongdoing.

■ President Andrew Johnson was *impeached;* this means that he was (a) guilty, (b) accused. (   )

■ If the governor has misused the funds, we should *imp*_____ him.

■ To *immobilize* a broken leg is (a) to exercise it, (b) to keep it from moving. (   )

■ The policeman pulled Nick's arms back so as to *imm*_____ him.

■ One columnist predicts that we will *imp*_____ Senator Swindle, convict him, and send him to a prison cell to *imm*_____ him.

---

23. **intimidate** (in-tim′i-dāt′): to make timid; to control action by inducing fear.
24. **laud** (lôd): to praise.

■ Bugsy's scowl and brass knuckles were enough to _____ [intimate / intimidate] me.

■ If the critics *laud* your performance, they are (a) praising it, (b) knocking it. (   )

■ Some artists have to die before anyone will *l*_____ them for their accomplishments.

■ Drive a compact car in heavy traffic and the huge trucks will *int*_____ you.

■ Belinda saved the hikers' lives, and our newspapers all *l*_____ her bravery. She did not let the grizzly bears *int*_____ her.

(marginal answers)

(b)

impeach

(b)

immobilize

impeach

immobilize

intimidate

(a)

laud

intimidate

laud
intimidate

Write the letter that indicates the best definition.

1. (a)
2. (c)
3. (f)
4. (e)
5. (b)
6. (d)

(   ) 1. haggle   a. to quibble about prices
(   ) 2. heckle   b. to control by fear
(   ) 3. immobilize   c. to annoy with sarcastic remarks
(   ) 4. impeach   d. to heap praises on
(   ) 5. intimidate   e. to accuse of misconduct
(   ) 6. laud   f. to eliminate movement

---

25. **orient** (ôr′ē-ənt): to adjust to a situation.
26. **ostracize** (os′trə-sīz′): to exclude from society; to banish.

■ When a person is shunned by others, he is said to be _____ [extradited / ostracized].

ostracized

■ In your first days of work at the stock exchange, you will try to _____ [alienate / orient] yourself.

orient

■ The new clerk at the department store didn't know a lace curtain from a lace panty. He was not yet _____*ed*.

oriented

■ Jasper was a sneak and a tattletale, so his fellow workers began to *os*_____ him.

ostracize

■ Every year this college must *or*_____ a new class of freshmen and must hope that each newcomer will be accepted, not _____*ed*, by campus groups.

orient

ostracized

---

27. **pander:** to help satisfy the base desires of others.
28. **procrastinate** (prō-kras′tə-nāt′): to delay, to postpone action.

■ Dope pushers, bootleggers, and prostitutes _____ [pander / don't pander] to the vices of others.

pander

■ No lust or desire is so low but that someone will *pa*_____ to it.

pander

■ Elmer *procrastinates*, repeating, (a) "Let's do it now," (b) "Let's wait." (   )

(b)

procrastinate

■ Huge term reports are due soon, so don't *pro*_____ .

procrastinate

pander

■ Our town drunkard gets up early; he does not *pr*_____ . By nine a.m. he has found a bartender to *pa*_____ to his thirst.

29. **prognosticate** (prog-nos'tə-kāt'): to predict; to foretell.
30. **rant:** to speak wildly; to rave.

(a)

■ Every day the newspaper *prognosticates* (a) the weather, (b) accidents and crimes. (   )

(b)

■ To *rant* is to speak (a) logically, (b) loudly and wildly. (   )

rant

■ Julius mounted the soapbox and began to fling his arms around and *ra*_____ .

prognosticate

■ Madame Zaza used a crystal ball to *pro*_____ the misfortunes ahead.

rant

prognosticate

■ Professor Schluck would glare at us and *r*_____ about our lack of discipline; then he would *pro*_____ our final reward—on the gallows.

Quiz

Write the letter that indicates the best definition.

1. (c)
2. (f)
3. (a)
4. (b)
5. (e)
6. (d)

(   ) 1. orient   a. to serve the low desires of others

(   ) 2. ostracize   b. to put off taking action

(   ) 3. pander   c. to adjust to surroundings

(   ) 4. procrastinate   d. to talk wildly and noisily

(   ) 5. prognosticate   e. to predict future events

(   ) 6. rant   f. to shut out from society

31. **raze** (rāz): to tear to the ground; to demolish.
32. **recant** (ri-kant'): to renounce formally one's previous statements.

■ To *recant* is (a) to add overwhelming evidence, (b) to take back one's words. ( )

(b)

■ To improve our city we should first _____ [raise / raze] more condemned tenements.

raze

■ Galileo asserted that the earth revolved around the sun, but he was forced by the church to re_____ .

recant

■ Let's *ra*_____ the old barn, Hiram, and build a new-fangled garage.

raze

■ Mayor Gronk promised to *ra*_____ all unsafe buildings, but when his own hotel was condemned, he decided to *re*_____ .

raze

recant

---

33. **simulate** (sim′yoo-lāt′): to pretend; to imitate; to counterfeit.
34. **slander:** to utter falsehoods injuring someone's reputation.

■ "Real simulated pearls," recently advertised for $15.95, are (a) genuine pearls, (b) imitations. ( )

(b)

■ Death and agony, says Emily Dickinson, are genuine and not easy to *sim*_____ .

simulate

■ To print damaging lies about somebody is to libel; to speak such lies is to *sla*_____ .

slander

■ Call the tax assessor a "bribe-happy reptile" and he'll sue you for *sl*_____ .

slander

■ Thomas Paine had many enemies, and when he died a few tried to *sim*_____ grief and others continued to *sl*_____ him.

simulate
slander

35. **smirk:** to smile in a conceited or affected manner.
36. **supersede** (sōō'pər-sēd'): to take the place of; to replace; to supplant.

■ As a news reporter you would be insulting the guest of honor if you wrote that he (a) smiled, (b) smirked. (   )

(b)

■ If Plan X *supersedes* Plan W, then (a) both plans are in effect, (b) only Plan X is in effect. (   )

(b)

■ Yesterday's orders are void because today's orders *sup*_____ them.

supersede

■ Posing for the camera, most tourists will stand in front of a museum and *sm*_____ .

smirk

■ When Dora told Moose, the big fullback, that he was going to *su*_____ everybody else in her affections, he could only scratch his ear and *sm*_____ .

supersede
smirk

Quiz

Write the letter that indicates the best definition.

1. (b)
2. (c)
3. (d)
4. (f)
5. (e)
6. (a)

(   ) 1. raze   a. to take the place of
(   ) 2. recant   b. to tear down
(   ) 3. simulate   c. to take back what was said
(   ) 4. slander   d. to imitate
(   ) 5. smirk   e. to smile in a silly way
(   ) 6. supersede   f. to utter defamatory remarks

REVIEW TEST

Write the word studied in this chapter that will complete the sentence.

_____ 1. Heat the iron! We must [ca-t-z-] the wound.

_____ 2. This passage in Homer is Greek to me. Please [el-d-t-].

_____ 3. Adding chicory will merely [ad-lt-] this pure coffee.

_____ 4. Calling him a dirty thief is [sl-d-].

_____ 5. My term paper is due. Oh, why did I [pr-c-t-]?

_____ 6. Our governor is corrupt. We must [imp-] him.

_____ 7. We ignore the live artist. He dies and we [l-d] his works.

_____ 8. In Morocco one is expected to [h-gl-] over rug prices.

_____ 9. I want a candid camera shot. Please don't [sm-k].

_____ 10. Sally sprayed the ants and managed to [dec-] them.

_____ 11. He'd become St. Buster if the church would [can-] him.

_____ 12. Your leg is broken. We'll use splints to [im-b-z-] it.

_____ 13. Praise your spouse in public. Never [dis-ge] her.

_____ 14. What a mimic! She can [sim-t-] the sound of a dog-cat fight.

_____ 15. "Trigger" Sloan is a killer. Why did the jury [a-q-t] him?

_____ 16. Ohio wants the fugitive and has asked Utah to [ex-d-] him.

_____ 17. At a new school you need a week to [or-t] yourself.

_____ 18. Never have so many economists tried to [prog-] future economic trends. We need an excess prophets' tax.

Matching. Write the letter that indicates the best definition.

( ) 19. blaspheme
( ) 20. canvass
( ) 21. condone
( ) 22. heckle
( ) 23. ostracize
( ) 24. pander
( ) 25. rant

a. to taunt and annoy a speaker
b. to put up a tent
c. to meditate
d. to excuse a fault
e. to satisfy vulgar desires of others
f. to swear profanely
g. to lease to a tenant
h. to check district opinions
i. to shun socially
j. to speak wildly

Key to Review Test

Check your test answers by the following key. Deduct 4% per error from a possible 100%.

1. cauterize	10. decimate	19. (f)
2. elucidate	11. canonize	20. (h)
3. adulterate	12. immobilize	21. (d)
4. slander	13. disparage	22. (a)
5. procrastinate	14. simulate	23. (i)
6. impeach	15. acquit	24. (e)
7. laud	16. extradite	25. (j)
8. haggle	17. orient	
9. smirk	18. prognosticate	

Score: _____%

NOTE: For a supplementary exercise on additional action words, see APPENDIX B, page 323.

PART TWO

13

Rhetoric

When you write English, you are like a G.I. crawling through a mined field. You have to recognize and avoid the traps and snares—clichés, redundancy, plagiarism, logical fallacies. You have to know and use the helpful devices, too—concreteness, analogy, parallelism, ellipsis, idioms. As a resourceful writer you study your craft to survive.

Chapter 13 defines terms that deal with writing. Most frames present two definitions and the usual choices and completions. As in previous chapters, choose the right words to fill the blanks. But you can do more than learn word meanings. You can, perhaps—without damage to your creativity—apply some concepts behind these terms to your own writing.

1. **rhetoric** (ret′ə-rik): the art of using words persuasively and effectively in writing and speaking. *Rhetoric* involves grammar, logic, style, figures of speech, and so forth.
2. **redundancy** (ri-dun′dən-sē′): wordiness; needless repetition; tautology; for example, "visible to the eye," "each and everyone," "7:00 p.m. in the evening," "Jewish rabbi."

rhetoric

■ The art of composition is called _____ [rhetoric / redundancy].

redundancy

■ Padded phrases like "red in color" are examples of *red_____* .

redundancy
rhetoric

■ The phrase "necessary essentials" also illustrates *red_____* and is poor *rh_____* .

(a)

■ Mere *rhetoric* without sound ideas usually results in (a) empty eloquence, (b) a literary masterpiece. (   )

redundancy

■ Terms like *tautology, pleonasm, verbiage, verbosity, circumlocution, diffuseness, periphrasis,* and *prolixity* refer to various aspects of wordiness, or *re_____* .

rhetoric

■ The master of effective writing, or *rh_____* , avoids *redundant* phrases such as (a) "a hot pastrami sandwich,"

(b)

(b) "edible food to eat." (   )

3. **malapropism** (mal′ə-prop-iz′əm): ridiculous misuse of a word for another one that sounds like it. Mrs. *Malaprop* in Richard Sheridan's play *The Rivals* (1775) spoke of "an allegory [instead of alligator] on the banks of the Nile."

malapropism

■ The misuse of a word for another one that sounds like it, as in "they won the world serious," is a *mal_____* .

■ Which of these two blunders involves a *malapropism?*
(a) "Us boys went," (b) "a lecher course in history." (   )

(b)

■ "Every morning my mother exercises her abominable muscles"—this sentence contains a *mal_____* .

malapropism

■ Cross out each ridiculous misuse, known as a
m_____ , and write the correct word above it:

malapropism

Thomas Edison invented the indecent lamp.

incandescent

The wise men brought gifts of myrrh and frankfurters.

frankincense

Our government put the Indians into reservoirs.

reservations

The government of England is a limited mockery.

monarchy

The equator is a menagerie lion that runs around the middle
of the earth.

an imaginary
line

---

4. **euphemism** (yōō′fə-miz′əm): a mild expression substituted
   for a distasteful one, for example, "a morals charge" for "rape,"
   "resting place" for "grave," "stylishly stout" for "fat."
5. **cliché** (klē-shā′): a trite phrase; a stale expression, for example, "sigh of relief," "sadder but wiser," "fair sex," "reigned
   supreme," "bouncing baby boy."

■ A mild, indirect expression to avoid a blunt, painful one is a
euph_____ .

euphemism

■ A phrase like "a lung condition" for "lung cancer" is a
eu_____ .

euphemism

■ A trite phrase like "last but not least" or "without further
ado" is a *cl_____* .

cliché

■ Such *clichés* as "nipped in the bud" should be (a) nipped,
(b) used often in themes. (   )

(a)

euphemism

■ A substitute expression like "by gosh" for "by God" or "comfort station" for "toilet" is a *eu*_____ .

stale
cliché

■ A phrase like "doomed to disappointment" or "conspicuous by his absence" is _____ [fresh / stale]; therefore it is called a *cl*_____ .

euphemism
cliché

■ An expression like "passed away" or "went to his reward" is a mild substitute for "died," and trite, too; therefore, it is both a *e*_____ and a *c*_____ .

Quiz

Write the letter that indicates the best definition.

1. (e)
2. (a)
3. (d)
4. (b)
5. (c)

(   ) 1. rhetoric   a. tautology; wordiness

(   ) 2. redundancy   b. a mild substitute expression

(   ) 3. malapropism   c. a much-overused phrase

(   ) 4. euphemism   d. a ridiculous word blunder

(   ) 5. cliché   e. art of effective communication

---

6. **acronym** (ak′rə-nim): a word made up from the initial letters or syllables of a title or phrase, for example, "CARE," "ASCAP," and "snafu."

acronym

■ A word like "WAC," made up from the initials of "Women's Army Corps," is an *ac*_____ .

initial
acronym

■ The word "AWOL" is made up basically from the _____ [initial / final] letters of "absent without leave" and is therefore called an *ac*_____ .

■ Write the *acronym* for each of the following titles or phrases:

UFO

_____ unidentified flying object

radar

_____ radio detecting and ranging

GASP

_____ Group Against Smoking Pollution

NATO

_____ North Atlantic Treaty Organization

7. **antonym** (an′tə-nim): a word of opposite meaning; for example, "tall" and "short," "fast" and "slow," "smart" and "stupid" are pairs of *antonyms*.

8. **homonym** (hom′ə-nim): a word that sounds like another word but has a different meaning and usually a different spelling; for example, "air" and "heir," "past" and "passed," "site" and "cite" are *homonyms*.

homonyms

■ Pairs of words like "principle" and "principal," "block" and "bloc," are called *hom*_____ .

antonyms

■ Pairs of words like "beautiful" and "ugly," "rich" and "poor," are called *ant*_____ .

antonyms
homonyms

■ "Dear" and "hateful" are *an*_____ ; "dear" and "deer" are *ho*_____ .

homonyms
antonyms

■ "Bare" and "bear" are *h*_____ ; "bare" and "clothed" are _____ .

---

9. **concreteness:** quality of being specific and of referring to particular things. *Concreteness* adds clarity and power to writing.

10. **connotation:** the suggestiveness and emotional associations of a word, apart from its denotation, or literal meaning. Propagandists often use words that seem honest but which, by their *connotations*, arouse prejudice.

concreteness

■ Clarity of detail is called *conc*_____ .

(b)

■ Choose the *concrete* phrase: (a) "some young fellow," (b) "a shambling newsboy." (   )

(b)

■ Choose the *concrete* phrase: (a) "an interesting animal," (b) "a blue-bottomed ape." (   )

connotation

■ The feeling that surrounds a word is its *conn*_____ .

steadfast
staunch
unflinching

■ Underline three words with favorable *connotations* to describe an ancestor who absolutely refused to change his opinions about anything: obstinate, pig-headed, steadfast, hidebound, bigoted, staunch, unflinching.

■ Which news headline has unfavorable *connotations*? (a) "Mayor and Wife Invite Friends to Housewarming," (b) "Facts Bared About Mayor's New Love-Nest." (   )

(b)

Quiz

Write the letter that indicates the best definition.

1. (d)
2. (e)
3. (b)
4. (a)
5. (c)

(   ) 1. acronym   a. exactness; specificness
(   ) 2. antonym   b. word with same sound
(   ) 3. homonym   c. suggestive qualities; overtones
(   ) 4. concreteness   d. word made from initials
(   ) 5. connotation   e. word with opposite meaning

---

11. **prose:** writing or speech which is not poetry. Most communication—whether of newspapers, magazines, or conversation—is *prose*.

(a)

■ *Prose* is the language of (a) ordinary conversation and writing, (b) Longfellow's "The Village Blacksmith." (   )

prose

■ All of your life you have been talking in _____ [poetry / prose].

prose

■ Essays by Michael Montaigne, Charles Lamb, and Robert Benchley are all written in _____ [poetry / prose].

(b)

■ A *prose* composition requires (a) rhyming, (b) no rhyming. (   )

---

12. **exposition:** writing which explains or informs. *Exposition* is one of four traditional types of discourse, the others being *description*, *narration*, and *argumentation*.

13. **précis** (prā'sē): a short condensed version of a piece of writing. The *précis* is shorter than the original but it maintains something of the same phrasing, tone, order, and proportion of ideas.

exposition

■ Writing that is explanatory is called _____ [narration / exposition].

précis

■ Summarizing a composition but preserving the original phrasing and tone results in a *pr*_____ .

(a)

■ The *précis* of a magazine article or essay (a) shortens it, (b) expands it. (   )

exposition
(b)

■ To set forth information is the function of *exp*_____ ; so the natural language of *exposition* is (a) poetry, (b) prose. (   )

(a)

■ A good subject for *exposition* might be (a) symbolism in Melville's *Billy Budd*, (b) an imaginary dialogue between two love-smitten Eskimos. (   )

(a)

■ Although the *précis* of a composition is much shorter than the original, it usually retains (a) some of the original phrasing and tone, (b) only the restated main ideas. (   )

14. **plagiarism** (plā'jə-riz'əm): copying the language or ideas of another author and presenting them as one's own; includes the lifting of phrases and sentences from research sources without using quotation marks. *Plagiarism* results in severe penalties at most colleges.

15. **paraphrase** (par'ə-frāz'): to restate a passage in different words. The researcher must *paraphrase* borrowed material or place it within quotation marks, and must credit the source in either case.

plagiarism

■ Copying somebody else's writing without giving proper credit is called *pl*_____ .

paraphrase

■ To restate a borrowed passage in one's own words is to *par_____* .

credit

■ Whether you *paraphrase* a passage or quote it, you should _____ [credit / ignore] the original source.

(a)

■ *Plagiarism* is (a) literary theft, (b) permissible borrowing. (   )

plagiarism

■ One way to avoid the serious offense of *pla_____* is to (a) change a word now and then in borrowed material, (b) use quotes around each borrowed passage and credit the original

(b)

writer. (   )

(b)
plagiarism

■ If a line is too individual or clever for easy *paraphrasing* the researcher should (a) steal it, (b) place it in quotation marks. (   ) Then, if he also credits the source, he will avoid *pl_____* .

Quiz

Write the letter that indicates the best definition.

1. (d)
2. (e)
3. (b)
4. (c)
5. (a)

(   ) 1. prose   a. a restatement in one's own words
(   ) 2. exposition   b. a condensation; a shortened version
(   ) 3. précis   c. literary theft
(   ) 4. plagiarism   d. ordinary nonpoetic language
(   ) 5. paraphrase   e. informative writing; one type of essay

---

16. **ellipsis** (i-lip′sis): the omission of words, as from quoted material, usually indicated by three dots or asterisks. *Ellipsis* may be used to shorten a quoted passage but not so as to change the meaning or to remove surgically any damaging evidence.

■ "But, in a larger sense, we cannot dedicate . . . this ground"—here the three dots indicate (a) an ellipsis, (b) a pause while

(a)

Lincoln sneezed three times. (   )

■ The omission of words from a quoted passage is called an

ellipsis

el_____ .

three

■ The *ellipsis* is indicated by _____ [three / seven] dots.

improper
ellipsis

■ If your research source says, "Poe drank, although very infrequently, during this period" and you write it as "Poe drank . . . during this period," you are making _____ [proper / improper] use of *el_____* .

---

17. **begging the question:** assuming what has yet to be proved. *Begging the question* is a fallacy of logic, as when we say, "Shouldn't all those crooks at City Hall be turned out of office?" or "It's a waste of money to give that murderer a trial. Just string 'im up!"
18. **post hoc** (pōst hok′): assuming that one thing caused another merely because it happened earlier. This term for a fallacy of logic is from the Latin phrase *post hoc, ergo propter hoc,* which literally means "after this, therefore because of this."

begging

■ To take something for granted without proof is called *b_____ the question.*

question
"useless"

■ "Why must a useless course like history be made compulsory?" Here the word that *begs the qu_____* and needs proving is _____ ["useless" / "course"].

post hoc

■ When an Indian dance gets credit for causing the rain that falls the next day, the reasoning behind such credit is called *po_____ ho_____* .

post hoc

■ The fallacy of assuming that two events that follow each other must have a cause-effect relationship is called *p_____ h_____* .

begs
(b)

■ "We must not permit a pornographic book like *The Catcher in the Rye* to be kept in our library." Here the word that *b_____ the question* and needs proving is (a) "permit," (b) "pornographic." (   )

(a)

■ A young pugilist wearing a certain bathrobe scored a knock-out in one round; thereafter he insisted on wearing that same robe, never cleaned, to every fight of his career. He believed in (a) *post hoc* reasoning, (b) hygiene. (   )

19. **ad hominem** (ad hom′ə-nəm): appealing to a person's prejudices or selfish interests rather than to his reason; attacking an opponent rather than sticking to the issue. The Latin phrase *argumentum ad hominem* means "argument at or to the man."

20. **non sequitur** (non sek′wi-tər): a conclusion that does not follow from the evidence presented. The Latin phrase *non sequitur* means "it does not follow."

hominem

■ In a debate about state lotteries, an attack on your moral character is *ad hom*_____ .

(a)

■ *Ad hominem* implies that the real issue of the argument gets (a) overlooked, (b) close attention. (   )

sequitur

■ "My husband loves Italian motion picture films, so I think he'll enjoy the chicken cacciatora I am going to cook for him." The reasoning here involves a *non seq*_____ .

does not

■ In a *non sequitur* the conclusion _____ [does / does not] follow from the evidence presented.

non sequitur

■ "Schopenhauer was very pessimistic and nobody should read his essays." The conclusion is not justified by the evidence, and we have a *n*_____ *seq*_____ .

ad hominem

■ "Better vote against this school bill, Smedley; your kids have graduated already and you'll just get soaked for more taxes." The argument here is *a*_____ *hom*_____ .

Quiz

Write the letter that indicates the best definition.

( ) 1. ellipsis
( ) 2. begging the
        question
( ) 3. post hoc
( ) 4. ad hominem
( ) 5. non sequitur

a. appeal to prejudice
b. an illogical conclusion
c. omission of words
d. assuming without proof
e. after this, therefore because of
   this

---

21. **bandwagon device:** persuasion to join the popular or winning side. "To climb aboard the bandwagon" means to shift one's vote to the apparent winner.

■ "Three out of four smoke Hempos!" Such ads suggesting that we join the majority use the *ba_____ device.*

■ The *bandwagon device* tells us to vote for Jim Snurd because he is going to _____ [lose / win] by a landslide.

■ "Three million sold already!" Whether this pitch refers to Klunker cars, to horseburgers, or to albums by the Five Lunatics, it uses the *b_____ device* and it urges you to do (a) the rational thing, (b) what the crowd is doing. ( )

---

22. **faulty dilemma** (di-lem′ə): the offering of only two alternatives when more than two exist. "We must wipe out the Pootzians or we will perish"—such talk illustrates the *faulty dilemma,* since it ignores the possibility of peaceful coexistence.

23. **analogy** (ə-nal′ə-jē): an extended comparison to clarify an idea; a comparison of things that are alike in certain ways and therefore presumably alike in other ways. *Analogies* can illustrate an idea but they do not prove it.

■ "Either the man is boss in a home or the woman will rule." Such logic presents a *faulty di_____* .

analogy

■ Comparing man to an eagle that must rule its own nest is an *an_____* .

illustrate

■ *Analogies _____* [prove / illustrate] ideas.

analogy

■ "The early bird catches the worm, so I'll be up at dawn and find a job." This is reasoning by *an_____* .

faulty
   dilemma

■ "Don't take up skiing or you'll break your legs." This choice is the *f_____ di_____* .

two

■ The *faulty dilemma* forces one to choose from _____ [two / all of the] possibilities.

analogy

■ In his *Ecclesiastical History* (eighth century), Bede says that our life is like the quick flight of a sparrow through a lighted hall at night. Bede has used an *an_____* .

---

24. **Socratic irony** (sǝ-krat′ik): the device of pretending to be ignorant and asking questions in order to trap the opponent into obvious error. Socrates uses *Socratic irony*, for instance, to refute a husky Athenian who argues that might makes right.

(b)

■ The man who uses *Socratic irony* asks a series of innocent-sounding questions (a) because he is stupid, (b) because he is leading his opponent into self-contradiction. ( )

Socratic

■ To employ *Soc_____ irony* one must (a) ask adroit questions to draw out the other fellow's ignorance, (b) talk constantly in an opinionated fashion. ( )

(a)

irony

■ If falsely accused of plagiarism you might use *Socratic i_____* to clear yourself by saying, (a) "I'm innocent, teacher; I swear I'm innocent!" (b) "Very interesting. Now where is this passage which I have stolen?" ( )

(b)

Write the letter that indicates the best definition.

1. (b)
2. (d)
3. (a)
4. (c)

( ) 1. bandwagon device   a. an extended comparison
( ) 2. faulty dilemma   b. argument for joining the popular side
( ) 3. analogy   c. refuting by means of clever but innocent-sounding questions
( ) 4. Socratic irony   d. offering two alternatives when more exist

---

25. **fragment:** an incomplete sentence. *Fragments* are often considered the unpardonable sin in freshman themes, though they are acceptable in exclamations, dialogue, and certain types of informal writing. *Fragment:* "Because I fell on my head."

26. **comma splice:** the use of a comma between main clauses where a period or semicolon should be used; for example, "Jack London wrote about supermen and superdogs, he became a rich socialist." (Worse even than the *comma splice* is the *fused sentence*, in which two sentences are run together with no punctuation at all between them. *Fused sentence:* "Horses are smart they don't bet on people.")

■ After each of the following write *fragment, comma splice,* or *correct:*

comma splice

H. L. Mencken was pungent and opinionated, I never thought he was dull. _____

fragment

Alexandre Dumas being about the most imaginative novelist I had ever read. _____

fragment

Because the *Bhagavad* teaches complete unselfishness, humility, and goodness. _____

correct

O. Henry fled. _____

■ After each of the following write *fragment, comma splice,* or *correct:*

comma splice

The British loved Kipling, however, he was never poet laureate. _____

fragment

A scholarly analysis, which reads like a detective story, of the Shakespeare sonnets, particularly those dealing with the Dark Lady. _____

correct

My brother can't write like Chaucer, but he spells like him. _____

---

27. **infinitive** (in-fin′i-tiv): a verbal form that consists usually of "to" plus a verb, as "to walk." The *infinitive* can do the work of a noun, adjective, or adverb.
28. **participle** (pär′ti-sip′əl): a verbal adjective. "Flying in a battered plane, I had some frightening moments." Here "flying," "battered," and "frightening" are *participles*.

infinitive

■ A phrase like "to paint" is an *in*_____ .

participle

■ A verbal adjective—like "honking" in "honking geese"—is a *par*_____ .

participle
infinitive
participle

■ "Attacking his critics, James Fenimore Cooper began to waste valuable writing time." Here "attacking" is a *p*_____, "to waste" is an *i*_____ , and "writing" is a *p*_____ .

infinitives

■ "To strive, to seek, to find, and not to yield." This final line of Tennyson's poem "Ulysses" (1842) contains four *i*_____ .

(a)

■ Inserting words between "to" and the verb in an *infinitive* results in a *split infinitive*, a phrasing which often sounds awkward. Which phrase has a split infinitive?—(a) "to as soon as possible analyze Chekhov's play," (b) "to analyze Chekhov's play as soon as possible." (   )

infinitive
participle

■ "Shakespeare was able to find several gripping themes in the chronicles of Holinshed." Here "to find" is an *in*_____ and "gripping" is a *pa*_____ .

■ A *participle* that does not clearly modify the right word is a *dangling participle*. After each of the following write *dangler* or *correct:*

dangler

Becoming six years old, my mother got a divorce.
_____

correct
dangler

Echoing Emerson, Walt Whitman spoke of man's divinity.
_____

If stewed, you will enjoy these prunes. _____

parallelism

yodeling

faulty

(b)

for
parallelism

idioms

(a)

idiom
(b)

(b)

29. **parallelism** (par′ə-lel-iz-əm): similarity of grammatical structure given to similar ideas. *Parallelism* in phrasing brings out *parallelism* in ideas.

■ Consider the sentence "Fritz loves fishing, climbing, and to yodel." It has faulty *par_____* but would become acceptable if the phrase "to yodel" were changed to the word *y_____* .

■ "Gunder has vowed to work, to save money, and that he will succeed in business." This sentence has _____ [acceptable / faulty] *parallelism*.

■ Which has better *parallelism*?—(a) "I came and after I saw the enemy they were conquered by me," (b) "I came, I saw, I conquered." (   )

■ Lincoln referred to "government of the people, by the people, _____ [for / to help] the people" and achieved structural *pa_____* .

---

30. **idiom:** an accepted phrase that is contrary to the usual language pattern. *Idioms* are natural, supple, and often very informal, for example, "catch cold," "give in," "hint at," "knock off work," "pick a fight."

■ Phrases like "comes in handy" and "takes after his father" are *id_____* .

■ Although *idioms* violate normal language construction they are (a) proper and acceptable, (b) colorful but unusable. (   )

■ Another peculiar English phrasing, known as an *id_____* , is (a) "walk with me," (b) "angry with me." (   )

■ Which is an *idiom*?—(a) "became a loafer," (b) "went to the dogs." (   )

204

idiomatic

■ Ernest Hemingway achieved vigor and naturalness in his stories by using _____ [formal / idiomatic] English.

Quiz

Write the letter that indicates the best example.

1. (e)
2. (c)
3. (a)
4. (d)
5. (f)
6. (b)

( ) 1. fragment
( ) 2. comma splice
( ) 3. infinitive
( ) 4. participle
( ) 5. parallelism
( ) 6. idiom

a. *To err* is human.
b. We grabbed a bite.
c. Here comes Lulu, get the hymn book.
d. "The Lottery" is a *terrifying* story.
e. Whereas Irving knew the Catskills.
f. He lived; he loved; he died.

REVIEW TEST

Write the word studied in this chapter that will complete the sentence.

1. Copying material without giving proper credit is *pl*_____ .

2. The ridiculous misuse of a word for another that sounds like it is a *ma*_____ .

3. A word like "WAVE," made up from the initials of a title, is an *ac*_____ .

4. A mild word substituted for a blunt one is a *eu*_____ .

5. Prose composition that explains or sets forth is *ex*_____ .

6. Ordinary writing that is not poetry is called *pr*_____ .

7. A word of opposite meaning is an *an*_____ .

8. A word with the same sound but different meaning is a *ho*_____ .

9. A conclusion which "does not follow" from the evidence is a *n*_____ *se*_____ .

10. Needless repetition or wordiness is *re*_____ .

11. An accepted phrase that defies normal language patterns is an *id*_____ .

12. The verbal "grinning" in "grinning faces" is a *pa*_____ .

13. An incomplete sentence is a *fr*_____ .

14. Propaganda urging one to follow the crowd is the *ba*_____ *device*.

15. An omission of words, indicated by three dots, is an *el*_____ .

Write *True* or *False*.

_____ 16. *Concreteness* refers to the use of clear, specific detail.

_____ 17. *Post hoc* logic is considered valid in science.

_____ 18. *Begging the question* means assuming without proof.

_____ 19. An argument *ad hominem* sticks to the main issue.

_____ 20. *Clichés* add color and vigor to one's style.

_____ 21. To use *Socratic irony* means to argue and fall into one's own trap.

_____ 22. In the *faulty dilemma* one must choose from an incomplete set of alternatives.

_____ 23. *Comma splice* refers to the omission of a comma.

_____ 24. The following contains *parallelism:* "We will fight with guns, with bombs, and with fists."

_____ 25. *Rhetoric* is the art of persuasive writing and speaking.

Write the letter that indicates the best completion.

( ) 26. An *analogy* is (a) a proof, (b) an exaggeration, (c) a comparison, (d) a stale expression.

( ) 27. An example of an *infinitive* is (a) "the critic Mencken," (b) "criticizing," (c) "to criticize," (d) "to critics."

( ) 28. A *précis* is (a) an explanation, (b) an expansion, (c) a quotation, (d) a condensation.

( ) 29. A *paraphrase* is (a) a restatement, (b) a quotation, (c) a line of poetry, (d) a wordy passage.

Match each word with its definition.

( ) 30. participle   a. a worn-out phrase
( ) 31. cliché   b. suggestiveness
( ) 32. connotation   c. verbal adjective
( ) 33. plagiarism   d. literary theft

Key to Review Test

Check your test answers by the following key. Deduct 3% per error from a possible 100%.

1. plagiarism	12. participle	23. False
2. malapropism	13. fragment	24. True
3. acronym	14. bandwagon	25. True
4. euphemism	15. ellipsis	26. (c)
5. exposition	16. True	27. (c)
6. prose	17. False	28. (d)
7. antonym	18. True	29. (a)
8. homonym	19. False	30. (c)
9. non sequitur	20. False	31. (a)
10. redundancy	21. False	32. (b)
11. idiom	22. True	33. (d)

Score: _____%

14

Figures of Speech

Abraham Lincoln said that a man should preach "like a man fighting off a swarm of bees" (simile); that "we must save the good old ship of the Union on this voyage" (metaphor); that we must "bind up the nation's wounds" (personification). Figures of speech are a trademark of the imaginative writer. A random survey of William Shakespeare, Emily Dickinson, Herman Melville, or Jim Murray would reveal a galaxy of similes, metaphors, hyperboles, oxymorons. Your familiarity with such terms can help you in two ways: As an analyst of literary passages you can more ably identify and appreciate the stylistic devices used; as a creative writer you can gain sparkle and vigor by using a greater variety of figures of speech.

COVER THIS STRIP

1. **simile** (sim′ə-lē): a figure of speech comparing two unlike things, usually with "like" or "as"; for example, "She has a figure like an hourglass—and not a minute of it wasted."

2. **metaphor** (met′ə-fôr′): a figure of speech in which one thing is said to be another thing, without "like" or "as," or in which a likeness is implied; for example, "All the world's a stage"; "My boss barked out his orders."

■ After each example write *simile* or *metaphor:*

"Boston was a beehive."_____

"Orville has a head like a granite block."_____

"Teacher's heart is as big and soft as an overripe pumpkin." _____

"My mother-in-law sailed into the room."_____

metaphor
simile

simile
metaphor

■ An expressed comparison between unlike things, with "like" or "as," is a _____ ; an implied comparison is a _____ .

simile
metaphor

■ Write *simile* or *metaphor:*

"Mabel was a dynamo, but she got short-circuited." _____

"He looks like a dishonest Abe Lincoln." _____

"The Buick purred down the freeway." _____

metaphor
simile
metaphor

3. **alliteration:** the repetition of an initial sound in words or accented syllables close together. *Alliteration* abounds in the big brutal battles of *Beowulf.*

4. **onomatopoeia** (on′ə-mat′ə-pē′ə): the use of words whose pronunciation suggests their meaning. *Onomatopoeic* words are common: *boom, hiss, murmur, zoom, moan, hum, chug, sizzle, cuckoo, glug.*

■ Using words that sound like what they mean is *on*_____ .

onomatopoeia

■ Using the same initial letter in neighboring words is *al*_____ .

alliteration

(b)

■ Which line of poetry by Robert Herrick contains *alliteration?*—(a) "The liquefaction of her clothes," (b) "I sing of brooks, of blossoms, birds and bowers." (   )

■ After each example write *alliteration* or *onomatopoeia:*
"The locomotive snorted and hissed—then went chug-ah!"

onomatopoeia

_____

"What a tale of terror now their turbulency tells!"

alliteration

_____

alliteration
"That lazy, lovable lunatic."_____

onomatopoeia
"He dived on his belly—plop, splash."_____

5. **hyperbole** (hī-pûr′bə-lē): a gross exaggeration for rhetorical effect; for example, "Wally swallows a barrel or two of vitamin pills and rattles off to work."

6. **litotes** (lī′tə-tēz′): a figure of speech in which a point is made by a denying of its opposite; a kind of understatement; for example, "It's no small matter"; "Rockefeller was no pauper"; "The prisoner approached the gallows without enthusiasm."

litotes

■ Denying the opposite of what you mean is *li_____* .

hyperbole

■ Gross exaggeration is *hy_____* .

(b)

■ A *hyperbole* might say that the village boozer (a) drank several bottles of beer, (b) made the local brewery go on a twenty-four hour shift. (   )

(b)

■ An example of *litotes* is (a) "The mackerel had a bad odor," (b) "The mackerel did not smell like Chanel No. 5." (   )

■ After each example write *hyperbole* or *litotes:*
"The mosquitoes were rangy and enterprising, and they'd siphon a quart of blood before you noticed them."

hyperbole

_____

"There's enough poetry on the boys' washroom walls to put

hyperbole
Shakespeare out of business."_____

"Gangster Al Capone did not exactly win the Best Citizen

litotes
award." _____

litotes
"Helen of Troy was no hag, you know."_____

Quiz

Write the letter that indicates the best example.

1. (c)
2. (e)
3. (f)
4. (d)
5. (b)
6. (a)

( ) 1. alliteration   a. a hairdo like an unmade bed
( ) 2. hyperbole   b. the *bar-r-room* of the trombones
( ) 3. litotes   c. lively lads and lasses
( ) 4. metaphor   d. Alice was sugar and cream.
( ) 5. onomatopoeia   e. Lulu has an army of suitors.
( ) 6. simile   f. Caruso was not a bad singer either.

---

7. **apostrophe** (ə-pos′trə-fē): addressing a personified object, or an absent person as though present; example from Francis Thompson: "O world invisible, we view thee."

8. **metonymy** (mi-ton′ə-mē): a figure of speech in which the name of a thing is used for something else associated with it; virtually synonymous with *synecdoche;* for example, "The sailor was warned to stay away from the skirts."

■ In *apostrophe* the poet is emotionally involved with some absent person or some personified object and speaks directly

to it

_____ [to it / of it].

metonymy

■ "He was addicted to the bottle" is *met*_____

(a)

because "bottle" is associated with (a) liquor, (b) glassware. ( )

■ After each example write *apostrophe* or *metonymy:*

metonymy
metonymy

"Dinner is $12.95 a plate."_____

"Melvin has read Tennessee Williams."_____

Robert Burns: "O Scotia! my dear, my native soil!"

apostrophe
metonymy

_____

"The White House announces . . ."_____

■ Which line involves *apostrophe*?—(a) William Wordsworth: "Milton! thou shouldst be living at this hour," (b) John Masefield:

(a)

"Oh London Town's a fine town." ( )

211

9. **oxymoron** (ok′si-mōr′on): a combination of two apparently contradictory words; for example, "dazzling darkness," "devout atheism," "lively corpse"; from a Greek word meaning extremely silly.

10. **antithesis** (an-tith′i-sis): the strong contrast of expressions, clauses, sentences, or ideas within a balanced grammatical structure; for example, "Life is short; art is long," "Give me liberty or give me death."

■ A seeming contradiction like "clever idiot" is an *ox_____* .

oxymoron

■ "We must all hang together, or assuredly we shall all hang separately." This famous utterance by Benjamin Franklin in 1776 illustrates *ant_____* , since it _____ [does / does not] present a contrast of ideas in a balanced pattern.

antithesis
does

■ Which ending results in *antithesis?*—"Johnny was in the church basement making taffy, and (a) wondering if Jimmy ever had so much fun," (b) Jimmy was in the theater balcony making love." (   )

(b)

■ "Militant pacifism" is an *ox_____* , and Sir Philip Sidney's reference to "living deaths, dear wounds, fair storms, and freezing fires" includes four *ox_____* .

oxymoron

oxymorons

■ An *oxymoron* might refer to a "_____ [strange / noisy] silence" or to an "_____ [attractive / unusual] repulsiveness."

noisy
attractive

■ A contrast of ideas expressed as a balanced sentence is known as *ant_____* .

antithesis

■ An example of *antithesis* is (a) "You do not have to cut off your fingers to write shorthand," (b) "A cat has its claws at the end of the paws; a comma has its pause at the end of the clause." (   )

(b)

11. **personification** (pər-son'ə-fə-kā'shən): the giving of human qualities to something that is not human; for example, "stern-faced Duty" and "the murmuring pines."

12. **pathetic fallacy** (fal'ə-sē): attributing human feelings to inanimate things—an aspect of personification. In *Modern Painters* (1856), John Ruskin objects to the *pathetic fallacy*, or falseness, in phrases like "the cruel crawling foam" or "weeping skies."

■ *Personification*, like "the brow of the hill," gives human qualities to (a) people, (b) non-human things. (　)

(b)

■ *Personification* is referred to as the *pathetic fa_____* when trees or skies are not merely likened to humans but are even endowed with (a) human feelings, (b) divine qualities. (　)

fallacy

(a)

■ Which line involves *personification?*—(a) Samuel Coleridge: "The one red leaf, the last of its clan, / That dances as often as dance it can," (b) Alfred Tennyson: "Comrades, leave me here a little, while as yet 'tis early morn." (　)

(a)

■ Which line involves *personification?*—(a) William Shakespeare: "Blow, winds, and crack your cheeks," (b) Christina Rossetti: "This Advent moon shines cold and clear." (　)

(a)

■ The type of *personification* which attributes feelings to things, known as the *pa_____ fallacy*, is suggested by (a) "in the teeth of the wind," (b) "the wailing wind." (　)

pathetic
(b)

Quiz

Write the letter that indicates the best example.

1. (d)
2. (b)
3. (c)
4. (a)
5. (f)
6. (e)

(　) 1. apostrophe   a. her bold shyness
(　) 2. antithesis   b. Man proposes; God disposes.
(　) 3. metonymy   c. The farmer hired three hands.
(　) 4. oxymoron   d. Here's to thee, oh Alma Mater!
(　) 5. pathetic fallacy   e. the eye of the storm
(　) 6. personification   f. the groaning branches of fruit (special type of personification)

---

13. **allusion** (ə-lōō′zhən): a passing reference to something; an indirect mention. Milton's poetry is peppered with classical *allusions*, that is, references to passages in world literature.

allusion

■ Mentioning Achilles or Sancho Panza or Blake's "The Tiger" would be a literary *al*_____ .

(a)

■ A man makes a Biblical *allusion* if he refers to his wife as his (a) "rib," (b) "ball and chain." ( )

allusion

■ "Everything that Tanya touches turns to gold." Here the writer has made a passing reference, or *al*_____ , to the story of King Midas.

allusion
(a)

■ "Well, I'll be a monkey's cousin!" This comment embodies an indirect reference, or *a*_____ , to (a) Darwinism, (b) Jeffersonian democracy. ( )

14. **irony** (ī′rə-nē), also known as *verbal irony:* saying the opposite of what is meant, by way of mockery; in general, the implying of a contrast between an obvious attitude or condition and a possible one. See also *Socratic irony* (Chapter 13, frame 24) and *irony of fate* (Chapter 15, frame 10). The modern poet tends to avoid the simple expression of love or indignation, preferring the complex, self-critical attitude of *ironic* statement.

(b)

■ When peace-loving Stephen Crane says, "War is kind," he is probably (a) serious, (b) ironic. ( )

irony
(b)

■ "That's right," says your father, "have a good time, forget your homework, become a bum!" His advice is an example of *i*_____ because he really means (a) exactly what he says, (b) the opposite of what he says. ( )

irony

■ In "A Modest Proposal" (1729), Jonathan Swift urges with tongue in cheek, or with *ir*_____ , that Englishmen should eat Irish infants.

(a)

■ *Verbal irony* is a form of (a) sarcasm, (b) eulogy. ( )

■ The baseball coach uses *irony* when he says, "You struck out five times—(a) such rotten luck!" (b) such a marvelous athlete!" (   )

---

15. **symbol** (sim′bəl): an object or a story element which has a basic meaning yet which also has another meaning; for example, a dove is a bird of the pigeon family yet it also stands for peace. In Hawthorne's *The Scarlet Letter*, the minister keeps putting his hand to his heart, a natural gesture but also a *symbol* of hidden guilt.

■ A flag, a cross, or a handclasp may stand for something beside themselves and thus each may be a *sy*———————— .

■ Appropriate *symbols* to suggest old age might be (a) withered leaves and dry ashes, (b) budding flowers and gushing waters. (   )

■ *Symbolism* in fiction can exist (a) only in concrete objects such as an ivory leg, a livid scar, a white whale, (b) in objects, characters, gestures, situations, etc. (   )

■ As the Hemingway hero lies mortally wounded, he sees the buzzards circle closer and closer. The buzzards are a *s*———————— of (a) death, (b) hope. (   )

Quiz

Write the letter that indicates the best definition.

(   ) 1. allusion   a. mockery by expressing opposites
(   ) 2. irony   b. that which stands for something else
(   ) 3. symbol   c. a casual reference to something

REVIEW TEST

Write the word studied in this chapter that will complete the sentence.

1. A gross exaggeration is a *hy*——————— .

2. The repetition of initial letters in words is *al*——————— .

3. Saying the opposite of what is really meant, in order to ridicule, is known as *ir*——————— .

4. A comparison using "like" or "as" is a *si*——————— .

5. Use of words that sound like what they mean is *on*——————— .

6. Addressing the absent as though present is known as *ap*——————— .

7. Naming of a thing to represent something closely associated with it is *me*——————— .

8. "I was a stricken deer." Cowper's figure of speech is a *me*——————— .

9. "The sun peered at me." This figure of speech is *pe*——————— .

10. "Darkness visible": Milton's contradictory phrase is an *ox*——————— .

Name the figure of speech in each example. The first letter of each answer is given.

11. lovely Lulu from Laredo   *a*———————

12. a head shaped like a Persian melon   *s*———————

13. Eat another plate.   *m*———————

14. a beach not without its beer cans and litter   *l*———————

15. Boom, crash, clang went the drum section.   *o*———————

16. Her brain is a storage vault.   *m*———————

17. the bitter sweetness of farewell   *o*———————

18. Kay's wardrobe closet is about fifty yards long.   *h*———————

19. The pansies closed their little eyes.   *p*———————

20. O Eve, Eve, why did you eat the forbidden fruit?   *a*———————

21. He generously gave the church all of two cents.   *i*———————

22. Sam spends much; he earns little.   *a*———————

23. Respect the sceptre, the sword, the flag.　　　　　　　s_____

24. We spoke of Plato, Chartres, Waterloo, Einstein's
    theory, and the art of Chaplin.　　　　　　　　　a_____

25. the grieving, melancholy clouds　　　p_____　f_____

Key to Review Test

Check your test answers by the following key. Deduct 4% per error from a possible 100%.

1. hyperbole	10. oxymoron	19. personification
2. alliteration	11. alliteration	20. apostrophe
3. irony	12. simile	21. irony
4. simile	13. metonymy	22. antithesis
5. onomatopoeia	14. litotes	23. symbols
6. apostrophe	15. onomatopoeia	24. allusions
7. metonymy	16. metaphor	25. pathetic fallacy
8. metaphor	17. oxymoron	
9. personification	18. hyperbole	

Score: _____%

15

General Literature

People read literature mainly for pleasure. As with music or painting or pizza-making, however, the more you know about a subject the more pleasure you derive from it. College students should be able to distinguish free verse from blank verse, comedy from farce, prologue from epilogue, biography from bibliography. They should be aware of narrative aspects such as plot, characterization, and suspense. Of course you can enjoy literature without knowing a myth from a moth, but you will appreciate literature better and discuss it more intelligently if you understand some technical terms associated with it.

Study the definitions carefully. Fill in the blanks without looking back to the top of the frame.

1. **novel:** a long fictitious prose story of some complexity, involving characters, scenes, and action. The first English *novel* is usually said to be Samuel Richardson's *Pamela*, published in 1740; the first American novel is William Hill Brown's *The Power of Sympathy* (1789).

2. **novelette:** a short novel, about fifty to a hundred pages long, for example, Ernest Hemingway's *The Old Man and the Sea* (1952); also sometimes referred to as a *novella*.

fictitious
does

■ A *novel* is a long _____ [factual / fictitious] story which _____ [does / does not] involve characters and action.

novelette (or
  novella)

■ A story about sixty pages long is usually called a *n_____* .

novel

■ Samuel Richardson's *Pamela*, a lengthy fictitious story, was the first English *n_____* .

novelette (or
  novella)

■ Herman Melville's fictitious story *Benito Cereno* (1856) is about seventy pages long and can be referred to as a *n_____* .

longer
shorter

■ A *novelette* is _____ [shorter / longer] than a short story and _____ [shorter / longer] than a novel.

3. **plot:** the central plan of action in a story or play; the author's arrangement of episodes. The story consists of certain events in chronological order, whereas the *plot* is the form into which the author organizes those events.

4. **coincidence** (kō-in′sə-dəns): the remarkable occurrence of certain events at the same time, apparently by chance. For example, Longfellow's *Evangeline* is separated from her lover Gabriel and, years later, as an old nurse, she finds him by chance just as he is dying in an alms-house.

(b)

■ By the *plot* of a novel we mean (a) its general subject, (b) its arrangement of action. ( )

■ When Huck Finn, by sheerest chance, arrives at a distant farmhouse on the very day when Tom Sawyer is expected there, it is *co*_____ .

coincidence

■ The overuse of *coincidences* in a story tends to make the *plot* _____ [more / less] believable.

less

■ Aristotle says in his *Poetics* that the most important element of tragedy is *plot,* by which he means (a) the plan of action, (b) the moral tone. (   )

(a)

■ O. Henry stresses the plan of action, or *p*_____ , but unfortunately his *plot* usually hinges on some incredible chance meeting, or *c*_____ .

plot

coincidence

---

5. **suspense:** uncertainty as to the outcome; anxiety caused by a tense situation. *Suspense* is an indispensable ingredient of the mystery thriller and the melodrama.
6. **flashback:** an interruption in a story or play to present action which occurred earlier. *Flashback* breaks up the orderly time sequence but often gains psychological values.

■ *Suspense* refers to (a) uncertainty, (b) pleasure. (   )

(a)

■ In the play *Death of a Salesman*, Willy Loman is shown remembering and reliving a hotel episode of an earlier period. This is a *fl*_____ .

flashback

■ The *flashback*, often very effective in drama, jumps to the _____ [past / future].

past

■ During the fourth act of his five-act plays Shakespeare has the unhappy problem of keeping alive the uncertainty and tension known as *su*_____ .

suspense

■ The maintaining of *suspense* is especially important in the (a) mystery story, (b) essay. (   )

(a)

suspense

flashback

■ The condemned killer is strapped to the electric chair in a scene fraught with *su*_____ ; then suddenly we see him, years earlier, as a boy scout winning a prize at Sunday school. This time shift is called *fl*_____ .

---

7. **anachronism** (ə-nak′rə-niz′əm): representing something as happening in the wrong historical period. An *anachronism* occurs in *Julius Caesar* when Cassius says, "The clock has stricken three."

anachronism

■ Raphael's depiction of the Holy Family in medieval clothing is an *an*_____ .

(b)

■ An *anachronism* is an error involving (a) bad grammar, (b) the wrong period of time. (   )

anachronism
(b)

■ In a western film, critics noticed a time-flaw, or *an*_____ : above the Indians could be seen (a) an eagle, (b) a commercial airplane. (   )

anachronism

(a)

■ It would also be a historical error, or *an*_____ , to show Abraham Lincoln using (a) an electric shaver, (b) a feather pen. (   )

Quiz

Write the letter that indicates the best definition.

1. (g)
2. (e)
3. (b)
4. (a)
5. (d)
6. (f)
7. (c)

(   ) 1. anachronism
(   ) 2. coincidence
(   ) 3. flashback
(   ) 4. novel
(   ) 5. novelette
(   ) 6. plot
(   ) 7. suspense

a. a full-length fictitious story
b. a shift to earlier events
c. anxiety as to how things will turn out
d. a fictitious story shorter than a novel but longer than fifty pages
e. the simultaneous occurrence of unrelated incidents
f. the pattern of story action
g. an event misplaced in history

8. **characterization** (kar′ik-tər-i-zā′shən): the portrayal of people, their physical and spiritual traits and peculiarities. Good *characterization* is consistent and three-dimensional, developed largely by action and dialogue rather than merely by flat abstract description.

9. **motivation:** that which causes a character to do what he does. What *motivations* cause Macbeth to murder Duncan?

character-
ization

■ The way people are portrayed is *ch*_____ .

motivation

■ The passion, grievance, or need which impels a character to act as he does is his *mo*_____ .

motivation

■ Men will not kill, seek divorces, or chase whales without sufficient *mo*_____ .

character-
ization

■ Thomas Wolfe portrayed people so that you came to know their yearnings, their impulses, and their warts. This was effective *ch*_____ .

motivation
character-
ization

■ The sudden reform of sinners and misers at the end of sentimental stories is usually without sufficient *mo*_____ . It suggests faulty *ch*_____ .

---

10. **irony of fate** (ī′rə-nē): the way that destiny twists or foils the plans of men. Thomas Hardy's characters get a glimpse of happiness but by some *irony of fate* they fail to achieve it.

fate
(b)

■ The *irony of f*_____ has a way of providing (a) the expected reward, (b) the unexpected disaster. (   )

(a)

■ In Stephen Crane's "The Open Boat" (1898) the unselfish oiler, who is possibly the most deserving of life, is the only man who drowns. This illustrates (a) the irony of fate, (b) that this is the best of all possible worlds. (   )

irony
(b)

■ The *i*_____ *of fate* would be illustrated if the fire department building (a) needed painting, (b) burned down. (   )

---

11. **social criticism:** the exposure of faults in various aspects of society. The *social criticism* of Sinclair Lewis hits at small town gossip, middle-class conformity, racial discrimination, and medical quackery.

social

■ Harriet Beecher Stowe's *Uncle Tom's Cabin* (1852) attacks slavery and therefore represents important *so_____ criticism.*

criticism

■ Another story involving *social cr_____* is (a) John Steinbeck's *The Grapes of Wrath* (1939), exposing the miserable plight of the Okies, (b) Henry W. Longfellow's *Hiawatha* (1855), depicting an Indian romance. (   )

(a)

social
  criticism
(b)

■ Columnist Art Buchwald indulges in *so_____ cr_____* when he describes (a) the pleasures of air travel, (b) excessive street crime in our major cities. (   )

12. **comedy:** an amusing play with a happy ending. Unlike tragedy, *comedy* does not stress the noble conception of life; instead it pleasantly satirizes human follies and incidents and, according to Aristotle, represents men as worse than in actual life.

13. **farce:** exaggerated comedy marked by ridiculous situations and horseplay. Whereas true comedy has an element of seriousness in it, *farce* aims to produce laughter merely for its own sake.

happily
wedding

■ An Elizabethan *comedy* was amusing, and it ended _____ [happily / unhappily], possibly with a _____ [wedding / funeral].

farce

■ If a play is full of absurd situations and tomfoolery, as, for example, in the Marx brothers' *Horsefeathers*, it may be described as a *f_____* .

cheerful

(b)

■ A *comedy* such as Shakespeare's *As You Like It* (1599) not only ends on a _____ [depressing / cheerful] note but the general tone throughout the play is (a) morbid, (b) amusing. (   )

223

ridiculous

■ George M. Cohan's *Seven Keys to Baldpate* (1913) is usually called a *farce* because of its slapstick, broad humor, and _____ [believable / ridiculous] action.

farce

■ Clowning and far-fetched situations are typical of a *f*_____ .

---

14. **prologue** (prō′lôg): an introduction to a play or poem. Shakespeare's *Pericles* (1607) begins with a *prologue* delivered by one of the actors.

15. **epilogue** (ep′ə-lôg′): a final comment added to a play, poem, or novel; for example, Shakespeare's *The Tempest* (1611) ends with an *epilogue*.

beginning

■ The *prologue* to a play or to an act comes at the _____ [beginning / end].

epilogue
(b)

■ Ben Jonson's *Bartholomew Fair* (1614) begins with a *prologue;* but its *ep*_____ follows (a) Act I, (b) Act V. (   )

epilogue

■ Elizabethan and Restoration dramas often ended with a speech to win the good will of the spectators; this was the *e*_____ .

(b)

■ The *epilogue* of a play is a speech delivered as (a) an introduction, (b) a farewell. (   )

prologue

■ Preliminary remarks are delivered as a *p*_____ .

Quiz

Write the letter that indicates the best definition.

1. (f)
2. (e)
3. (a)
4. (c)
5. (b)
6. (h)
7. (g)
8. (d)

(   ) 1. characterization   a. farewell speech in a play
(   ) 2. comedy   b. unexpected twist of destiny
(   ) 3. epilogue   c. exaggerated comedy; slapstick
(   ) 4. farce   d. exposure of people's faults
(   ) 5. irony of fate   e. amusing play with a happy ending
(   ) 6. motivation   f. how people are portrayed
(   ) 7. prologue   g. introduction to a play
(   ) 8. social criticism   h. the cause of a character's actions

16. **bibliography:** a list of books and other writings which deal with a particular subject. Building a *bibliography* is an early step in writing a research paper.

17. **biography:** a person's life story, written by another person (if written by himself it is called autobiography). Modern *biography* began with James Boswell's *Life of Samuel Johnson* (1791), with its honest details about an eccentric, talented man.

biography
(a)

■ Carl Sandburg's account of Lincoln's life is a *bi*_____ , because it is a product of (a) facts, (b) fiction. (   )

is not

■ *The History of Tom Jones* (1749) is the product of Henry Fielding's fertile imagination, so it _____ [is / is not] a *biography*.

bibliography

■ A scholarly writer lists his research sources in a *bi*_____ .

biography

■ If you consulted A. O. Tate's *bi*_____ of Thomas Alva Edison, your term paper should list that life story

bibliography

in its *bi*_____ .

bibliography

■ To avoid plagiarism, you should footnote every borrowed line or idea, in addition to listing the general sources in the *bi*_____ of your research paper.

---

18. **epic:** a long narrative poem that describes heroic adventures in an exalted style. The *folk* or primitive *epic*, such as *Beowulf* or the *Iliad*, was originally recited by a bard to nobility; the *literary epic*, such as Virgil's *Aeneid* or Milton's *Paradise Lost*, is a more unified and polished work intended for reading.

poem

■ An *epic* is a lengthy, dignified _____ [essay / poem] which deals with (a) the beauty of flowers, (b) the adventures

(b)

of heroes. (   )

epic
(a)

■ A long narrative poem in exalted style is known as an *e*_____ ; an example of an *epic* is (a) Homer's *Odyssey*, (b) Whittier's "The Barefoot Boy." (   )

■ An *epic* such as Milton's *Paradise Lost* has a length of several hundred (a) words, (b) pages. (   )

■ The tone of an *epic* poem by Homer or Milton is (a) lofty and dignified, (b) vulgar and uninspiring. (   )

■ A long, dignified narrative poem, called an *e_____* , deals with (a) humorous family situations, (b) heroic adventures. (   )

---

19. **iambic pentameter:** a line of poetic verse consisting of five *iambic* feet. An *iambic* foot is a unit of poetic rhythm consisting of two syllables, with the stress on the second syllable; for example: "tonĭght," "dĕný," "aňd nów," "mў lov́e."

■ As death approached, John Keats wrote a poem with the opening line: "When I have fears that I may cease to be." This verse is written in *ia_____ pen_____* .

Let us further examine the line by Keats:

■ The first *iambic* foot is "When I," with the stress on "I." The second *iambic* foot is "*h_____ f_____* ," with the stress on the word "*f_____* ."

■ The fifth *i_____* foot is "*_____ _____* ," with the stress on the word "_____."

■ Since the line by Keats consists of _____ [3 / 5 / 6] *ia_____* feet, it is said to be written in *i_____ p_____* .

---

20. **sonnet:** a fourteen-line poem in iambic pentameter with a prescribed rhyming and structural pattern. The *English,* or *Shakespearean, sonnet* consists of three quatrains and a couplet, rhyming *abab cdcd efef gg.* The *Italian,* or *Petrarchan, sonnet* consists of an octave (having eight lines) followed by a sestet (having six lines) and rhymes *abba abba cde cde* (the rhyme scheme of the sestet may vary).

fourteen (a)	■ The *sonnet* is _____ [twelve / fourteen] lines long and is in iambic (a) pentameter, (b) hexameter. ( )
sonnet (a)	■ If its fourteen lines consist of three quatrains and a couplet, the *so*_____ is (a) English, (b) Italian. ( )
sonnet (b)	■ If its fourteen lines consist of an octave and a sestet, the *s*_____ is (a) English, (b) Italian. ( )
sonnet	■ Shakespeare and Petrarch were masters of the beautifully structured fourteen-line poem known as a *s*_____ .

21. **blank verse:** unrhymed iambic pentameter. *Blank verse* is used in the dramas of Shakespeare and Marlowe and in other serious English poetry such as Milton's *Paradise Lost*.
22. **free verse:** rhythmical lines of irregular length without fixed metrical pattern and usually without rhyme; also called *vers libre*. *Free verse* has the rhythms and cadences of natural speech.

(b)	■ The magnificent *blank verse* of *Macbeth* and *Julius Caesar* is (a) rhymed, (b) unrhymed. ( )
(a)	■ *Blank verse* consists of lines that are unrhymed and (a) in iambic pentameter, (b) of various lengths and stresses. ( )
free	■ On the other hand, unrhymed lines of irregular length are *f*_____ *verse*.
free (b)	■ A line of *vers libre*, or *f*_____ *verse*, has (a) five stresses, (b) no fixed metrical pattern. ( )
free	■ Walt Whitman, Amy Lowell, and Carl Sandburg often use lines of irregular length and rhythm, known as _____ *verse*.
is blank verse	■ "For who would bear the whips and scorns of time"—this representative line from *Hamlet*_____ [is / is not] in iambic pentameter, and so this unrhymed drama is in *bl*_____ *v*_____ .

Quiz

Write the letter that indicates the best definition.

1. (f)
2. (c)
3. (a)
4. (g)
5. (d)
6. (e)
7. (b)

(   ) 1. bibliography
(   ) 2. biography
(   ) 3. blank verse
(   ) 4. epic
(   ) 5. free verse
(   ) 6. iambic
           pentameter
(   ) 7. sonnet

a. poetry in unrhymed iambic pentameters
b. a fourteen-line structured poem
c. a life story
d. poetry with lines of irregular length
e. a line with five iambic feet
f. list of sources
g. a long poem about heroic adventure

REVIEW TEST

Write the word studied in this chapter that will complete the sentence.

1. The portrayal of an event or object in the wrong historical period is an an_____ .

2. A remarkable chance occurrence of events at the same time is a co_____ .

3. Bringing out the personalities and individual traits of people in a story is ch_____ .

4. An exaggerated comedy with horseplay is a fa_____ .

5. The life story of an eminent person is a bi_____ .

6. A long narrative poem describing heroic deeds is an ep_____ .

7. An introduction to a play or poem is a pr_____ .

8. Sources of your research paper are listed in a bi_____ .

9. A novel that is sixty or seventy pages long is usually referred to as a no_____ .

10. An interruption in a story or drama to present earlier action is called fl_____ .

Write *True* or *False*.

_____ 11. A *sonnet* includes fourteen lines in iambic pentameter.

_____ 12. *Blank verse* uses an irregular number of metrical feet to the line.

_____ 13. A short final speech to the play audience is an *epilogue*.

_____ 14. *Motivation* is the moving about or traveling which takes place in a story.

_____ 15. The *irony of fate* implies that man usually gets what he expects and deserves.

_____ 16. *Social criticism* refers to a critical review of the style, merits, and shortcomings of a book.

_____ 17. *Pentameter* verse has five metrical feet to the line.

_____ 18. *Suspense* is a desirable quality in a mystery story.

_____ 19. Remarkable *coincidences* contribute to the realism of a story.

_____ 20. Magazine sources as well as book sources should be listed in the *bibliography* of a research paper.

Write the letter that indicates the best completion.

( ) 21. An example of an *iambic* foot is (a) "favor," (b) "depend," (c) "the farmer," (d) "tenderly."

( ) 22. *Free verse* has (a) regular meter, (b) rhyming restrictions, (c) speech rhythms, (d) five-stress lines.

( ) 23. A *novel* is a lengthy (a) life story, (b) essay, (c) moral lesson, (d) fictitious story.

( ) 24. The *plot* of a novel is its (a) plan of action, (b) moral, (c) background, (d) social criticism.

( ) 25. A *comedy* is (a) suspenseful, (b) educational, (c) amusing, (d) musical and poetic.

Key to Review Test

Check your test answers by the following key. Deduct 4% per error from a possible 100%.

1. anachronism	11. True	21. (b)
2. coincidence	12. False	22. (c)
3. characterization	13. True	23. (d)
4. farce	14. False	24. (a)
5. biography	15. False	25. (c)
6. epic	16. False	
7. prologue	17. True	
8. bibliography	18. True	
9. novelette (*or* novella)	19. False	
10. flashback	20. True	

Score: _____%

NOTE: For supplementary exercises on additional terms relating to literature, see APPENDIX B, page 324.

16

Name Derivatives

1. aphrodisiac
2. boycott
3. chauvinism
4. cynic
5. Darwinism
6. Frankenstein monster
7. herculean
8. jabberwocky
9. laconic
10. Lilliputian
11. machiavellian
12. maudlin
13. maverick
14. mentor
15. nimrod
16. odyssey
17. Pyrrhic victory
18. quixotic
19. robot
20. solon
21. spoonerism
22. stentorian
23. tantalize
24. utopian
25. vandal

The names of people and places are imbedded in our language. The commonest forms are simple adjectives like "Shakespearean" or "Siamese." But when someone like Louis Pasteur or John L. McAdam discovers or develops something of wide use, we get words like "pasteurize" or "macadamize." From literature and mythology come a horde of words such as "cereal" (from "Ceres," goddess of the grain), "jovial" (from "Jove"), and "yahoo" (from Jonathan Swift's *Gulliver's Travels*, 1726).

The name words in Chapter 16 are a cultural heritage and are sure to turn up in your reading. Learning their source will make it easier to remember their meaning. Four supplementary exercises on name words are included in Appendix B.

COVER THIS STRIP

1. **aphrodisiac** (af'rǝ-diz'i-ak): arousing sexual desire. An *aphrodisiac* is any drug, food, or agent which excites lust; it is named after *Aphrodite*, the goddess of love.
2. **boycott:** to refuse to deal or associate with, in order to coerce or punish. Captain Charles *Boycott* was shunned by the Irish Land League in 1880 for refusing to reduce land rents.

■ An *aphrodisiac* increases one's (a) beauty, (b) sexual desire. (   )

(b)

■ Any music, perfume, or food which increases sexual desire is an *aph_____* .

aphrodisiac

■ When Aldous Huxley refers to a certain juice as "tart and *aphrodisiac*," he means the drink will arouse (a) hostility, (b) lustfulness. (   )

(b)

■ To *boycott* is to _____ [trade with / shun].

shun

■ Those who *boycott* a restaurant (a) avoid the place, (b) hold luncheon meetings there. (   )

(a)

■ Grandfather claims that most so-called adult movies merely act as an *aph_____* ; obviously he should stay away from such motion pictures—that is, he should *bo_____* them.

aphrodisiac
boycott

3. **chauvinism** (shō'vin-iz'ǝm): fanatical or blind patriotism. Nicolas *Chauvin* became ridiculous with bragging about his superloyalty to Napoleon and France.
4. **cynic** (sin'ik): one who has a sneering disbelief in human sincerity and goodness. The *Cynics* were ancient Greek philosophers who maintained that virtue was the goal of life and who, as a result, became very critical of other people and their motives.

■ The Nazi conviction that Hitler and Germany could do no wrong was *ch_____* .

chauvinism

(a)

■ The patriotism of a *chauvinist* is (a) extreme, (b) moderate. (   )

chauvinism

(b)

■ The intense national spirit known as *ch*_____ is manifested in most countries by (a) impartial criticism of national policy, (b) much flag-waving. (   )

(a)

■ A *cynical* person is (a) suspicious and sarcastic, (b) agreeable and innocent. (   )

(b)

■ The *Cynic* Diogenes, who kept looking for an honest man, obviously thought that most people are (a) virtuous, (b) lacking in virtue. (   )

cynic

chauvinism

chauvinism

■ One who sneers at our motives is a *cy*_____ , and such a person would have a low opinion of fanatical patriotism, known as national *ch*_____ , or, possibly, of the delusion that males are the superior sex, known as male *c*_____ .

---

5. **Darwinism:** the theory of evolution that plants and animals transmit slight hereditary variations to future generations and that those forms survive and develop that are best suited to their environment. *Darwinism* involves, in brief, the concepts of natural selection and of the survival of the fittest.

Darwinism

(a)

■ According to the theory of evolution, known as *Dar*_____ , species of plants and animals (a) have been changing and developing from earlier species, (b) have always been as they are now. (   )

(b)

■ Nature permits a species to survive, according to *Darwinism*, if that species (a) has moral goodness, (b) adapts itself to its environment. (   )

Darwinism

(b)

■ Those species that have the necessary claws or fins or teeth, according to _____*ism*, will (a) be punished, (b) survive. (   )

Write the letter that indicates the best definition.

1. (d)
2. (c)
3. (a)
4. (b)
5. (e)

( ) 1. aphrodisiac   a. fanatical patriotism
( ) 2. boycott   b. a suspicious, sarcastic pessimist
( ) 3. chauvinism   c. refuse to deal with
( ) 4. cynic   d. tending to excite lust
( ) 5. Darwinism   e. evolution of species through the survival of the fittest

---

6. **Frankenstein monster** (frank′ən-stīn′): anything that becomes a danger to its creator. In Mary Shelley's novel *Frankenstein* (1818) a natural philosopher named *Frankenstein* creates a repulsive monster which gets out of control and murders him.

(a)

■ A *Frankenstein monster* becomes (a) a threat to its inventor, (b) a faithful, useful servant. ( )

Frankenstein

■ The monster gets out of control and kills *Fr_____* . One must remember that *Frankenstein* is the name of (a) the treacherous monster, (b) the scientist who created the mon-

(b)

ster. ( )

Frankenstein
(a)

■ A *Fr_____* monster among us today, threatening its creators, is (a) the thermonuclear bomb, (b) the bicycle. ( )

---

7. **herculean** (hur′kyoo-lē′ən): very powerful and courageous. *Hercules*, son of Zeus, performed twelve tremendous labors which Hera imposed on him.

(a)

■ A *herculean* task demands (a) power and courage, (b) wit and grace. ( )

herculean
herculean
(a)

■ The job of digging the Panama Canal was *her_____* ; another tremendous, *h_____* job was construction of (a) Hoover Dam, (b) Mabel's new earrings. ( )

(b)

■ Like all *herculean* heroes, steel-drivin' John Henry was courageous and (a) highly educated, (b) powerful. ( )

---

8. **jabberwocky:** nonsensical talk. "Jabberwocky" is an amusing nonsense poem in Lewis Carroll's *Through the Looking Glass* (1872).

■ Nonsense talk is called *jab_____* . To understand *jabberwocky* is (a) easy, (b) almost impossible. (   )

■ Which of the following lines is *jabberwocky?*—(a) "He did not wear his scarlet coat," (b) " 'Twas brillig, and the slithy toves. . . ." (   )

■ To accuse a congressman of *jab_____* is to imply that his talk is (a) meaningless, (b) unpatriotic. (   )

9. **laconic** (lə-kon′ik): brief; pithy. The *Laconians* were thrifty with words; they replied to an enemy ultimatum with one word: "If."
10. **Lilliputian** (lil′ə-pū′shən): very small; a tiny person. On the island of *Lilliput*, described in Swift's *Gulliver's Travels*, the men and women are six inches tall.

■ Most classified ads are _____ [laconic / prolix].

■ A *laconic* answer is _____ [verbose / brief].

■ To say that a presidential candidate is "*Lil_____* in talents" is (a) insulting to him, (b) flattering to him. (   )

■ A *Lilliputian* house is _____ [huge / tiny].

■ Political candidates tend to be wordy rather than *la_____* .

■ Gulliver meets the Brobdingnagians, a race of highly intelligent giants who are quite the opposite of the tiny *Li_____s.*

Quiz

Write the letter that indicates the best definition.

1. (d)
2. (e)
3. (b)
4. (a)
5. (c)

( )	1. Frankenstein monster	a.	brief; concise
		b.	gibberish; doubletalk
( )	2. herculean	c.	tiny
( )	3. jabberwocky	d.	a threat to its own inventor
( )	4. laconic	e.	powerful; requiring great strength
( )	5. Lilliputian		and bravery

---

11. **machiavellian** (mak′i-ə-vel′i-ən): crafty and deceitful in political strategy. In *The Prince* (1513), Niccolo *Machiavelli*, a Florentine diplomat, describes ways to grasp and maintain political power.

12. **maudlin** (môd′lin): tearfully emotional or sentimental; foolishly drunk. Mary *Magdalen* was depicted by medieval painters with her eyes red and swollen from weeping.

■ Sentimental people often revel in their tearful memories and become *mau*_____ .

maudlin

■ One who is *maudlin* is emotionally _____ [stable / unstable] and perhaps inclined to _____ [dissect / weep over] a dead bird.

unstable
weep over

■ Bribes, double dealing, and false promises are common to *mac*_____ diplomacy.

machiavellian

■ The *machiavellian* politician is hard-boiled and _____ [honorable / unscrupulous] with no time for tearful loyalties and *m*_____ sentiment.

unscrupulous

maudlin

■ The woman who weeps softly into her beer is *ma*_____ .

maudlin

■ The diplomat who thinks "Anything goes" is *ma*_____ .

machiavellian

---

13. **maverick** (mav′ĕr-ik): a person of unorthodox ideas who tends to act independently of parties and factions. Samuel *Maverick* (circa 1850), a Texas rancher, would not brand his calves, and they were called *mavericks*.

maverick	■ An independent-minded congressman who can't be counted on to vote with his party is sometimes called a *mav*_____ .
(b)	■ A *maverick* is (a) a conformist, (b) a nonconformist. ( )
maverick	■ Henry David Thoreau, who defied his government by refusing to pay his poll tax, was a *m*_____ .
defend maverick	■ Ralph Waldo Emerson believed in self-reliance and genuine individualism, and so his essays tend to _____ [defend / attack] a man's right to be a *m*_____ .

14. **mentor** (men′tər): a wise and loyal adviser; a trusted teacher. In Greek legend, *Mentor* gives wise counsel to Odysseus and his son Telemachus.

mentor	■ A head football coach is sometimes referred to as a _____ [monitor / mentor].
counselor	■ A *mentor* is a trusted _____ [wife / counselor].
mentor (a)	■ You might refer to your English professor as your *m*_____ . After all, *Mentor* was Telemachus' (a) wise teacher, (b) mortal enemy. ( )

15. **nimrod:** a hunter. *Nimrod*, the grandson of Ham, is described as a mighty hunter in Genesis, 10:8.

(a)	■ A store for *nimrods* sells (a) shotguns, (b) women's purses. ( )
Nimrod hunter	■ The Bible mentions *Nim*_____ , who was a mighty _____ [wrestler / hunter].
nimrods	■ Our western elk have been decimated by _____ [nimrods / hotrods].

Write the letter that indicates the best definition.

1. (b)
2. (a)
3. (e)
4. (c)
5. (d)

( ) 1. machiavellian
( ) 2. maudlin
( ) 3. maverick
( ) 4. mentor
( ) 5. nimrod

a. weakly or tearfully emotional
b. politically crafty; unscrupulous
c. a counselor
d. a hunter
e. a nonconformist

---

16. **odyssey** (od′ə-si): a long eventful journey. Homer's *Odyssey* describes ten adventurous years of wandering by *Odysseus* on his homeward voyage after the fall of Troy.

odyssey

■ In Steinbeck's *The Grapes of Wrath* (1939) the Joads make an adventurous *od*_____ from Oklahoma to California.

odyssey

(b)

■ A long journey, such as was made by Lewis and Clark, is called an *o*_____ if it is (a) quick and direct, (b) wandering and with unexpected delays. ( )

odyssey

(a)

■ Colorful wanderings such as those of Odysseus are known as an _____—and one would probably use the word *odyssey* to describe one's (a) two-year trip across Asia by donkey, (b) overnight flight to Chicago. ( )

---

17. **Pyrrhic victory** (pir′ik): a too costly victory. *Pyrrhos* defeated the Romans at Asculum, 279 B.C., but lost so many men that he exclaimed, "One more such victory and we are undone!"

Pyrrhic

(b)

■ A *Pyr*_____ *victory* is (a) an overwhelming success, (b) extremely expensive. ( )

Pyrrhic

■ A baseball team which wins a practice game but loses its shortstop and its star pitcher in a bone-breaking collision has won a *P*_____ *victory*.

victory
hollow

■ A nation which drains its resources to win a small military objective has won a *Pyrrhic v*_____ , that is, a rather _____ [wonderful / hollow] triumph.

---

18. **quixotic** (kwik-sot'ik): idealistic but ridiculously impractical. Don *Quixote*, the hero of a novel by Cervantes (1615), is a romantic visionary, a tilter at windmills, but one of God's fools.

quixotic

(b)

■ Idealists like Don Quixote are *qu*_____ ; they tend to be (a) level-headed and conventional, (b) impulsive and romantic. (   )

quixotic
(a)

■ Critics condemned Woodrow Wilson's plan for a League of Nations as *qu*_____ , that is, (a) visionary, (b) cynical. (   )

quixotic
impractical

■ The American Transcendentalists were full of visionary and *q*_____ schemes, such as the Brook Farm experiment, a truly _____ [practical / impractical] undertaking.

---

19. **robot** (rō'bət): a human-like machine or a machine-like human. *R.U.R.*, *Rossum's Universal Robots* (1923), a satiric play by Karel Kapek, introduced the word *robot* into our language.

20. **solon** (sō'lən): a wise lawmaker. *Solon* is referred to in Plato's "The Symposium" as "the revered father of Athenian Laws."

solons

■ Legislators are often called *so*_____ .

robots

■ Automatons are *ro*_____ .

Congress
factories

■ Normally one might expect to see *solons* in _____ [factories / Congress] and *robots* in _____ [factories / Congress].

robot

■ A person who must perform the same simple mechanical operation day after day becomes a kind of *r*_____ .

■ *Robots* have (a) passions and free will, (b) only automatic reactions. (   )

■ Our laws are formulated by s_____ .

■ The word *solon* has traditionally suggested a _____ [wise / featherheaded] lawmaker.

Quiz

Write the letter that indicates the best definition.

(   ) 1. odyssey   a. a wise lawmaker
(   ) 2. Pyrrhic victory   b. a costly triumph
(   ) 3. quixotic   c. visionary; impractical
(   ) 4. robot   d. a wandering journey
(   ) 5. solon   e. an automaton

---

21. **spoonerism:** an accidental transposition of sounds in adjacent words. The Rev. W. A. *Spooner* of New College, Oxford, used to make comic blunders like "our queer old dean" for "our dear old queen."

■ *Spoonerisms* like "nosey little cook" for "cozy little nook" involve (a) transposed sounds, (b) gross exaggerations. (   )

■ "It is kistumary to cuss the bride" is a *sp_____* .

■ Another _____*ism* is "half-warmed fish" for (a) "half-formed wish," (b) "half-hearted kiss." (   )

■ The phrase "tons of soil" is a *spoonerism* for "sons of toil," and "well boiled icicle" is a *sp_____* for "well _____ _____ ."

---

22. **stentorian:** extremely loud. *Stentor* is described by Homer in *The Iliad* as a Greek herald with the voice of fifty men.

■ Challenging the Trojans in the distance required a *st_____* voice.

■ A *stentorian* voice is like (a) a whisper, (b) a bellow. (   )

■ Of course, *st*_____ tones are quite acceptable in (a) a football stadium, (b) a college library. (   )

■ The Greek herald named Stentor _____ [was / was not] silent as the Sphinx.

---

23. **tantalize:** to tease and torment by withholding what is offered. *Tantalus* was tormented in Hades by water and fruit that he could never quite reach.

■ A hungry cat is *tantalized* when it is allowed to _____ [eat / smell] a roast chicken.

■ We usually tease, or *tan*_____ , by (a) giving gifts, (b) withholding satisfactions. (   )

■ A famished beggar is _____*zed* as he walks (a) through a forest, (b) past a bakery. (   )

---

24. **utopian** (ū-tō′pi-ən): impossibly ideal, especially in social organization. Sir Thomas More's *Utopia* (1516) describes a flawless government and society—imaginary, of course.

■ Dreamers envision a *utopian* social order in which everything will be (a) lousy, (b) practically perfect. (   )

■ A nation without wars, without crime, without poverty? That would be *ut*_____ .

■ Edward Bellamy's *Looking Backward* (1887) describes a *u*_____ society of the year 2000, wherein conditions will presumably be vastly (a) improved, (b) worse. (   )

■ Ivor Brown speaks of H. G. Wells' "charting of Utopias," meaning that Wells explored (a) African jungles, (b) plans for ideal societies. (   )

241

25. **vandal:** a person who willfully or ignorantly mars or destroys property, especially what is beautiful or valuable. The *Vandals* were a Germanic people who ravaged Gaul and Spain and sacked Rome in A.D. 455.

vandals

(b)

■ Window smashers and tire slashers are *van*_____ ; in short, they are public (a) benefactors, (b) menaces. (   )

vandal

■ Whoever painted those vulgar words all over our elementary school is a *va*_____ , and a poor speller, too.

vandal

■ A beauty-defacing rascal, or *v*_____ , might be found (a) drawing a famous ruin, (b) ruining a famous draw-

(b)

ing. (   )

vandal

■ Were Venus de Milo's arms broken off by a *v*_____ , or did she chew her fingernails too much?

Quiz

Write the letter that indicates the best definition.

1. (e)
2. (d)
3. (a)
4. (c)
5. (b)

(   ) 1. spoonerism   a. to tease and torment
(   ) 2. stentorian   b. a destroyer of property
(   ) 3. tantalize   c. ideal; existing only in theory
(   ) 4. utopian   d. loud as a trumpet
(   ) 5. vandal   e. turned-around syllables

REVIEW TEST

Write the word studied in this chapter that will complete the sentence.

1. A voice of Homeric loudness is *st*_____ .

2. A hunter is sometimes called a *ni*_____ .

3. A slip of the tongue involving transposed syllables is a *sp*_____ .

4. A general refusal to deal with somebody is a *bo*_____ .

5. Winning a contest at tremendous cost is a *Py*_____ *v* _____ .

6. To be tearfully, drunkenly sentimental is to be *ma*_____ .

7. A drug or other agent which excites lust is an *ap*_____ .

8. An automaton or mechanical person is a *ro*_____ .

9. One who maliciously defaces public property is a *va*_____ .

10. A wise lawmaker is a *so*_____ .

11. A device that becomes a threat to its own creator is a *Fr*_____ *m*_____ .

12. Patriotism carried to a fanatical extreme is *ch*_____ .

13. A long wandering journey is an *od*_____ .

14. A nonconformist acting independently of party is a *ma*_____ .

15. The concepts of natural selection and of the survival of the fittest are basic to *Da*_____ .

Write *True* or *False*.

_____ 16. A *Lilliputian* would probably be an effective basketball center.

_____ 17. A *herculean* task requires great strength and endurance.

_____ 18. *Jabberwocky* is clear, standard English.

_____ 19. A *mentor* is a wise counselor or teacher.

_____ 20. A *cynic* tends to distrust people's motives.

Write the letter that indicates the best completion.

( ) 21. A *utopian* plan is (a) economical, (b) practical, (c) democratic, (d) visionary.
( ) 22. A *machiavellian* leader is (a) unscrupulous, (b) honorable, (c) self-sacrificing, (d) naive.
( ) 23. A *laconic* comment is (a) flattering, (b) windy, (c) short, (d) amusing.
( ) 24. A *quixotic* undertaking is (a) expensive, (b) impractical, (c) popular, (d) dull.
( ) 25. To *tantalize* is (a) to inoculate, (b) to tickle, (c) to tease, (d) to eat.

Key to Review Test

Check your test answers by the following key. Deduct 4% per error from a possible 100%.

1. stentorian	6. maudlin	11. Frankenstein	16. False	21. (d)
2. nimrod	7. aphrodisiac	monster	17. True	22. (a)
3. spoonerism	8. robot	12. chauvinism	18. False	23. (c)
4. boycott	9. vandal	13. odyssey	19. True	24. (b)
5. Pyrrhic victory	10. solon	14. maverick	20. True	25. (c)
		15. Darwinism		

Score: _____%

NOTE: For supplementary exercises on additional name derivatives, see APPENDIX B, page 328.

17

Psychology

A cynic has said that psychology "tells us what everybody knows, in language that nobody understands." His comment is more witty than accurate. Actually, psychology, which is the study of human behavior, tells us many things we don't know about ourselves and in language we can learn to understand quite well. In fact, the terms of psychology must be understood if we are to qualify in such diverse areas as social work, law, and medicine; or if we are to analyze the fiction of Faulkner, the poetry of Jeffers, the dramas of O'Neill.

Chapter 17 stresses twenty-five basic terms of psychology, and presents fifty more definitions in a supplementary list. As you fill in the frames, try to relate the terms to people you have known or read about. Can you think of anyone with a *neurosis*, a *psychosomatic* illness, or a trace of *narcissism*? Have you yourself had a *traumatic* experience? Are you a *sibling* (or would you knock a person down for calling you that)? Words become more meaningful when you see how they apply to the life around you.

1. **ambivalence** (am-biv′ə-ləns): conflicting feelings, such as love and hate, toward the same person or thing. You may have a deep affection for your parents and yet be angry because they interfere with your decisions; your attitude toward them, then, is one of *ambivalence*.

■ A child wants to pet a strange "doggie" but is fearful. The conflict of feelings is called *amb*_____ .

ambivalence

■ Felix wants to order the giant hot fudge sundae but he doesn't want to get fat. His attitude toward the sundae is one of *am*_____ .

ambivalence

■ A star basketball player has *ambivalent* feelings toward his coach. This means that the athlete (a) can shoot with either hand, (b) has contradictory emotions. (   )

(b)

■ Wilmer wants to ask Alice for a date but worries that she will turn him down; Alice loves Jerry but has fits of jealousy when he talks to other girls; Jerry craves alcohol but realizes that it can ruin him. These conflicting attitudes illustrate *am*_____ .

ambivalence

■ It is _____ [possible / impossible] for a person to be both attracted and repelled by something. The condition is called *a*_____ .

possible

ambivalence

2. **aptitude** (ap′tə-tood′): the natural ability to acquire a skill or type of knowledge. A test of musical *aptitude*, for example, does not measure achievement but predicts future performance.

■ A high score in a mechanical-*aptitude* test means (a) that you have unusual ability as a mechanic, (b) that you could be trained to be a good mechanic. (   )

(b)

246

aptitude	■ An achievement test measures what you can do now; an *apt*_____ test predicts what you will be able to do with training.
aptitude	■ Glenna is extremely athletic, and although she has never played tennis she probably has an *ap*_____ for it.
does aptitude	■ Harvey is an excellent speller and scores high in a finger-dexterity test; apparently he _____ [does / doesn't] have an *a*_____ for typewriting.

3. **claustrophobia** (klô′strə-fō′bē-ə): morbid fear of being in enclosed or narrow places.

claustrophobia	■ Linus feels stifled and fearful in an elevator or a closet. He has *cl*_____ .
(a)	■ *Claustrophobia* manifests itself in an abnormal fear of (a) small rooms, (b) heights. ( )
claustrophobia	■ A phobia involves excessive fear in the absence of real danger. The excessive fear and anxiety of a clerk who must work in a small, windowless office may be due to *cl*_____ .
(a)	■ A person with *claustrophobia* would probably feel comfortable (a) in a meadow, (b) in a trunk. ( )

4. **compensation:** an attempt to make up for an undesirable trait by exaggerating a socially approved one.

compensation	■ A student who is weak in academic courses may try to excel in athletics—an example of *com*_____ .
inferiority	■ *Compensation* is an effort to excel in one activity in order to make up for a feeling of _____ [inferiority / accomplishment] in another.
compensation	■ Napoleon, Hitler, and Stalin were of short stature, and their drive for political power was probably a form of *co*_____ .

success
compensation

■ Igor was embarrassingly poor in athletics, so he tried doubly hard to become a _____ [success / failure] as a debater, an effort known as c_____ .

5. **dipsomania:** an abnormal craving for alcoholic liquors.
6. **kleptomania:** an abnormal tendency to steal.

kleptomania
dipsomania

■ An irresistible impulse to steal is *klep*_____ ; an insatiable desire for alcohol is *di*_____ .

drink
steal

■ Emotional disturbances have been cited as a cause of *dipsomania*, or the tendency to _____ [steal / drink], and *kleptomania*, or the tendency to _____ [steal / drink].

dipsomania

■ Alcoholics Anonymous is an excellent organization for those whose problem is *di*_____ .

kleptomania

■ "Stealing lingerie?" said the judge. "Looks like a case of *kl*_____ . Ten days should be enough. After all, this is your first slip."

(b)

■ *Kleptomania* is associated with (a) overeating, (b) shoplifting. (   )

(a)

■ *Dipsomania* is associated with (a) boozing, (b) pocket picking. (   )

Quiz

Write the letter that indicates the best definition.

1. (e)
2. (c)
3. (a)
4. (f)
5. (b)
6. (d)

(   ) 1. ambivalence   a. fear of small enclosures
(   ) 2. aptitude   b. alcoholism
(   ) 3. claustrophobia   c. capacity to learn
(   ) 4. compensation   d. irresistible stealing
(   ) 5. dipsomania   e. conflicting feelings
(   ) 6. kleptomania   f. making up for a shortcoming

7. **ego** (ē′gō): the conscious part of the personality, which has to deal with the id, the superego, and external reality, according to Freud. The *ego* does our logical thinking.

8. **id:** the primitive, instinctive, aggressive part of our personality. The pleasure-loving *id*, with which we are born, seeks immediate gratification regardless of consequences, but it is later held in check by the superego and ego, says Freud.

9. **superego:** the moralistic part of the personality which acts as a conscience to control the ego and the id. The *superego* is a product of parental and social training, and it sets up standards of right and wrong.

■ A baby is like a little animal; it is swayed by the raw, instinctive part of its personality, the *i*＿＿＿＿＿ .

id

■ From its environment the child absorbs a sense of what is right and wrong. This developing conscience has been called the *su*＿＿＿＿＿ .

superego

■ The self-aware, thinking part of the mind is called the *e*＿＿＿＿＿ .

ego

■ The unconscious parts of the mind include the primitive drives, or *i*＿＿＿＿＿ , and the conscience, or *su*＿＿＿＿＿ . The conscious part of the mind, which does our thinking, is the *e*＿＿＿＿＿ .

id
superego
ego

■ The uncontrolled impulses of the *id* are likely to be ＿＿＿＿＿ [encouraged / condemned] by society. Such uncontrolled impulses would probably produce (a) rapists, burglars, gluttons, (b) priests, teachers, saints. (   )

condemned

(a)

■ Traditional values and ideals of society are represented by the *su*＿＿＿＿＿ . The *superego* strives for (a) pleasure, (b) perfection. (   )

superego
(b)

■ The conscious, thinking part of you is called the *e*＿＿＿＿ . The *ego* operates according to the ＿＿＿＿＿ [reality / pleasure] principle.

ego
reality

id
superego
ego

■ Personalities can be distorted, says Freud, if either the animalistic i_____ or the moralistic s_____ is too strong. One's behavior should be controlled by the conscious aspect of the mind, the e_____ .

(a)

■ The concept of an *id*, *ego*, and *superego* was first developed by (a) Sigmund Freud, (b) Charles Darwin. (   )

---

10. **extrasensory perception** (ESP): ability to gain knowledge without use of the known senses. *ESP* refers to telepathy, clairvoyance, or any other means of perceiving external events or communicating by mental rather than physical means.

(a)

■ *Extrasensory perception* would be operative if you could send a message by (a) brain waves, (b) Western Union. (   )

extrasensory
  perception

■ *ESP* is an acronym for *ex_____ per_____* .

extrasensory
  perception

■ You dream that your best friend is calling for help, and the next day he falls down a well. Precognition, as illustrated here, is a type of *ex_____ p_____* .

ESP

■ Most psychologists do not as yet believe in *extrasensory perception* (usually abbreviated _____).

(d)

■ The term *ESP* does *not* refer to (a) clairvoyance, (b) precognition, (c) telepathy, (d) short-wave radio. (   )

---

11. **free association:** the free, unhampered, rambling talk by a patient by which his repressions are discovered.
12. **psychoanalysis** (sī′kō-ə-nal′ə-sis): a system of mental therapy, devised by Freud, whereby through free association and dream analysis certain conflictual material is released from the unconscious.

psychoanalysis

■ Freud's technique of treating mental illness is known as *psy_____* .

free association psychoanalysis	■ Rambling from one topic to another is called *fr*_____ *as*_____ . This activity is common during sessions of *psy*_____ .
(a)	■ The purpose of *psychoanalysis* is to help the patient overcome problems that are basically (a) mental, (b) physical. ( )
psychoanalysis free association	■ A mental shock that occurred in infancy might be disclosed during a session of *ps*_____ by means of *fr*_____ *as*_____ .
(b)	■ Through *free association* one's unconscious wishes find (a) concealment, (b) verbal expression. ( )
psychoanalysis	■ Psychologists do not accept all of Freud's theories, but he is respected as the father of *p*_____*sis*.

Quiz

Write the letter that indicates the best definition.

1. (f) 2. (d) 3. (b) 4. (e) 5. (c) 6. (a)	( ) 1. ego a. Freud's system of treatment ( ) 2. id b. conscience, or moral control ( ) 3. superego c. rambling monologue ( ) 4. ESP d. seat of animalistic impulses ( ) 5. free association e. thought transference ( ) 6. psychoanalysis f. thinking part of the mind

---

13. **hallucination** (hə-lōō′sə-nā′shən): the apparent witnessing of sights and sounds that do not exist.

hallucination	■ "Yesterday upon a stair / I saw a man who wasn't there. . . ." The poet seems to have had a *hal*_____ .
(a)	■ The sights and sounds of a *hallucination* are (a) imaginary, (b) actual. ( )
hallucination	■ Macbeth imagines that he sees the murdered Banquo sitting in front of him; Macbeth is experiencing a *ha*_____ .

251

■ *Hallucinative* drugs make one's sense impressions more (a) dependable, (b) undependable. (　)

---

14. **hypochondria** (hī′pə-kon′drē-ə): excessive worry about one's health; anxiety about minor or imaginary ailments.
15. **psychosomatic** (sī′kō-sō-mat′ik): referring to a physical disorder caused by emotional stress.

hypochondria

■ Every morning Wilhelm gets up worried, looks at his tongue, and swallows thirty pills; his problem is *hyp*_____ .

(a)

■ A *hypochondriac* usually believes that his health is (a) failing, (b) perfect. (　)

psychosomatic

■ Gus's ulcers act up when he works under pressure; his illness is probably *psy*_____ .

psychosomatic
(a)

■ Disorders such as asthma, dermatitis, and high blood pressure are sometimes *ps*_____ , that is, caused by (a) emotional stress, (b) bacterial infection. (　)

hypochondria

■ Julius with his imaginary illnesses suffers from *hy*_____ ; he caught his last disease from the *Reader's Digest*. His wife Lydia, overfearful of germs, boils dishes three times before using them; she also suffers from

hypochondria

*h*_____ .

psychosomatic

■ Soldiers have sometimes developed a paralysis from fear of combat; such paralysis is _____*ic*.

---

16. **narcissism** (när′si-siz′əm): abnormal self-love; erotic pleasure obtained from admiration of one's own body or mind.
17. **Oedipus complex** (ed′ə-pəs): sexual attraction to the parent of the opposite sex and hostility for the parent of the same sex.

narcissism

■ *Narcissus* admired his own physical features; thus, Freud refers to such self-love as *nar*_____ .

(b)

■ *Narcissism* involves a lack of concern for other people and extreme concern for (a) narcotics, (b) one's self. (　)

Oedipus
    complex

■ *Oedipus* loved his mother and hated his father; thus, Freud refers to a similar stage in child development as the *Oed*_____ *com*_____ .

Oedipus
    complex

■ Little Jasper is competing with his father for the love of his mother; Jasper's feelings are referred to as the *O*_____ *c*_____ .

narcissism

■ The pretty people in TV commercials often say, "I love my hair—so soft and fragrant," "My skin is baby-smooth," "My breath is twenty-four hours sweet and fresh, thanks to Putro"; such conceited lines suggest *nar*_____ .

(b)

■ The *Oedipus complex* involves rivalry for the love of the parent of (a) the same sex, (b) the opposite sex. (   )

narcissism

■ A person who is obsessed with his or her own handsome appearance is exhibiting *na*_____ .

Quiz

Write the letter that indicates the best definition.

1. (e)
2. (d)
3. (a)
4. (c)
5. (b)

(   ) 1. hallucination   a. of illness caused by emotions
(   ) 2. hypochondria   b. love-mother, hate-father phase
(   ) 3. psychosomatic   c. self-love
(   ) 4. narcissism   d. anxiety about one's health
(   ) 5. Oedipus complex   e. seeing what is nonexistent

18. **psychosis** (sī-kō′sis): a mental disorder such as paranoia or schizophrenia that involves very serious disorganization of the personality; insanity.
19. **paranoia** (par′ə-noi′ə): a mental disorder marked by delusions of persecution or of grandeur.
20. **schizophrenia** (skit′sə-frē′nē-ə): a mental disorder marked by splitting of the personality, a retreat from reality, and emotional deterioration.

(a)
(b)

■ *Psychotic* people are (a) irrational, (b) rational. (   ) They tend to (a) cope with reality, (b) withdraw from reality. (   )

paranoia	■ The delusion that people are plotting behind your back and are "out to get you" is a symptom of *par*_____ .
(a)	■ Another common symptom of *paranoia* is the delusion of (a) grandeur, (b) inferiority. ( )
schizophrenia	■ Stanley sits silently for hours, possibly in a fixed position. Such withdrawal from reality is usually known as *sc*_____ .
(a)	■ A *schizophrenic* tends to be (a) withdrawn and mute, (b) the life of the party. ( )
paranoia	■ Delusions of grandeur ("I am Napoleon," "I am Jesus Christ") are symptoms of *pa*_____ .
(b)	■ A major mental disorder is (a) a neurosis, (b) a psychosis. ( )
psychosis	■ Hardening of blood vessels in the brain of an elderly person may result in a serious mental disorder, or *ps*_____ .
schizophrenia

paranoia | ■ The *psychotic* who is rigid and unresponsive probably suffers from *sc*_____ ; the *psychotic* who shouts "They conspire against me—I'll kill them—I'll rule the world!" probably suffers from *pa*_____ . |

---

21. **rationalization** (rash'ən-ə-liz-ā'shən): justifying of unreasonable behavior by presenting false but plausible reasons to oneself or to others.

conceal	■ To *rationalize* one of our misdeeds is to _____ [reveal / conceal] the real motives behind it.
rationalization	■ Whenever Buster, who is overweight, orders another double banana split, he says: "I have to keep up my strength." Buster's excuse is an example of *rat*_____ .

(b)
■ Big Country invades rich Little Country, saying, "We will restore better government." Big Country is probably indulging in (a) pure altruism, (b) rationalization. (   )

rationalization

(b)
■ Self-justification, known as *ra*_____ , is probably being used when a football coach explains a 79-6 loss this way: "We lost because (a) we were outplayed"; (b) them umpires was prejudiced." (   )

---

22. **regression:** going back to earlier, less mature behavior as an escape from a present conflict.

regression
■ Six-year-old Wilmer sees his new baby sister get all the attention, so he begins to wet his pants again. He is trying to solve his conflict by *reg*_____ .

less
■ *Regression* involves a change to _____ [more / less] mature behavior.

regression
■ A young housewife keeps running back to the security of her parental home. This, too, is probably *reg*_____ .

child
regression
■ A man loses his wife or his job and gets drunk. His escape to the irresponsible condition of a _____ [child / adult] is *r*_____ .

---

23. **sibling:** a brother or sister.

siblings
■ The Grunches have three sons and two daughters, a total of five *sib*_____ .

siblings
■ Suppose you have an older sister and a younger brother. This means that you have two *si*_____ .

are not
■ Your cousins _____ [are / are not] your *siblings*.

is not
■ Wally, an only child, _____ [is / is not] a *sibling*.

■ Competition and jealousy between two brothers, between two sisters, or between a brother and a sister are aspects of s_____ rivalry.

---

24. **trauma** (trou′mə): an emotional shock which has a lasting effect.

■ A trauma is a _____ [minor / major] emotional shock.

■ Nellie has nightmares ever since her car accident. Its effect has been (a) traumatic, (b) salutary. (   )

■ Incest or other forms of sexual molestation can cause serious tr_____ in children.

■ The effects of an emotional shock, or t_____ , are (a) temporary, (b) lasting. (   )

---

25. **voyeur** (vwä-yûr′): a Peeping Tom; one who obtains sexual gratification by looking at sexual objects or acts, especially secretively.

■ A *voyeur* peeks into windows hoping to see (a) sexual acts, (b) television programs. (   )

■ A Peeping Tom, also known as a *vo_____* , derives particular pleasure from (a) exhibiting his body, (b) peeking in secret at the nakedness of others. (   )

■ Two men are using telescopes. The *voyeur* is the fellow peering (a) at Jupiter, (b) into bedrooms. (   )

■ Children go through a stage of intense curiosity about sex. Consequently, *voyeurism* is considered to be _____ [a mature / an immature] way of achieving sexual fulfillment.

Quiz

Write the letter that indicates the best definition.

1. (e)
2. (c)
3. (h)
4. (b)
5. (g)
6. (d)
7. (a)
8. (f)

( ) 1. psychosis
( ) 2. paranoia
( ) 3. schizophrenia
( ) 4. rationalization
( ) 5. regression
( ) 6. sibling
( ) 7. trauma
( ) 8. voyeur

a. a lasting emotional shock
b. justifying with false reasons
c. delusions of grandeur and persecution
d. a brother or sister
e. serious mental disorder (general term)
f. a Peeping Tom
g. escape via less mature behavior
h. splitting of personality

REVIEW TEST

Write the word studied in this chapter that will complete the sentence.

1. Abnormal self-love is *na*_____ .

2. Morbid fear of small, enclosed places is *cl*_____ .

3. That part of the unconscious mind that acts as a conscience is the *su*_____ .

4. A brother or sister is a *si*_____ .

5. A splitting of the personality and withdrawal from reality is *sc*_____ .

6. Conflicting feelings, like love and hate, for the same person are known as *amb*_____ .

7. A son's desire for his mother and rivalry with his father is the *Oed*_____ *c*_____ .

8. Physical illness caused by emotional stress is *ps*_____ .

9. Reverting to less mature behavior as an escape is *reg*_____ .

10. Excessive desire for alcohol is *di*_____ .

11. Abnormal anxiety about one's imagined illnesses is *hy*_____ .

12. A compulsion to do shoplifting is *kl*_____ .

13. A lasting emotional shock is a *tr*_____ .

14. One who peeks into windows to see sex acts is a *vo*_____ .

15. Uncle Fritz claims he is General Grant and that the neighbors are plotting to poison him. Fritz has symptoms of *pa*_____ .

Write *True* or *False*.

_____ 16. The purpose of an *aptitude* test is to measure achievement.

_____ 17. The *ego* is the conscious part of the personality.

_____ 18. *Hallucinations* can be caused by drugs.

_____ 19. *Free association* is a technique used in psychoanalysis.

_____ 20. A *psychosis* is a fairly common, minor nervous ailment.

_____ 21. Unusually keen vision and hearing are referred to as *extra-sensory perception (ESP)*.

_____ 22. The *id*, which is powerful during one's infancy, passes out of existence when one reaches maturity.

_____ 23. A certain blind girl tries doubly hard to master the piano; her efforts are a form of *compensation*.

_____ 24. *Rationalization* means logical reasoning, the avoidance of fallacy.

_____ 25. *Psychoanalysis* is a method of treating mental illness.

Key to Review Test

Check your test answers by the following key. Deduct 4% per error from a possible 100%.

1. narcissism	10. dipsomania	19. True
2. claustrophobia	11. hypochondria	20. False
3. superego	12. kleptomania	21. False
4. sibling	13. trauma	22. False
5. schizophrenia	14. voyeur	23. True
6. ambivalence	15. paranoia	24. False
7. Oedipus complex	16. False	25. True
8. psychosomatic	17. True	
9. regression	18. True	

Score: _____%

SUPPLEMENTARY LIST

1. **abnormal psychology:** the study of abnormal behavior, including neurosis, psychosis, and other mental disorders.
2. **acrophobia** (ak′rə-fō′bē-ə): a fear of high places.
3. **aggression:** behavior that aims to hurt someone or what he stands for.
4. **amnesia** (am-nē′zhə): partial or total loss of memory; specifically, forgetting one's own identity.
5. **atavism** (at′ə-viz′əm): reversion to an earlier ancestral characteristic.
6. **behaviorism:** the doctrine that man reacts automatically, like a machine, to stimuli.
7. **clairvoyance** (klâr-voi′əns): the alleged ability to see objects or to know things beyond the range of the senses.
8. **compulsion:** an irresistible impulse to perform an irrational act.

9. **conditioned reflex:** a response set off by a second stimulus associated with the primary stimulus; for example, secretion of saliva set off in Pavlov's dog by a dinner bell.

10. **defense mechanism** (mek′ə-niz′əm): an unconscious adjustment to block out unpleasant memories, feelings, or knowledge.

11. **dementia praecox** (di-men′shə prē′koks): former term for schizophrenia.

12. **dissociation** (di-sō′sē-ā′shən): a splitting apart of mental elements, involving loss of control over memory and motor processes.

13. **dualism:** the state of being twofold; the theory that a man consists of two entities—body and mind.

14. **Electra complex:** a daughter's unconscious sexual attachment to her father and hostility to her mother.

15. **empathy:** one's participating in the feelings and spirit of another person or thing.

16. **exhibitionism:** a tendency to behave so as to attract attention; self-exposure.

17. **extrovert** (eks′trō-vûrt): a person actively interested in his environment and other people rather than in himself.

18. **fixation:** an abnormal attachment to some person, object, or idea.

19. **Freudian** (froi′dē-ən): pertaining to Sigmund Freud's methods of psychoanalysis, which emphasize the techniques of free association and transference and try to give the patient an insight into his unconscious conflicts and motives.

20. **gustatory** (gus′tə-tôr′ē): relating to the sense of taste.

21. **hysteria** (hi-ster′ē-ə): emotional frenzy marked by sensory and motor disturbances.

22. **identification:** the putting of oneself in the place of someone else and unconsciously sharing his admirable qualities.

23. **infantilism** (in-fan′tə-liz′əm): extreme immaturity of mind and body in an adult.

24. **inhibition** (in′i-bish′ən): the blocking of one impulse by another.

25. **intelligence quotient** (I.Q.): the mental age multiplied by 100 and then divided by the actual age.

26. **introspection:** analysis of one's own mental and emotional states.

27. **intuition** (in′too-ish′ən): awareness of something without conscious reasoning.

28. **kinesthetic** (kin′is-thet′ik): pertaining to muscle sense or the sensation of position, movement, and tension in the body.

29. **libido** (li-bē′dō): the drive for sex gratification.

30. **masochism** (mas′ə-kiz′əm): the deriving of sexual pleasure from being hurt or humiliated.

31. **maturation** (mach′oo-rā′shən): completion of growth process in the body and the accompanying behavioral changes.

32. **megalomania** (meg′ə-lō-mā′nē-ə): delusions of wealth, power, and self-importance.

33. **melancholia** (mel′ən-kō′lē-ə): a mental disorder characterized by extreme gloominess and depression of spirits.

34. **neurasthenic** (nūr′əs-then′ik): afflicted with fatigue, worry, pains, etc., because of emotional conflicts.

35. **neurosis** (nū-rō′sis): an emotional disorder, less severe than a psychosis, characterized by anxieties, obsessions, compulsions, and physical complaints.

36. **obsession:** an idea or desire that haunts the mind.

37. **parapsychology** (par′ə): the study of clairvoyance, telepathy, and other apparently supernatural phenomena.

38. **phobia** (fō′bē-ə): any irrational or morbid fear.

39. **pleasure principle:** automatic adjustment of one's thoughts to secure pleasure and to avoid pain.

40. **projection:** ascribing one's own motives to someone else, thus relieving one's ego of guilt feelings.

41. **psychedelic** (sī′ki-del′ik): of a mental state, usually drug-induced, marked by entrancement and blissful aesthetic perceptiveness.

42. **psychodrama:** the acting out of situations related to one's problem, as a form of cathartic therapy.

43. **Rorschach test** (rôr′shäk): the analysis of personality by means of responses to ink-blot designs.

44. **sadism** (sad′iz-əm): the deriving of sexual pleasure from hurting one's partner.

45. **stimulus** (stim′yoo-ləs): anything that excites an organism, organ, or part into activity.

46. **subjective:** reflecting a person's feelings and thinking rather than objective reality.

47. **sublimation:** the channeling of psychic energy into socially acceptable activities.

48. **subliminal** (sub-lim′ə-nəl): below the level of consciousness but perceptible by the subconscious.

49. **synapse** (si-naps′): the point where a nerve impulse passes from one neuron to the next.

50. **xenophobia** (zen′ə-fō′bē-ə): fear or hatred of strangers and foreigners.

18

Business and Law

This chapter is recommended to only two groups of students:

1. Those going into business or law
2. Those *not* going into business or law

All citizens, in short, must wet their feet in commercial law. In the words of the jurist Sir William Blackstone, good citizens "cannot, in any scene of life, discharge properly their duty either to the public or to themselves, without some degree of knowledge in the laws" (1753).

Pick up a newspaper and you read of *indictments, injunctions, libel suits,* and *felonies.* Buy a house and you must talk of *realty, collateral, mortgages,* and *easements.* Open a pizza parlor and you bandy words like *franchise, prospectus, solvent,* and *vouchers.* Inescapably you live in a world of business law.

First, master the twenty programed words, then get acquainted with the fifty terms in the supplementary list. You will meet these words again—possibly during life's crises—and you will be grateful that you recognize them.

COVER THIS STRIP

1. **actuary** (ak'choo-er'ē): a person who calculates risks, premiums, etc., for insurance purposes.

■ The insurance company mathematician who uses statistical records to figure out what rates to charge is called an *ac*_____ .

actuary

■ If you wanted to insure your outdoor music festival against rain, the *actuary* would first consult (a) the probabilities of rain on that date, (b) an astrology book. ( )

(a)

■ The statistical expert of an insurance company, who is known as an *a*_____ , must be especially qualified in (a) poetry, (b) mathematics. ( )

actuary
(b)

■ If an insurance company keeps charging too low a premium for the company to make a profit (an unlikely situation), the fault is probably that of (a) the filing clerks, (b) the actuaries. ( )

(b)

2. **affidavit** (af-i-dā'vit): a sworn, written statement, witnessed by an authorized person.
3. **notarize** (nō'tə-rīz'): to authenticate or certify a document through a notary public.

■ A public official known as a notary public will put his seal and signature on your wedding certificate, that is, he will *not*_____ it.

notarize

■ An *affidavit* is a sworn legal statement (a) spoken in court, (b) written and witnessed. ( )

(b)

■ A hit-and-run motorist has smashed your parked car. If your star witness is too ill to testify in court for you, his testimony should be submitted in the form of an *af*_____ , that is, a sworn statement that a notary public would *no*_____ .

affidavit
notarize

■ It is necessary to *notarize* (a) your English composition, (b) a birth certificate. (   )

(b)

■ To avoid having to pay out-of-state tuition, a college student sometimes needs a sworn, written statement, or *af_____* , testifying that he has been a resident of the state for a full year. This *affidavit* must be by (a) a member of congress, (b) somebody who has known the student for the past year. (   )

affidavit

(b)

■ An important function of a notary public is to certify, or *n_____* , a sworn statement known as an *a_____* , which deals as a rule with (a) legal matters, (b) doctors' prescriptions. (   )

notarize
affidavit
(a)

---

4. **collateral** (kə-lat′ər-əl): any security, such as stocks and bonds, that guarantees the payment of a loan.
5. **negotiable** (ni-gō′shē-ə-bəl): legally transferable to a third party: said of checks, promissory notes, and securities.

■ *Collateral* is (a) security that guarantees payment of a debt, (b) a tricky football maneuver. (   )

(a)

■ A *negotiable* instrument, such as most personal checks, _____ [can / cannot] be made payable to a third party.

can

■ If a bill of exchange or a promissory note uses a phrase such as "pay to bearer" or "pay to the order of," that financial instrument is *neg_____* .

negotiable

■ Most people who buy a house must borrow money from a bank and must guarantee repayment of that bank loan with some sort of *col_____* , usually a mortgage on the house.

collateral

■ If transferable, your shares of stock are said to be *ne_____* and they may be used as *co_____* to secure a loan.

negotiable
collateral

■ A farmer might use his crop or his farm equipment as security for a loan, in other words, as *co_____* .

collateral

Quiz

Write the letter that indicates the best definition.

1. (c)
2. (a)
3. (e)
4. (d)
5. (b)

(   ) 1. actuary   a. a written statement made on oath
(   ) 2. affidavit   b. transferable to a third party
(   ) 3. notarize   c. an expert on insurance risks
(   ) 4. collateral   d. security for a loan
(   ) 5. negotiable   e. to certify a document officially

---

6. **felony** (fel′ə-nē): a major crime such as murder or burglary, usually punished in the United States by more than a year of imprisonment.

7. **larceny** (lar′sə-nē): theft. Stealing property valued above a certain amount, possibly $500 or as fixed by state law, is *grand larceny;* stealing a lesser amount is *petit* (or *petty*) *larceny.*

(b)

■ A *felony* is a major crime such as (a) overtime parking, (b) rape. (   )

(a)

■ *Larceny* refers to (a) theft, (b) wife-beating. (   )

felony

■ The crime of kidnapping is a *fel*_____ .

felony
larceny

■ The plant manager who misappropriates (steals) several thousand dollars in company funds is guilty of a *f*_____ , specifically, grand *lar*_____ .

larceny

■ The girl who stole a brassiere worth six dollars from a department store was guilty of petty *l*_____ .

(e)

■ Which of the following is *not* a *felony*? (a) burglary, (b) forgery, (c) murder, (d) hijacking, (e) failure to get a dog license for Rover. (   )

---

8. **franchise** (fran′chīz): the right to vote; also, a special privilege granted by the government or by a corporation: as, a *franchise* to operate a bus line, a *franchise* to operate a McDonald's Restaurant.

(b)

■ To exercise one's *franchise* means (a) to jog, (b) to vote. (   )

■ The root *franc*, from Old French, means "free." Thus, the *franchise* granted by the city council to the telephone company or to the waterworks is (a) a special, exclusive privilege, (b) a heavy tax. (   )

(a)

■ The competition of two or three gas companies in the same town would result in excessive digging and inefficiency; therefore, one company is usually granted the exclusive right to operate, known as a *fra_____* .

franchise

■ Since a *franchise* restrains others from entering the same business or trade, it tends to establish (a) a legal monopoly, (b) open competition. (   )

(a)

■ Suppose you want to be the only distributor of Wingding Waterbeds in Snorkelville; you might apply for the local *fr_____* .

franchise

■ In 1920 the Nineteenth Amendment to the Constitution gave women the *f_____* , also known as suffrage, which means (a) the right to suffer in the kitchen, (b) the right to vote. (   )

franchise

(b)

---

9. **indictment** (in-dīt′mənt): a formal accusation by a grand jury.
10. **injunction** (in-jungk′shən): a legal order requiring that certain people do, or refrain from doing, certain things.

■ Amanda's fickle boy friend is found shot to death. The grand jury prepares an *indictment* against Amanda. This means that she (a) is found guilty, (b) must face trial. (   )

(b)

■ The formal accusation by a grand jury is an *ind_____* .

indictment

■ To prevent a neighbor from erecting a "spite" fence that would shade your yard, you would file an *inj_____* .

injunction

■ An *injunction* is (a) a word like *and, but, or, for,* and *nor,* (b) a court order to prevent or to enforce action. (   )

(b)

■ The grand jury has reason to believe that the city manager accepted "payola" (bribes); therefore, the jury brings him to trial by means of an *ind*_____ .

indictment

■ The Dingle Duo signed a contract to play exclusively for your night club, yet they intend to play for your competitor next week. You can stop them by means of a court order known as an *inj*_____ .

injunction

■ Each night a certain insecticide factory pours lethal wastes into the air; this unneighborly practice is stopped by a court order known as an _____ . Later the manager apparently sets fire to the factory for insurance purposes. To bring him to trial, the grand jury issues an _____ .

injunction

indictment

Quiz

Write the letter that indicates the best definition.

1. (d)
2. (c)
3. (a)
4. (b)
5. (e)

( ) 1. felony   a. a special privilege
( ) 2. larceny   b. accusation by a grand jury
( ) 3. franchise   c. theft
( ) 4. indictment   d. a crime such as murder or forgery
( ) 5. injunction   e. a legal restraining order

11. **libel** (lī′bəl): the writing or printing of something false or damaging about someone.
12. **subpoena** (sə-pē′nə): a legal order directing a person to appear in court to testify.

■ You would be guilty of *libel* if you spread lies about a person (a) in your writing, (b) in your speeches. ( )

(a)

■ Defaming your sheriff by word of mouth would be slander; defaming him in a magazine article would be *li*_____ .

libel

■ A *subpoena* is a legal order that requires a person (a) to go back to work, (b) to testify in court. ( )

(b)

267

subpoena

◼ You are accused of a felony, but the witness who could clear you says he is too busy to come to your trial. You may have to *sub_____* him.

libel
wrote

◼ You might be sued for *l_____* if you _____ [said / wrote] that the new scoutmaster was (a) "a remarkable shaper of boys' character," (b) "a drunken pervert who sells dope to the boys." (   )

(b)

libel

◼ In a so-called letter of recommendation to Mr. Shoat, your boss refers to you as "a paranoiac pickpocket and a stinking swindler." You instigate a *l_____* suit against your boss and, since Shoat is somewhat reluctant to testify, you request the court to issue a *s_____* for Shoat. If Shoat ignores the *subpoena* he is in *contempt of court*.

subpoena

---

13. **lien** (lēn): a claim on a property as security against payment of a debt.
14. **realty** (rē′əl-tē): real estate; land and buildings.

(b)

◼ Real estate is known as (a) reality, (b) realty. (   )

realty
(a)

◼ A realtor deals in *re_____* ; that is, he helps you buy or sell (a) house and land, (b) stocks and bonds. (   )

(b)

◼ A *lien* on a property is (a) a building or fence that leans against it, (b) a claim against it. (   )

lien

◼ The right of a creditor to control another person's property in order to satisfy a debt is a *li_____* .

realty
lien

◼ When you buy a home or other *re_____* , you should be aware of any claim, or *li_____* , of creditors against that property.

lien

◼ Suppose you build a garage for Mr. Grob and he refuses to pay for your labor. You can protect your claim by taking out a *l_____* on Grob's property.

---

15. **perjury** (pûr′jə-rē): the telling of a lie by a witness under oath; false testimony in court, considered a felony.

■ *Perjury* is (a) lying, (b) stealing. (   )

■ Sonya testifies falsely in court that Bill was playing checkers with her at her apartment at the time of the bank robbery. She has committed *per*_____ .

■ *Perjury* refers to (a) ordinary fibbing, (b) lying about a vital matter in court while under oath to tell the truth. (   )

■ Suppose you see your friend Fleegle speed through a red light and cause a three-car smashup, yet you swear in court that the light was green. You are guilty of *p*_____ , an offense regarded by the court as (a) a felony, (b) fairly trivial. (   )

Quiz

Write the letter that indicates the best definition.

( ) 1. libel a. legal order to appear in court
( ) 2. subpoena b. a claim on property
( ) 3. lien c. written defamation of character
( ) 4. realty d. the telling of lies at a trial
( ) 5. perjury e. real estate

---

16. **precedent** (pres′ə-dənt): a legal decision that may serve as an example for a later one.

■ A *precedent* is an earlier law case that is (a) similar to the present one, (b) different from the present one. (   )

■ Lawyers like to cite prior legal decisions that can serve as a *pre*_____ for the present case.

■ Sometimes the divorced father is given custody of the children. Let us consider the case of *Spatz v. Spatz* as a *pr*_____ .

■ The lawyer said that Ringo's lawsuit was without *precedent*. This means that (a) Ringo would lose the case, (b) no case like it had ever been tried in court. (   )

(b)

---

17. **prospectus** (prə-spec′təs): a statement outlining a proposed business undertaking or literary work.
18. **speculation:** making risky business investments in the hope of big profits.

■ A *prospectus* for a business venture is a review of (a) past achievements, (b) future possibilities. (   )

(b)

■ Before offering a contract, a publishing company will expect to see at least an outline, or *pro_____* , of your proposed book.

prospectus

■ *Speculation* refers to a kind of (a) ornamenting of garments, with specks, (b) business gambling. (   )

(b)

■ Much frantic *speculation* has taken place (a) in Wall Street, (b) in the Grand Canyon. (   )

(a)

■ Buying and selling for quick profit is known as *spec_____* . *Speculation* very commonly involves dabbling in (a) bathtubs, (b) real estate. (   )

speculation
(b)

■ The new Low-Cal Pizza Company has painted a rosy picture of its prospects in its initial *pr_____* . Better buy shares of its stock if you are interested in *sp_____* .

prospectus
speculation

---

19. **solvent** (sol′vənt): able to pay all one's debts.
20. **voucher:** a receipt showing payment of a debt.

■ A business firm is *solvent* (a) if it has some money in the bank, (b) if it can pay all of its bills. (   )

(b)

■ A firm may go bankrupt when it is no longer *sol_____* .

solvent

(a)

■ A *voucher* is (a) a receipt showing that a debt has been paid, (b) a stinging insect. (   )

voucher

■ When you take an all-expenses-paid trip, you had better hang on to every *vou*_____ .

solvent

■ The Clumpy Cleaners haven't been able to pay salaries for ten weeks. "We're almost clean out of funds," says Mr. Clumpy. "Our company isn't *so*_____ ."

voucher

■ If the Internal Revenue agent doubts any expense in your income tax statement, show him a *vo*_____ .

voucher
solvent

■ The accountant for our Mucilage Manufacturing Company has gone over every bill, asset, and *v*_____ . She says that our future is sticky but that we are still *s*_____ .

Quiz

Write the letter that indicates the best definition.

1. (d)
2. (b)
3. (e)
4. (c)
5. (a)

(   ) 1. precedent a. evidence of payment
(   ) 2. prospectus b. an outline of a future undertaking
(   ) 3. speculation c. able to meet financial responsibilities
(   ) 4. solvent d. an earlier, similar law case
(   ) 5. voucher e. risky investment for fat profit

REVIEW TEST

Write the word studied in this chapter that will complete the sentence.

1. To tell a lie in court while sworn to tell the truth is *pe_____* .

2. A firm that can pay all its debts is *so_____* .

3. A receipt showing that a payment has been made is a *vo_____* .

4. A judicial decision that furnishes a model for deciding a later, similar case is a
   pr_____ .

5. A major crime such as armed robbery or embezzlement is a *fe_____* .

6. In most towns an electric company is given an exclusive privilege to operate,
   known as a *fr_____* .

7. A claim on someone's property, such as a mortgage or a bill for unpaid taxes,
   is a *li_____* .

8. You can make a reluctant witness attend a trial by serving him a court order
   called a *su_____* .

9. The insurance expert who calculates risks and premiums is an *ac_____* .

10. The grand jury brings a possible criminal to trial by issuing a formal accusation
    known as an *in_____* .

Write *True* or *False*.

_____ 11. An *affidavit* requires the signature of an authorized witness.

_____ 12. *Negotiable* bonds can be cashed only by the original purchaser.

_____ 13. If you make false accusations in a radio speech, defaming another person, you are guilty of *libel*.

_____ 14. To secure a loan a person could use his house as *collateral*.

_____ 15. Buying farmland and buildings in the hope of selling at a profit is a form of *speculation*.

_____ 16. *Larceny* is a sexual offense.

_____ 17. *Realty* means "not imaginary."

_____ 18. A *prospectus* might describe a proposed business venture or a proposed literary production.

_____ 19. A notary public is able to *notarize* an affidavit.

_____ 20. An *injunction* is a highway intersection.

Key to Review Test

Check your answers by the following key. Deduct 5% per error from a possible 100%.

1. perjury	6. franchise	11. True	16. False
2. solvent	7. lien	12. False	17. False
3. voucher	8. subpoena	13. False	18. True
4. precedent	9. actuary	14. True	19. True
5. felony	10. indictment	15. True	20. False

Score: _____%

SUPPLEMENTARY LIST

1. **ad valorem** (ad və-lôr′əm): in proportion to the value: said of a duty on imports.
2. **amortization** (am′ər-ti-zā′shən): gradual settling of a debt by installment payments.
3. **annuity** (ə-nū′i-tē): a sum of money paid yearly to a person during his lifetime.
4. **beneficiary** (ben′ə-fish′ə-rē): a person who is to receive funds or other property under a trust, will, or insurance policy.
5. **broker:** a person who buys and sells securities for his customers.
6. **cartel** (kär-tel′): an international syndicate that aims at monopoly and price-fixing.
7. **cashier's check:** a check backed by the bank's own funds and signed by the cashier.
8. **caveat emptor** (kā′vē-at emp′tôr): L., let the buyer beware, implying that one buys at his own risk.
9. **codicil** (kod′ə-sil): an addition or supplement to a will.
10. **copyright:** the exclusive right for a limited period to print and dispose of a literary or artistic work.
11. **covenant:** a solemn agreement; a formal, sealed contract.
12. **de facto** (dē fak′tō): L., in fact; actually existing, whether legal or not; distinguished from *de jure* (dē joor′i), according to law.
13. **deflationary:** characterized by a decline in prices caused by a decrease in spending.
14. **easement:** the right or privilege of making a special, limited use of someone else's property: as, a right of way.
15. **eminent domain:** the right of a governmental body to take private property for public use upon giving just compensation to the owner.
16. **encumbrance:** a claim or lien upon a property.
17. **ex post facto** (eks pōst fak′tō): L., having retroactive effect: as an *ex post facto* law.
18. **foreclosure:** public sale by court order of property on which the mortgage has not been paid.
19. **habeas corpus** (hā′bē-əs kôr′pəs): L., a writ that would free a prisoner who is held without legal charges; literally, "have the body."
20. **intestate** (in-tes′tāt): having made no will before death.
21. **ipso facto** (ip′sō fac′tō): L., by that very fact.
22. **jurisprudence:** a system or philosophy of law.
23. **kangaroo court:** *colloq.* an unauthorized and irregular court which ignores or perverts normal legal procedure.
24. **lame duck:** a lawmaker or officeholder who continues in office for a time after his defeat for reelection.
25. **legal tender:** money which may be lawfully used in payment of debts.
26. **litigation** (lit′ə-gā′shən): legal action; a lawsuit.

27. **misdemeanor** (mis′di-mē′nər): a minor offense; a crime less serious than a felony.
28. **moratorium** (môr′ə-tôr′ē-əm): legal authorization to delay the payment of debts, as in an emergency.
29. **mortgage** (môr′gij): the pledging of property as security for payment of a debt.
30. **negligence** (neg′li-jəns): the failure to exercise such care as one would ordinarily expect of a reasonable, prudent person.
31. **plenary** (plē′nə-rē): full; attended by all members: as, a *plenary* session.
32. **pocket veto:** veto of a congressional bill, at the end of a session, for lack of presidential action.
33. **preferred stock:** shares which receive dividends or distributed assets first, before common stock gets any.
34. **probate** (prō′bāt): the process by which a will is proved to be authentic or valid.
35. **proviso** (prə-vī′zō): a stipulation or condition that is attached to a contract or a statute.
36. **quitclaim:** a deed giving up one's claim to some property or right of action.
37. **ratification:** approval; confirmation.
38. **requisition:** a formal written order or request, as for certain equipment.
39. **respondent:** the defendant.
40. **restitution:** reimbursement for loss or damage.
41. **scrip:** a temporary paper to be redeemed later for money or other benefits.
42. **statute** (stach′o͞ot): an established law or rule.
43. **stipend** (stī′pend): a salary, pension, or allowance.
44. **submarginal:** unprofitable; unproductive; not worth cultivating.
45. **syndicate** (sin′də-kit): an association of individuals formed to conduct a business enterprise requiring much capital.
46. **tort:** any injury or damage for which a civil suit can be brought.
47. **usury** (yo͞o′zhə-rē): lending money at an unlawfully high rate of interest.
48. **venue** (ven′yo͞o): the locality where a legal case is tried.
49. **waiver:** the voluntary giving up of a right.
50. **working capital:** the excess of current assets over debts and obligations.

19

Computers

A few decades ago a marvelous device was born—the computer. Though simple enough in its infancy, the computer has developed and grown more sophisticated until it has now revolutionized science, industry, and publishing.

Computers are everywhere. For instance, you (1) look at your digital watch, (2) withdraw some cash at the bank, (3) buy fish at the supermarket, (4) bake the fish in a microwave oven—and computers have been working for you every step of the way. And if that fish smells old enough to vote, you can use a word processor, also computerized, to write a letter of complaint to the store manager.

Since computers are becoming increasingly important, the ambitious student will not shun an acquaintance with a few words that relate to computers. . . . Incidentally, what's the word for that bunch of parallel lines on your box of granola?

This chapter presents twenty-seven terms of "computerese" in programed form, as well as a supplementary list of definitions.

1. **computer:** electronic equipment that handles input/output information. It can (a) take in elements of information, known as data, (b) store data, (c) manipulate data, and (d) turn out meaningful results.
2. **CPU:** central processing unit. The *CPU* of a computer is the "thinking" part that manipulates the data.

does

■ A *computer* _____ [does / does not] include devices for input and output of information.

computer

■ Banks keep track of your deposits, withdrawals, dividends, and balance by means of a *com_____* .

CPU

■ The central processing unit, which manipulates the data within a *computer*, is usually referred to by its three initials: _____ .

brain

■ If a computer is compared to a human being, the CPU (central processing unit) inside the computer would correspond to our _____ [ears / mouth / brain].

central
  processing
  unit

CPU stands for *c_____ pr_____ u_____* .

CPU

■ The central processing unit, abbreviated _____ , is made up of integrated circuits that are the "thinking" part of

computer

the *co_____* .

3. **hardware:** the physical equipment of a computer system. *Hardware* includes such things as the keyboard, display screen, and printer.
4. **software:** computer programs. *Software* tells the computer how to respond to various commands.

software

■ A program of instructions to the computer may be stored on a floppy disk. The program is _____*ware*.

hardware	■ Electro-mechanical equipment such as your printer and CPU are _____ *ware*.
hardware software	■ Your hi-fi set is, in some ways, like a computer. Your receiver, amplifier, and speakers are _____*ware*, and your music and voice are _____*ware*.
software hardware	■ Punched cards that are fed into a computer carry instructions known as _____*ware;* whereas the disk drive, containing the motor, is _____*ware*.
hardware software	■ The finest CPU, keyboard, and other _____*re* are useless unless they are fed a program of instructions known as _____*re*.

---

5. **RAM:** Random Access Memory. *RAM* stores up information in such a way that you can add to it or change it at any time.
6. **ROM:** Read Only Memory. *ROM* is stored information that you ordinarily cannot alter. [Remember: RAM cAn change; ROM cannOt.]

RAM ROM	■ Random Access Memory is referred to by its initials: ____ . Read Only Memory is referred to by its initials: _____ .
cAn	■ *RAM* is temporary storage, and you _____ [cAn / cannot] change the information in it.
cannOt	■ *ROM* is permanent storage, and you _____ [can / cannOt] change the information in it.
ROM	■ A _____ [ROM / RAM] program is like a phonograph record made by a manufacturer. You use it but you cannot change it.
RAM	■ One advantage of _____ [ROM / RAM] is that you can easily make changes in it if you are composing a story or document.

Write the letter that indicates the best definition.

1. (e)
2. (a)
3. (f)
4. (c)
5. (d)
6. (b)

( ) 1. computer
( ) 2. CPU
( ) 3. hardware
( ) 4. software
( ) 5. RAM
( ) 6. ROM

a. the "brains" of a computer
b. permanent, unerasable memory storage
c. a program of instructions to the computer
d. temporary, changeable memory storage
e. components that handle input and output
f. physical equipment

---

7. **display screen:** the TV-like screen where you can see the text as it enters the system.
8. **terminal:** a work station consisting of a keyboard and a display screen. Data can enter or leave a communication system from a *terminal*.

display screen

■ What you type on the keyboard you can read on the *dis*_____ *sc*_____ .

display screen
terminal

■ A work station with a keyboard and a *dis*_____ *sc*_____ is referred to as a *ter*_____ .

terminal

■ Each bank teller sits next to a *ter*_____ of the computer system.

display screen

■ The bank teller types data into the keyboard and then views the data on the *d*_____ *sc*_____ .

terminal

■ In businesses with a large computer system, the users may each sit at some distant *t*_____ and still share the same data.

---

9. **floppy disk:** an information storage device. The *floppy disk* is a flexible, magnetic plate commonly used for storing information.

10. **word processing:** an efficient system of preparing documents by computer. Components include the keyboard, the display, the disk drive, and the printer.

■ A *floppy disk* is (a) a device to store information, (b) a faulty backbone. (   )

■ Processing of numerical data by computer is called data processing; processing of words is called *w_____ pr_____* .

■ Changes in the wording and layout of a term paper can be made quickly and efficiently with (a) a portable typewriter, (b) a word processor. (   )

■ The information storage device known as the *fl_____ d_____* is used in *w_____ pr_____* .

■ Typed information can easily be edited and improved if it is stored in RAM. Once editing is finished, the document can be stored on a *fl_____ d_____* .

11. **cursor:** a blinking light on the display screen that shows where the next keystroke will appear. It can be moved by special keys or by a device called a "mouse."
12. **merge:** combining a document with a list of variables. A word processor can "personalize" a standard letter by *merging* it with names on a mailing list.

■ The term *cursor* refers to (a) a blinking light, (b) an angry typist. (   )

■ You can move the blinking light, or *cu_____* , to the spot on the display screen where you want to type or make some kind of a change.

■ To *merge*, on a word processor, is to _____ [combine / destroy] printed materials from different files.

merge

■ When a bill collector combines his standard threatening letter with listed names and amounts overdue, he uses _____ [merge / scotch tape].

cursor

■ Looking at the screen, you know your next typing will appear where you see the blinking *c*_____ .

(b)

■ Advertisements in the mail that print your very own name in six places and say you've (almost) won a Cadillac are the result of (a) a miracle, (b) merge. (   )

_____

Quiz

Write the letter that indicates the best definition.

1. (b)
2. (e)
3. (f)
4. (a)
5. (d)
6. (c)

( )	1. display screen	a. writing documents by computer
( )	2. terminal	b. where text can be read
( )	3. floppy disk	c. to blend sources of text
( )	4. word processing	d. a movable blinker
( )	5. cursor	e. a keyboard and screen
( )	6. merge	f. a device to store information

_____

13. **bar code:** machine-printed stripes that give information such as the product ID and size/model.
14. **binary:** belonging to a numbering system to the base 2. *Binary* numbers are expressed in the *binary* digits 0 and 1.

■ Numbers in the decimal system, such as 1776, are to the base 10; numbers in the *binary* system, such as 10110, are to the base _____ [2 / 13].

2

■ Because electronic impulses can be either on or off, the digital computer uses the *b*_____ system to transmit numbers and letters.

binary

■ The machine-printed stripes on a can of beans are a _____ [symbol of purity / bar code].

bar code

bar code
bar code

(b)

binary

(a)

1000

250

kilobyte
bytes

1000
kilobytes

bytes
(c)

■ You buy some chocolate googoos, and on the box is a bunch of parallel stripes known as a *b*_____ *c*_____ . The supermarket computer scans this *b*_____ *c*_____ and promptly (a) takes your picture, (b) prints the price of the googoos. (   )

■ Although a digital computer operates on the *b*_____ mathematics system (base 2), it translates the results for us into the decimal system.

---

15. **byte:** the storage space needed to represent one letter or digit such as "g" or "6." A computer's memory is measured by the number of *bytes* it can hold.
16. **kilobyte:** approximately 1000 bytes, referred to as "K." For example, 128K memory capacity equals about 128,000 bytes.

■ A *byte* is (a) a unit of computer memory, (b) a canine's revenge. (   )

■ A *kilobyte* equals _____ [100 / 1000] *bytes*.

■ It takes about 2K of storage to handle the words on a typewritten page, double-spaced. Therefore, a floppy disk with a capacity of 512K can "remember" about _____ [250 / 1000] pages.

■ The symbol *K* stands for a *ki*_____ of computer memory, which is equal to 1000 *b*_____ .

■ The symbol *M* stands for a *megabyte*, which is equal to a million *bytes*, or _____ [100 / 1000] _____ [characters / kilobytes].

■ A large internal memory is desirable in a computer. A machine with a rated capacity of 256K (which is equal to 256,000 *b*_____) can remember approximately 125 (a) letters of the alphabet, (b) words, (c) typewritten pages. (   )

---

17. **printer:** a device that prints the paper copy. Dot-matrix *printers* make characters from patterns of dots; daisy-wheel *printers* produce letter-quality characters.
18. **proportional spacing:** giving space to letters according to their width. An "M" or "W" is given more space than an "i" or "r."

hardware

(b)

■ The *printer*, which is computer _____ [hardware / software], puts information on (a) the display screen, (b) paper. (   )

unequal

■ A *printer* with *proportional spacing* gives _____ [equal / unequal] space to "l" and "L."

proportional
spacing

■ Typewriters ordinarily print exactly ten letters (pica) or twelve letters (elite) to the inch. This suggests that they do *not* produce *prop*_____ *sp*_____ .

(a)

■ Numbers and letters made from patterns of dots are the product of a (a) dot-matrix printer, (b) letter-quality printer. (   )

faster

■ One daisy-wheel *printer* turns out 200 cps (characters per second); an electronic *printer* turns out two pages per second. Such computer *printers* are _____ [faster / slower] than the average freshman stabbing away with two fingers on a portable typewriter.

proportional
spacing

■ If a printer gives more horizontal space to "W" than to "i," we say it has *prop*_____ *sp*_____ .

---

19. **format:** the layout of a document page. *Format* involves the predetermined arrangement of margin settings, tabs, print size, captions, lines, page numbers, and so on.
20. **justify:** to produce text with an even right-hand margin. Some printers can vary the space between words, and even between letters, so that lines are of equal length (*justified*).

(b)

■ When printers *justify* they produce (a) a ragged right-hand margin, (b) an even right-hand margin, (c) legal documents. (   )

format

■ Indentations, double-spacing, number of lines to the page, margins—these are matters of _____ [cursors / format].

before

■ *Format* should be decided _____ [before / after] a document is printed.

justify

■ Books and newspapers turn out neat, flush right-hand margins because their printers *ju*_____ the copy.

format
justify

■ A good word processing printer produces a handsome page arrangement, or _____ [doormat / format], because the printer has proportional spacing and also can _____ [justify / typify] the lines.

Quiz

Write the letter that indicates the best definition.

1. (e)
2. (d)
3. (g)
4. (f)
5. (b)
6. (a)
7. (h)
8. (c)

(   ) 1. bar code   a. giving "W" extra space
(   ) 2. binary   b. maker of paper copy
(   ) 3. byte   c. to make even margins
(   ) 4. kilobyte   d. numbering to the base 2
(   ) 5. printer   e. stripes indicating product
(   ) 6. proportional   f. storage for 1000 letters
      spacing   g. storage space for one digit
(   ) 7. format   h. page layout
(   ) 8. justify

---

21. **BASIC:** a computer language—Beginner's All-purpose Symbolic Instruction Code. Program instructions in BASIC are directly usable, without translation, by the computer.
22. **COBOL:** a computer language—COmmon Business Oriented Language. COBOL is used in business data computing.
23. **FORTRAN:** a computer language—FORmula TRANslation. FORTRAN is used in scientific computing.

■ The easiest computer language to learn and use is the Beginner's All-purpose Symbolic Instruction Code, which is referred to by its initials as *B*_____ .

BASIC

■ The high-level computer language COmmon Business Oriented Language is usually referred to as *C*_____ .

■ The high-level FORmula TRANslation is usually referred to as *F*_____ .

■ COBOL was designed to handle the data of (a) business, (b) sports, (c) science. (   )

■ FORTRAN was designed to handle the data of (a) business, (b) music, (c) science. (   )

■ BASIC was designed for easy computer operation by (a) businessmen, (b) beginners, (c) scientists. (   )

■ Although BASIC language is directly understood by the computer, *CO*_____ and *FOR*_____ require translation into machine language.

---

24. **bug:** a mistake in the coding of a computer program. A program tells a computer what things to do to solve a problem. A faulty program is "debugged" if possible by an analyst.
25. **flowchart:** graphic representation of a computer program. The *flowchart* uses special symbols to spell out an entire series of operations.

■ Those who design a complex computer program generally picture their plan by means of a *fl*_____ .

■ A *bug* is an _____ [insect / error] in a computer program.

■ If a computer program fails to work properly, an analyst revises the _____ [terminal / flowchart] to eliminate _____ [bugs / bytes].

■ A *flowchart* depicts a series of operations, using special _____ [cursors / symbols / bar codes].

debugged

■ A faulty computer program should be _____
[merged / sprayed / debugged].

---

26. **interface:** a link that permits different types of systems to work together. For example, an *interface* is needed between a computer and a printer.
27. **modem:** an interface between a computer or terminal and a telephone line. A *modem* is a MOdulator-DEModulator.

link

■ An *interface* is a _____ [conflict / link] between different kinds of equipment.

telephone

■ A *modem* links a computer or terminal to a _____ [telephone / clothes] line.

interface
modem

■ Two computers can "communicate" over a long distance telephone line if each uses a special *int*_____ called a *mo*_____ .

modem

■ Computer signals are modulated into audible tones for telephone transmission by a *m*_____ , then demodulated into computer signals at the receiving end by another

modem

*m*_____ .

interface

■ A computer can be connected to other equipment by means of an _____ [interfuse / interface / interlard].

Quiz

Write the letter that indicates the best definition.

1. (d)   (   ) 1. BASIC   a. a coupler between different systems
2. (e)   (   ) 2. COBOL   b. Formula Translation
3. (b)   (   ) 3. FORTRAN c. an error in a computer program
4. (c)   (   ) 4. bug   d. a beginner's computer code
5. (g)   (   ) 5. flowchart   e. Common Business Oriented Language
6. (a)   (   ) 6. interface   f. Modulation-Demodulation
7. (f)   (   ) 7. modem   g. pictorial of program operations

REVIEW TEST

Supply the missing words. The opening letters are given.

1. The *cu*_____ blinks where typing will next appear.

2. A *ter*_____ consists of a keyboard and a display screen.

3. A *fl*_____ *d*_____ is a flexible plate that stores information.

4. A *mo*_____ is an interface between computer and telephone line.

5. In the *bi*_____ system, the numbering is to the base two.

6. *For*_____ refers to page layout.

7. As text enters the system, we read it on the *dis*_____ *sc*_____.

8. To produce an even right-hand margin, a printer must be able to *ju*_____ .

9. *W*_____ *pr*_____ is a system for preparing documents.

10. The keyboard and printer are _____*ware.*

Write *True* or *False*.

_____ 11. A *bug* is an error in a computer program.

_____ 12. The *bar code* is a list of ingredients on a candy wrapper.

_____ 13. The *printer* puts printed words on the display screen.

_____ 14. Computer programs are *software.*

_____ 15. *Merging* can help to "personalize" a master letter.

_____ 16. Ordinary typewriters print with *proportional spacing.*

_____ 17. A *flowchart* is a water duct to cool the printer.

_____ 18. A *byte* is a unit of computer memory.

Give the abbreviation associated with each definition.

19. a thousand bytes _____

20. the "brains" of a computer _____

21. computer code for beginners   _____

22. changeable stored information   _____

23. computer code for science   _____

24. computer code for business   _____

25. unchangeable stored information   _____

Key to Review Test

Check your answers by the following key. Deduct 4% per error from a possible 100%.

1. cursor	10. hardware	19. K
2. terminal	11. True	20. CPU
3. floppy disk	12. False	21. BASIC
4. modem	13. False	22. RAM
5. binary	14. True	23. FORTRAN
6. format	15. True	24. COBOL
7. display screen	16. False	25. ROM
8. justify	17. False	
9. word processing	18. True	

Score: _____%

SUPPLEMENTARY LIST

1. **acronym:** a word formed from the opening letters of a series of words, as COBOL from COmmon Business Oriented Language.
2. **algorithm:** the logical steps by computer that will solve a problem.
3. **boilerplate:** standard paragraphs or passages that can be inserted, for example, into contracts and "personalized" form letters.
4. **camera copy:** copy in shape to be photographed for offset printing.
5. **card readers:** devices that accept data from punched or marked cards.
6. **character:** a single letter, number, punctuation mark, or symbol.
7. **chip:** a tiny slice of silicon carrying integrated circuits.
8. **collate:** to place the pages of a document in proper order.
9. **continuous form:** connected sheets that are accordion folded and fed non-stop into the printer.
10. **daisy wheel:** a wheel of spokes that print information at high speed.
11. **data:** basic elements of information.
12. **data base:** the interrelated information stored in a computer system.
13. **delete:** to remove letters, words, or longer passages, after which the gap is automatically closed.
14. **disk drive:** a piece of hardware that spins the magnetic disks so that information can be added to them or read from them.
15. **file:** a collection of data in storage.
16. **file protection:** a method of making sure that a file is not accidentally erased.
17. **function keys:** keys that do special jobs: "delete," "move," "search," etc.
18. **input:** data put into the computer for processing.
19. **menu:** a list of choices offered on the screen to the computer user.
20. **microcomputer:** a small computer.
21. **microprocessor:** the brains of a microcomputer; integrated circuits on a chip.
22. **microsecond:** one millionth of a second.
23. **Murphy's Law:** *Humorous.* If anything can go wrong, it will. Dropped bread lands with the peanut butter facing the rug.
24. **nanosecond:** one billionth of a second.
25. **output:** data put out by the computer, normally to the printer or screen.
26. **peripherals:** devices such as the keyboard, printer, and disk drive that are used by the central processing unit but are not physically a part of it.
27. **repagination:** renumbering the pages because of changes in the copy.
28. **scrolling:** moving the data on the screen up and down or sideways.
29. **search and replace:** the ability of a program to find specific words throughout a page or a document and replace them with certain other words.
30. **storage:** the part of the computer that holds information.

20

Foreign Expressions

1. *a cappella*
2. *ad nauseum*
3. *aficionado*
4. *à la carte*
5. *avant-garde*
6. *bête noir*
7. *c'est la vie*
8. *con amore*
9. *déjà vu*
10. *faux pas*
11. *hoi polloi*
12. *Homo sapiens*
13. *laissez faire*
14. *magnum opus*
15. *par excellence*
16. *persona non grata*
17. *potpourri*
18. *savoir-faire*
19. *sine qua non*
20. *status quo*
21. *sub rosa*
22. *tour de force*
23. *tout de suite*
24. *vox populi*
25. *Wunderkind*

English has become a *smörgäsbord* (Swedish: "a buffet of assorted foods") of terms taken from at least fifty languages.

Many imported words have been used so much that they are now completely absorbed into the English language. Here are a few examples:

American Indian: moccasin, moose
Arabic: algebra, magazine
Chinese: tea, typhoon
Dutch: cole slaw, sleigh
French: buffet, chauffeur
German: kindergarten, waltz
Greek: acrobat, alphabet

Hebrew: amen, kosher
Irish: slogan, whiskey
Italian: ballot, piano
Latin: cereal, report
Persian: pajamas, sugar
Russian: samovar, vodka
Spanish: alligator, cigar

A second group of foreign expressions are often used but are not yet generally regarded as adopted. Such terms are written in italics until our language assimilates them. Meanwhile the status and popular pronunciation of these words keep changing. When in doubt, consult a good dictionary for current practice as to how best to pronounce a foreign expression and whether to italicize it.

Abbreviations used in this chapter include *Fr.* (French), *G.* (German), *Gk.* (Greek), *It.* (Italian), *L.* (Latin), *Sp.* (Spanish).

Master the twenty-five foreign expressions that are programed in this chapter. Then warm your acquaintanceship with the forty terms in the supplementary list.

COVER THIS STRIP

1. **a cappella** (ä′kə-pel′ə) *It.* singing without instrumental accompaniment. "The church choir sang *a cappella*."
2. **ad nauseum** (ad′nô′zē-əm) *L.* to a disgusting degree. "One tourist complained about food and plumbing and prices *ad nauseum*."

■ The chorus will now sing *a cappella*, so the orchestra will be (a) silent, (b) sawing away. (   )

(a)

■ My pianist was in jail that evening. Consequently, I sang my solo *a cap*——————— .

a cappella

■ Our football captain kept referring *ad nauseum* to his own heroic achievements. He should probably have been more (a) modest, (b) detailed. (   )

(a)

■ The biology assistant, who hated snakes, had to handle them day after day *a*—— *na*——————— .

ad nauseum

■ When the sergeant took a shower, he sang *a ca*———————; and, ignorant of sharps and flats, he bellowed "Sorrento" tunelessly and endlessly *a*—— *n*——————— .

a cappella

ad nauseum

3. **aficionado** (ə-fish′yə-nä′də) *Sp.* a devoted follower of some sport or art. "Jose was an *aficionado* of bullfighting until he got trampled."
4. **à la carte** (ä lə kärt′) *Fr.* with a separate price for each dish on the menu; lit., according to the card. "Our guests, with an eye for expensive items, ordered *à la carte*."

■ An *aficionado* of soccer ——————————— [hates / loves] the game.

loves

■ The baseball sailed into the bleachers, where it was gloved by a young *af*_____ .

aficionado

■ It's wise to order *à la carte* if you want (a) the standard full meal, (b) two or three special items. (   )

(b)

■ Bill has a barrel of allergies and had to select his dishes *à la c*_____ .

à la carte

■ No, Joey, I won't push the fat worms onto your fishhooks. Better ask that *af*_____ of fishing to help you.

aficionado

■ My plump friend, with a tear in his eye, selected a spinach salad *à* _____ _____ .

à la carte

---

5. **avant-garde** (a-vänt gärd') *Fr.* the leaders in new artistic movements. "Walt Whitman was among the *avant-garde* to throw off the shackles of rhyme."
6. **bête noir** (bāt nwär') *Fr.* a person or thing that one fears and dislikes; lit., black beast. "Algebra had always been his *bête noir*."

■ Rudy sometimes chased me home from school. He was my _____ [*avant-garde / bête noir*].

bête noir

■ No fashions are too bizarre, if only they are created by the *av*_____-*ga*_____ among Parisian designers.

avant-garde

■ If not the first, Schonberg was among the *av*_____-*ga*_____ to compose in the twelve-tone technique.

avant-garde

■ Speak softly and carry a big stick, especially if the neighborhood dogs are your *b*_____ *no*_____ .

bête noir

■ By the time my ancestor Gaspar started fooling around with impressionism, the *av*_____-*g*_____ was already into cubism. Gaspar might have painted ceilings, but he was deathly afraid of ladders. They were his *b*_____ *n*_____ .

avant-garde

bête noir

Write the letter that indicates the best definition.

1. (b)
2. (d)
3. (c)
4. (a)
5. (f)
6. (e)

(   )   1. *a cappella*   a. each dish priced separately
(   )   2. *ad nauseum*   b. without accompaniment
(   )   3. *aficionado*   c. an ardent fan
(   )   4. *à la carte*   d. to a sickening degree
(   )   5. *avant-garde*   e. something one fears
(   )   6. *bête noir*   f. the leaders in art

---

7. **c'est la vie** (sā la vē′) *Fr.* Such is life. "The prisoner had been making big money—a half-inch too big. *C'est la vie.*"

8. **con amore** (kän ä-mō′rä) *It.* with love; tenderly (used as a direction to musicians). "The lullaby is to be sung *con amore.*"

■ The musical instruction *con amore* is usually seen in sheet music involving (a) military marches, (b) love songs. (   )

(b)

■ Sophia kissed the gift box of chocolates where Giuseppe had written "c_____ am_____ ."

con amore

■ *C'est la vie* seems to suggest that we must (a) fight hard for improvements, (b) accept the things that happen. (   )

(b)

■ The sheepherder gambled his life savings on one throw of the dice—and lost. "C_____ l_____ v_____," he shrugged. "Too ba-a-a-ad."

C'est la vie

■ "Yesterday Giuseppe nibbled my ear c_____ am_____ ," muttered Sophia. "Today he eloped with my best friend. Well, c_____ ____ v_____ ."

con amore

c'est la vie

---

9. **déjà vu** (dā-zha vü′) *Fr.* the feeling that a new situation has happened before. "He first saw Lisa with a sense of *déjà vu*, as though he was reliving a dream."

10. **faux pas** (fō pä′) *Fr.* a social blunder; lit., a false step. "Asking the hostess how much she weighed was a *faux pas*, Clarence."

■ We entered Pokeville, and *déjà vu!* It was as though I had (a) been here before, (b) never seen such a lousy town. (   )

(a)

■ Kay had seen so many pictures of Mt. Fujiyama that her first sighting of it filled her with d_____ v_____ .

déjà vu

■ A *faux pas* is (a) a pathway for forest beasts, (b) an error in etiquette such as a tactless remark. (   )

(b)

■ Spilling soup on his necktie was bad enough but wiping his tie on the linen tablecloth was a definite f_____ p_____ .

faux pas

■ With a terrible sense of d_____ v_____ , I was sure that Uncle Louie was now going to tell Father Clancy the one about the priest and the rabbi—what a f_____ p_____!

déjà vu

faux pas

---

11. **hoi polloi** (hoi′ pə-loi′) *Gk.* the common people: a somewhat contemptuous term. "The king sneered at the ignorance and sweat of the *hoi polloi*."

12. **Homo sapiens** (hō′mō sā′pē-enz) *L.* modern man; human being; lit., wise man. "Of all creatures, *Homo sapiens* is the only one who writes symphonies."

■ The scientific term *Homo sapiens* suggests that human beings have (a) wisdom, (b) a drinking problem. (   )

(a)

■ No animals had enough brains and ability to pollute the air, water, and earth except Ho_____ sap_____ .

Homo sapiens

■ The masses, known as *hoi polloi*, were held in _____ [high regard / contempt] by royalty.

contempt

■ A truly democratic country has neither lofty aristocrats nor lowly h_____ po_____ .

hoi polloi

■ Ignorant ho_____ po_____ are, nevertheless, members of Ho_____ sa_____ , and with education they can reach the stars.

hoi polloi
Homo sapiens

Write the letter that indicates the best definition.

1. (c)
2. (a)
3. (f)
4. (e)
5. (d)
6. (b)

( ) 1. *c'est la vie*   a. lovingly
( ) 2. *con amore*   b. thinking man
( ) 3. *déjà vu*   c. That's life.
( ) 4. *faux pas*   d. the masses
( ) 5. *hoi polloi*   e. a breach of etiquette
( ) 6. *Homo sapiens*   f. the illusion of a replay

13. **laissez faire** (les′ā fâr′) *Fr.* the policy of non-interference in business or in individual conduct; lit., let do. "Government should try to keep its nose out of industrial or private affairs, according to the doctrine of *laissez faire*."

14. **magnum opus** (mag′nəm ō′pəs) *L.* the masterpiece of a writer or artist; lit., a great work.

■ Under *laissez faire* our industries would operate with _____ [very few / numerous] government controls.

very few

■ Some parents lay down rigid rules; others, more permissive, tend to practice *la_____ fa_____ .*

laissez faire

■ A *magnum opus* is (a) a huge wine bottle, (b) an artist's masterpiece. ( )

(b)

■ John Roebling and his son built several suspension bridges, but Brooklyn Bridge (1883) was certainly their *mag_____ op_____ .*

magnum opus

■ Adam Smith wrote on economic theory, and in *Wealth of Nations*, his *m_____ op_____ ,* he developed the "let alone" doctrine of *la_____ fa_____ .*

magnum opus
laissez faire

15. **par excellence** (pär ek′sə-läns′) *Fr.* excellent beyond comparison. "Benjamin Franklin and the others framed a constitution *par excellence*."

16. **persona non grata** (pər-sō′nə nän grät′ə) *L.* an unwelcome person; esp., a diplomat unacceptable to another government. "His cigar smoking made him *persona non grata* at the theater."

■ To be *persona non grata* means that one is (a) not a great big person, (b) not welcome. (   )

■ Anna Pavlova was a ballet dancer *par excellence*. This means her dancing was (a) up to par, (b) exceptionally good. (   )

■ If a diplomatic representative from Slobbovia is found to be operating a spy ring in Washington, D.C., our State Department would call him *per_____ n_____ gr_____* .

■ Jeff went to the men's room whenever a restaurant bill arrived, and soon he was *per_____ n_____ gr_____* at the dinner parties.

■ My barber is a mediocre stylist but he is a conversationalist *p_____ exc_____* .

■ Show me a freshman who reads one library book a week, and I'll show you a student *p_____ ex_____* .

---

17. **potpourri** (pō-pōō-rē′) *Fr.* a miscellany or mixture of unrelated things. "Buster's pockets held a *potpourri* of his treasures."
18. **savoir-faire** (sav′wär fâr′) *Fr.* a ready knowledge of what to say or do in any situation; lit., knowing how to do. "Always smooth, always at ease, my friend was not lacking in *savoir-faire*."

■ "Our junior high band will now perform a musical *potpourri*." This announcement means we'll have the doubtful pleasure of hearing (a) a medley of tunes, (b) a symphony. (   )

■ At noon Times Square was crowded with clerks, shoppers, laborers, bankers, and pickpockets—a regular *pot_____* .

■ A person with *savoir-faire* tends to be (a) tactful, skillful, and adaptable; (b) flustered, awkward, and naive. (   )

(a)

savoir-faire

■ I was a country boy in Manhattan. I didn't have *sav_____-f_____* . In fact, I didn't have bus fare.

■ Pierre stepped into the room where a woman was taking a bubble bath. "Sorry, sir," he said, retreating. Pierre had *s_____-f_____* .

savoir-faire

potpourri

■ The *Reader's Digest* mixes short articles, anecdotes, quips, quotes, and quizzes; it presents a *po_____* .

Quiz

Write the letter that indicates the best definition.

1. (e)
2. (c)
3. (d)
4. (a)
5. (f)
6. (b)

( )	1.	*laissez faire*	a.		an undesirable person
( )	2.	*magnum opus*	b.		knowing always how to act
( )	3.	*par excellence*	c.		one's masterpiece
( )	4.	*persona non grata*	d.		supremely good
( )	5.	*potpourri*	e.		non-interference
( )	6.	*savoir-faire*	f.		a miscellany

---

19. **sine qua non** (sī′nē quā non′) *L.* something absolutely essential; lit., without which not. "The telephone has become a *sine qua non* of teenage romance."
20. **status quo** (stā′təs quō′) *L.* the existing condition; lit., state in which. "An ambitious executive will try to do more than maintain the *status quo*."

■ Defenders of the *status quo* in a society are likely to be (a) the underprivileged, (b) the wealthier class. (   )

(b)

status quo

■ Women were kitchen slaves until they decided to rebel against the *sta_____ q_____* .

sine qua non

■ A well-stocked library is the very _____ [*laissez faire* / *sine qua non*] of a college.

sine qua non
■ "Idiot!" bawled bakery foreman Schultz, a slow man with a compliment. "You forgot caraway seeds! They're the *sin_____ q_____ n_____* of a pumpernickel."

sine qua non
status quo
■ Our labor union says that a paid vacation on Ground Hog's Day is a *si_____ q_____ n_____* of a new contract; but company officials support the *st_____ q_____* .

---

21. **sub rosa** (sub rō′zə) *L.* secretly; confidentially; lit., under the rose, which was a symbol of secrecy. "The delicatessens agreed *sub rosa* to raise the price of salami."
22. **tour de force** (tōōr də fors′) *Fr.* a remarkable achievement; a stroke of genius; lit., a feat of skill. "Lindbergh's flight was a *tour de force* that won him instant admiration."

(b)
■ The phrase *tour de force* describes an accomplishment that is (a) rather boring, (b) sensational. (   )

tour de force
■ To ride a unicycle on a high wire and juggle five oranges— what a *t_____ d_____ f_____* !

(a)
■ A *sub rosa* transaction is one that takes place (a) in secret, (b) on a TV network. (   )

sub rosa
■ Clym pops his cork when he learns that his wife Eustacia has been meeting *s_____ ro_____* with her old flame Wildeve.

sub rosa
tour de force
■ "That's George Koltanowski," said an onlooker to me *s_____ ro_____* . "He once played thirty-four simultaneous games of chess blindfolded, a real *t_____ d_____ f_____* ."

---

23. **tout de suite** (tōōt swēt′) *Fr.* immediately; right away; lit., all in succession. "I'm neck-deep in quicksand! Help me *tout de suite!*"
24. **vox populi** (voks pop′yə-lī′) *L.* public opinion; lit., the voice of the people; abbrev., *vox pop.* "Congress must not ignore *vox populi.*"

(c)
■ *Vox populi* refers to (a) a popular song, (b) our growing population, (c) public sentiment. (   )

■ "The sergeant returned *tout de suite*." This means he came back (a) with his sweetheart, (b) to the sound of bugles, (c) right away. ( )

■ Letters written to the editors of American newspapers are fairly representative of *vo_____ po_____* .

■ Coach Cardiac was fuming: "We're trailing 14-13 with a minute to go. Let's try that trick play *to_____ d____ s_____* ."

■ Governor Goofov expresses contempt for our state laws and for *v____ pop_____* . He should be impeached *t_____ d____ s_____* .

25. **Wunderkind** (voon'dər kint') *G*. a child prodigy; lit., a wonder child. "This baby reads? She's a *Wunderkind!*"

■ A *Wunderkind* is (a) a brilliant youngster, (b) a thunderstorm along the Rhine. ( )

■ Wolfgang Amadeus Mozart was composing music at age four and giving piano concerts at seven. Austria hailed him as a *Wun_____* .

■ She sang, she danced, she acted; and tiny Shirley Temple quickly became Hollywood's *W_____* .

Quiz

Write the letter that indicates the best definition.

( )	1. *sine qua non*	a. secretly
( )	2. *status quo*	b. the voice of the people
( )	3. *sub rosa*	c. an indispensable thing
( )	4. *tour de force*	d. a remarkable accomplishment
( )	5. *tout de suite*	e. a wonder child
( )	6. *vox populi*	f. the current condition
( )	7. *Wunderkind*	g. immediately

REVIEW TEST

Supply the missing words. The opening letters are given.

1. The Greek aristocrats sneered at the lowly *h_____ pol_____* .

2. Saying "Hi, babe!" to the mayor's wife was a horrible *f_____ p_____* .

3. The rich get richer and the poor get babies. *C_____ la v_____* .

4. A country's leaders must listen to *v_____ pop_____* .

5. Nothing rattles Ronald. He has *sav_____-f_____* .

6. This wedding song must be sung sweetly and *c_____ am_____* .

7. I don't know soccer rules. Better ask an *afi_____* .

8. One official met *s_____ ro_____* with members of the Mafia.

9. *War and Peace* was Leo Tolstoi's *mag_____ o_____* .

10. I don't want the full meal. I'll order *à l_____ c_____* .

11. Your accompanist has passed out. Just sing *a ca_____* .

12. *High Noon* was a western movie *p_____ exc_____* .

13. The closet held a *pot_____* of shoes, tools, wigs, and apples.

14. Some old people resist change. They prefer the *st_____ q_____* .

15. I asked the boss for a raise and was turned down *to_____ de s_____* .

Write *True* or *False*.

_____ 16. A *Wunderkind* is a kid who wonders what's going on.

_____ 17. Hitting three home runs in one game is a *tour de force*.

_____ 18. A gorilla is a member of *Homo sapiens*.

_____ 19. The *avant-garde* often experiment with new art forms.

_____ 20. The *laissez faire* policy is permissive, not restrictive.

Write the foreign expression for each definition. The opening letters are given.

Definitions

21. *ad* n_____   to a disgusting degree

22. *b*_____ *no*_____   something feared

23. *d*_____ *v*_____   the feeling of reliving a scene

24. *p*_____ *n*____ *g*_____   an unwelcome individual

25. *s*_____ *qua n*_____   an indispensable thing

Key to Review Test

Check your test answers by the following key. Deduct 4% per error from a possible 100%.

1. *hoi polloi*	10. *à la carte*	19. True
2. *faux pas*	11. *a cappella*	20. True
3. *C'est la vie*	12. *par excellence*	21. *ad nauseum*
4. *vox populi*	13. *potpourri*	22. *bête noir*
5. *savoir-faire*	14. *status quo*	23. *déjà vu*
6. *con amore*	15. *tout de suite*	24. *persona non grata*
7. *aficionado*	16. False	25. *sine qua non*
8. *sub rosa*	17. True	
9. *magnum opus*	18. False	

Score: _____%

SUPPLEMENTARY LIST

1. **ad hoc** (ad hok′) *L.* for this purpose only. "She appointed an *ad hoc* committee which later made its report and was dissolved."

2. **ad infinitum** (ad in-fə-nī′təm) *L.* to infinity. "Every creature has smaller creatures inside 'im, and so on and so on *ad infinitum.*"

3. **au courant** (ō kōō-räṅ′) *Fr.* well informed on current matters; up to date. "The old man read news magazines and so kept *au courant.*"

4. **bona fide** (bō′nə fid′) *L.* in good faith; genuine. "Two park benches for ten dollars? Was this nice man making me a *bona fide* offer?"

5. **bon vivant** (bōṅ vē-väṅ′) *Fr.* a person who enjoys good food, drink, and luxury. "I have all the requirements of a *bon vivant* except money."

6. **carte blanche** (kärt′ bläṅsh′) *Fr.* full authority to do as one thinks best. "The governor of the island gave us *carte blanche* to shoot film anywhere."

7. **cause célèbre** (kôz′ sə-leb′r) *Fr.* a famous legal case or controversy. "The Watergate affair was a *cause célèbre* during the early seventies."

8. **caveat emptor** (kā′vē-at emp′tôr) *L.* Let the buyer beware; buy at your own risk. "Flea market sales are final, so it's *caveat emptor.*"

9. **coup de grâce** (kōō də gräs′) *Fr.* death blow; lit., stroke of mercy. "Our shop was losing money, and the workers' strike was the *coup de grâce.*"

10. **coup d'état** (kōō dā-ta′) *Fr.* a sudden, powerful political stroke, esp. the forcible overthrow of government. "In a bloody *coup d'état* the army leaders seized command of the young republic."

11. **cul-de-sac** (kul′də-sak′) *Fr.* a passage closed at one end; a blind alley. "Trapped in a *cul-de-sac!* They'd put all their Basques in one exit."

12. **de facto** (dē fak′tō) *L.* actually existing though possibly without legal sanction. "The *de facto* government is ruled by a tyrant and two lunatics."

13. **de jure** (dē joor′ē) *L.* legally so. "Democratic processes have set up a *de jure* government."

14. **dernier cri** (der-nyā krē′) *Fr.* the latest fashion; the newest thing. "Olga's gown is the *dernier cri* from Paris—from Paris, Texas, that is."

15. **e.g.** (abbrev. of *exempli gratia*) *L.* for example. "Grandpa collects various items, *e.g.*, beer bottle caps."

16. **entre nous** (äṅ-trə nōō′) *Fr.* between us; confidentially. "Let's settle this fender-scratching accident *entre nous.*"

17. **esprit de corps** (es-prē′də kôr′) *Fr.* enthusiastic spirit and loyalty of a group. "Football games contributed to the *esprit de corps* at Acne Junior High."

18. **ex officio** (eks ə-fish′ē-ō) *L.* because of one's office or position. "The vice president is the *ex officio* president of the Senate."

19. **ex post facto** (eks pōst fak′tō) *L.* having retroactive effect. "Congress is not allowed to pass *ex post facto* laws."

20. **fait accompli** (fe-ta-koṅ-plē′) *Fr.* an accomplished fact, a thing already done, so that opposition is useless. "Mother hated the colors, but our paint job was a *fait accompli.*"

21. **gemütlich** (gə-mūt′lish) *G.* cheerful; agreeable. "The tavern was cozy and the atmosphere *gemütlich.*"

22. **hic jacet** (hik jā′sit) *L.* here lies. "*Hic jacet* Hy Fee, dentist, filling his last cavity."

23. **hors de combat** (ôr də koṅ-ba′) *Fr.* put out of the fight; disabled. "In six minutes our 'indestructible' fullback was *hors de combat.*"

24. **hors d'oeuvre** (ôr dûrv′) *Fr.* an appetizer. "I nibbled an *hors d'oeuvre* with my little finger extended."

25. **in absentia** (in ab-sen′shē-ə) *L.* in absence; although not present. "The philanthropist was awarded his honorary degree *in absentia.*"

26. **ipso facto** (ip′sō fak′tō) *L.* by that very fact. "A driver with high alcoholic blood level is *ipso facto* a lawbreaker."

27. **modus operandi** (mō′dəs op′ə-ran′dē) *L.* method of operating. "Zelda studied the new computer to figure out its *modus operandi.*"

28. **nom de plume** (nom də plōōm′) *Fr.* a pen name; pseudonym. "George Sand is the *nom de plume* of a Frenchwoman who wrote novels."

29. **nouveau riche** (nōō-vō rēsh′) *Fr.* a newly-rich person, possibly lacking in taste and culture. "One of the *nouveau riche* nailed up a Picasso in the bathroom."

30. **op. cit.** (abbrev. of *opere citato*) *L.* in the work cited. "The footnote reads 'Dingle, *op. cit.*, p. 99.' "

31. **pièce de résistance** (pyes də rā-zē-stäṅs′) *Fr.* the main dish of a meal; the principal work of a group. "The *pièce de résistance* of the program was 'Concerto for Tuba in Six Flats and a Basement.' "

32. **prima facie** (prī′mə fā′shē) *L.* at first sight before investigation. "Fudd's possession of the stolen jewels is *prima facie* evidence of his guilt."

33. **pro bono publico** (prō bō′nō pub′li-kō) *L.* for the public good. "Gumbo Center has dedicated its town hall *pro bono publico.*"

34. **pro tem** (abbrev. of *pro tempore*) *L.* for the time being. "Harpo will be chairman *pro tem*, until we get organized."

35. **quid pro quo** (kwid prō kwō′) *L.* one thing in exchange for another. "The oil companies got you elected and now they want their *quid pro quo.*"

36. **raison d'être** (rā′zōṅ det′rə) *Fr.* reason for existing. "The exploration of nature was John Muir's *raison d'être.*"

37. **rara avis** (rer′ə ā′vis) *L.* a very unusual person; lit., a rare bird. "Our new plumber is a *rara avis.* He brought all the necessary tools."

38. **sotto voce** (sot′ō vō′chē) *It.* in an undertone. "Moosehead explained his escape plan *sotto voce* to his cellmate."

39. **table d'hôte** (tab′əl dōt′) *Fr.* a complete meal as detailed on the menu. Cf., *à la carte.* "Vegetarian Vivian ordered *à la carte*; Hungry Harry, *table d'hôte.*"

40. **tête-à-tête** (tāt′ə tāt′) *Fr.* a private chat between two persons. "Ben and Agatha enjoyed their *tête-à-tête* at the Greasy Platter."

APPENDIX A

Academic Terms

FINE ARTS

1. **a cappella** (ä′kə-pel′ə): sung without instrumental accompaniment.
2. **aesthetics** (es-thet′iks): the study of beauty, especially as found in the fine arts.
3. **allegro** (ə-lä′grō): lively; faster than *allegretto* but not so fast as *presto*.
4. **andante** (än-dän′tā): a moderately slow movement in music.
5. **aria** (ä′ri-ə): a melody for solo voices, as in an opera or oratorio, usually with instrumental accompaniment.
6. **atonality** (ā′tō-nal′i-tē): *music.* a lack of key or tonal center; a condition wherein no one tone holds a primary position.
7. **avant-garde** (ə-vänt′gärd′): Fr., the vanguard; especially, in art, those regarded as advanced, daring, and experimental.
8. **baroque** (bə-rōk′): involving fantastic ornamentation and theatrical effects, as in seventeenth-century art, architecture, and music.
9. **bas-relief** (bä′ri-lēf′): sculpture in which the figures project only slightly from the background.
10. **cadenza** (kə-den′zə): a showy musical passage, often improvised, by an unaccompanied instrument in a concerto.
11. **cantata** (kən-tä′tə): a composition involving arias, choruses, and recitatives, to be sung but not acted.
12. **ceramics** (sə-ram′iks): the art of making pottery, earthenware, tile, etc.
13. **chamber music:** music suitable for a small hall, as by an instrumental trio or quartet.
14. **coloratura** (kul′ə-rə-tyoor′ə): brilliant runs, trills, etc., to show off a singer's talents.
15. **connoisseur** (kon′ə-sûr′): an expert in some field, especially fine arts, or in matters of taste.
16. **crescendo** (krə-shen′dō): a gradual increase in loudness.
17. **cubism** (kū′biz-əm): art which uses cubes, cones, and other abstract geometric forms instead of representing nature realistically.

18. **decadent** (dek′ə-dənt): deteriorating, as in morals, art, and literature; a writer of a late nineteenth-century group which leaned toward artificial style and abnormal subjects.

19. **dilettante** (dil′ə-tänt′): one who cultivates an art or science superficially as a pastime.

20. **dynamics:** *music.* the various degrees of softness and loudness in performance.

21. **étude** (ā′tōōd): a technical study for solo instrument.

22. **finesse** (fi-nes′): refined skill; adroitness in handling a delicate situation.

23. **forte** (fôr′tā): *music.* loud.

24. **fresco:** the art of painting on wet plaster.

25. **Hellenic** (he-len′ik): Grecian; pertaining to the ancient Greeks.

26. **impresario** (im-pri-sär′ē-ō): the organizer or manager of an opera company or of concert artists.

27. **intaglio** (in-tal′yō): a design carved below the surface, as on a gem: opposed to *cameo*, a design that stands out in relief.

28. **lapidary** (lap′i-der′ē): pertaining to cutting and engraving precious stones.

29. **little theater:** amateur or community theater; experimental or avant-garde drama playing to a limited audience.

30. **lyric** (lir′ik): a songlike outpouring of emotions and sentiment, as in sonnets, odes, elegies, and hymns.

31. **mimesis** (mi-mē′sis): *drama.* the imitation of human speech and behavior.

32. **mural** (myoor′əl): a painting done on a wall.

33. **nocturne** (nok′tûrn): a dreamy, romantic musical composition appropriate to night.

34. **ode:** a dignified lyric poem which does honor to some person or thing.

35. **oratorio** (or′ə-tōr′ē-ō′): an extended composition for voice and orchestra, usually on a religious theme, without acting or scenery.

36. **overture** (ō′vər-chər): the orchestral introduction to an opera or other large work.

37. **percussion instrument** (pər-kush′ən): an instrument which produces its tone when a part is struck; for example, drums, triangles, piano.

38. **perspective:** the drawing of objects, exhibiting distance and depth.

39. **pointillism** (pwan′tə-liz′əm): a method of painting by placing small points of pure color on a canvas to produce a blended, luminous effect.

40. **sonata** (sə-nä′tə): a composition for a small instrumental group.

41. **statuary** (stach′ōō-er′ē): a collection of statues.

42. **Stradivarius** (strad′ə-var′ē-əs): a violin or other stringed instrument made by the Stradivari family.

43. **string quartet:** a music group usually playing first and second violin, viola, and cello; a composition for such a group.

44. **surrealism:** the depiction of irrational, incongruous workings of the subconscious mind, especially as manifested in dreams.

45. **symmetry** (sim′ə-trē): a balanced arrangement of parts.

46. **syncopation:** the beginning of a tone on the last half of a beat and holding it through the first part of the next beat.

47. **tapestry** (tap'is-trē): a wall-hanging textile with a decorative design.

48. **tempo:** the rate of speed of a musical passage.

49. **vignette** (vin-yet'): a short literary piece; a decorative design or a shaded drawing.

50. **virtuoso** (vûr'chōō-ō'sō): one who is eminently skilled in an art such as music.

NATURAL SCIENCE

1. **absolute zero:** the lowest possible temperature, theoretically -273.18 degrees C., at which molecular motion ceases.

2. **acceleration:** the rate of change in velocity.

3. **acoustics** (ə-kōōs'tiks): the laws of sound; the sound-transmitting qualities of a room or hall.

4. **adaptation** (ad'əp-tā'shən): a change in structure or function by which an organism adjusts better to its environment.

5. **aerodynamics** (âr'ō-dī-nam'iks): the branch of physics that studies gases in motion, including their mechanical effects and other properties.

6. **alchemy** (al'kə-mē): medieval chemistry which sought mainly to change lead into gold and to find the elixir of perpetual youth.

7. **ampere** (am'pēr): the standard unit of electric current, equal to the current sent by one volt through a resistance of one ohm.

8. **aneroid barometer** (an'ə-roid'): an instrument which measures atmospheric pressure by its effect on the flexible top of a metal box containing a partial vacuum.

9. **anticyclone:** a high pressure area in which the spiral currents flow clockwise in the northern hemisphere.

10. **asexual** (ā-sek'shōō-əl): without sex; reproducing itself without sexual union.

11. **ballistics** (bə-lis'tiks): the science dealing with the flight behavior and impact of projectiles.

12. **Bessemer process** (bes'ə-mər): making steel by forcing a blast of air through molten pig iron to remove impurities.

13. **Bohr theory** (bōr): the theory of Niels Bohr that electrons absorb or radiate energy when changing orbits.

14. **Brownian movement:** the zigzag movement of microscopic particles suspended in fluids, caused by collisions with molecules.

15. **cardiac** (kär'dē-ak'): pertaining to the heart.

16. **catalyst** (kat'ə-list): a substance which speeds up a chemical reaction but itself undergoes practically no change.

17. **centrifugal force** (sen-trif'yə-gəl): the force impelling a thing outward from the center of rotation.

18. **centripetal force** (sen-trip′ə-təl): the force tending to draw a thing inward toward the center of rotation.

19. **congenital** (kən-jen′ə-təl): existing from birth.

20. **cretinism** (krē′tən-iz′əm): idiocy and deformity resulting from a congenital thyroid deficiency.

21. **cybernetics** (sī-bər-net′iks): a comparative study of computers and the human nervous system to help explain brain processes.

22. **cyclotron** (sī′klə-tron′): an apparatus that gives high velocity and energy to protons and deuterons so they can smash nuclear targets.

23. **decibel** (des′ə-bel′): a measure of the volume of a sound; one tenth of a bel.

24. **dominant:** *genetics*. designating a hereditary character which prevails over and masks a *recessive* character.

25. **electrolysis** (i-lek′trol′ə-sis): the decomposition of a chemical solution by means of an electric current.

26. **electrostatics:** a branch of physics that deals with electricity at rest known as static electricity.

27. **fission** (fish′ən): the splitting of an atom, with release of energy.

28. **foot-pound:** a unit of work, enough to raise a one-pound mass a distance of one foot.

29. **fulcrum** (ful′krəm): the support on which a lever turns.

30. **galvanic** (gal-van′ik): of electricity from a battery; convulsive; startling.

31. **gene** (jēn): an element in the chromosomes that transmits hereditary characters.

32. **generic** (jə-ner′ik): pertaining to a genus or class; having a broad general application.

33. **geocentric** (jē′ō-sen′trik): regarding the earth as center of the universe.

34. **geophysics** (jē′ō-fiz′iks): the physics of the earth, dealing with tides, winds, earthquakes, magnetic fields, etc.

35. **gynecology** (gī′nə-kol′ə-jē): the branch of medicine dealing with women's diseases.

36. **gyroscope** (jī′rə-skōp′): a rotating device, used to stabilize ships and planes.

37. **hermetic** (hûr-met′ik): airtight; completely sealed to keep air and liquids from getting in or out.

38. **histology** (hi-stol′ə-jē): the microscopic study of tissue structure.

39. **horticulture:** the cultivation of garden plants.

40. **humus** (hū′məs): organic matter in soils, produced by decay of vegetable and animal stuff.

41. **hybrid** (hī-brid): the offspring of two plants or animals of different varieties.

42. **hydraulic:** using water or other liquid: as, a *hydraulic* brake.

43. **hygrometer** (hī-grom′ə-tər): an instrument for measuring humidity.

44. **immunology:** the branch of medicine which deals with immunity to disease.

45. **inertia** (in-ûr′shə): that tendency of matter to retain its state of rest or of uniform rectilinear motion unless acted upon by an external force.

46. **isobar** (ī′sə-bär′): a line on a weather map connecting points having the same barometric pressure.

47. **isotope** (ī′sə-tōp′): any of two or more forms of a chemical element, each with its individual mass number and radioactive behavior.

48. **kinetic energy** (ki-net′ik): energy resulting from the motion of a body: opposed to *potential* energy.

49. **Lamarckism** (lə-mär′kiz-əm): Lamarck's evolutionary theory that acquired characteristics can be inherited.

50. **malleable** (mal′ē-ə-bəl): pliable; capable of being hammered and shaped without breaking: said of metals.

51. **materia medica** (mə-tēr′ē-ə med′ə-kə): drugs and other remedial substances.

52. **maturation** (mach′oo-rā′shən): attainment of maturity; completion of growth.

53. **megaton** (meg′ə-tun′): the explosive power of one million tons of TNT.

54. **Mendelism** (men′də-liz′əm): Gregor Mendel's principles of heredity, which predict characteristics of the offspring in cross-breeding.

55. **metabolism** (mə-tab′ə-liz′əm): the sum of physical and chemical processes which supply energy to the body.

56. **metallurgy** (met′ə-lûr′jē): the science of separating metals from ores and refining them for use.

57. **mutation** (myoo-tā′shən): a sudden, transmissible variation from the parent type.

58. **natural selection:** the adaptation of a species to its environment through survival of the fittest.

59. **oscillation** (os′ə-lā′shən): the fluctuation between maximum and minimum values, as of an alternating current.

60. **osmosis** (oz-mō′sis): the passing of a fluid through a membrane to equalize pressures.

61. **periodic table:** an arrangement of chemical elements by atomic number to exhibit groups and families.

62. **pituitary** (pi-too′ə-ter′ē): a gland at the base of the brain that secretes hormones affecting growth and metabolism.

63. **qualitative analysis:** the determining of the ingredients in a substance.

64. **quantum theory** (kwon′təm): the theory that radiant energy is not smooth flowing but discontinuous, and emitted in definite units called *quanta*.

65. **rectifier:** any device, such as a vacuum tube, which converts alternating current into direct current.

66. **resonance** (rez′ə-nəns): reinforced vibration due to the vibration, at the same frequency, of another body.

67. **seismic** (sīz′mik): pertaining to earthquakes.

68. **serology** (si-rol′ə-jē): the science of serums.

69. **sextant** (seks′tənt): a navigational instrument used in determining latitude at sea.

70. **simian** (sim′ē-ən): pertaining to monkeys or anthropoid apes.

71. **solar** (sō′lər): pertaining to the sun.

72. **solstice** (sol′stis): the time when the sun is furthest from the equator, at about June 21 and December 22.

73. **spectrum:** a band of colors observed when a beam of white light passes through a prism.

74. **speleology** (spē′lē-ol′ə-jē): the science of exploring caves; spelunking.

75. **spirochete** (spī′rə-kēt′): any of a genus of spiral-shaped bacteria some of which cause syphilis, trench mouth, and yaws.

76. **spontaneous generation:** the discredited theory that living organisms can originate in nonliving matter.

77. **stalactite** (stə-lak′tīt): an icicle-shaped rocky deposit hanging from the roof of a cave: distinguished from a *stalagmite*, which projects upward from the floor of a cave.

78. **supersonic:** greater than the speed of sound; faster than 738 miles per hour.

79. **taxidermy** (tak′sə-dûr′mē): the art of stuffing animals.

80. **tetanus** (tet′ə-nəs): an infectious, often fatal disease, marked by muscle spasms and lockjaw.

81. **therapy** (ther′ə-pē): the treatment of disease.

82. **thrombosis** (throm-bō′sis): a clotting of blood, forming an obstruction to circulation.

83. **topography** (tə-pog′rə-fē): mapping the surface features of a region.

84. **torque** (tôrk): a force tending to produce rotation.

85. **toxemia** (tok-sē′mē-ə): blood poisoning.

86. **toxicology** (tok′sə-kol′ə-jē): the science of poisons.

87. **trajectory** (trə-jek′tə-rē): the path described by something hurtling through space, especially the path of a projectile.

88. **troposphere** (trop′ə-sfēr′): the atmosphere that contains clouds and winds, below the stratosphere.

89. **Ursa Major** (ur′sə mā′jər): the constellation of the seven stars that form the Big Dipper; literally, the *Great Bear*.

90. **valence** (vā′ləns): the combining capacity of an atom or radical compared with that of a hydrogen atom.

91. **vector** (vek′tər): a quantity, such as force or velocity, that has both magnitude and direction.

92. **ventral** (ven′trəl): pertaining to the belly; abdominal: opposed to *dorsal*, pertaining to the back.

93. **ventricle** (ven′tri-kəl): one of the two lower chambers of the heart.

94. **vernier** (vûr′nē-ər): an auxiliary device which makes possible a more precise setting of a measuring instrument or a tool.

95. **viable** (vī′ə-bəl): physically fitted to live: said of a fetus or of a seed.

96. **viscera** (vis′ər-ə): the internal organs such as the lungs and intestines.

97. **vivisection** (viv′i-sek′shən): cutting into a living animal body in the interests of experimental research.

98. **watershed:** a ridge of high land separating two river drainage basins.

99. **woofer:** a large loudspeaker used to reproduce low-frequency sound waves: distinguished from *tweeter*, used to reproduce high-frequency sound waves.

100. **zenith** (zē′nith): the point in the sky directly above an observer: opposed to *nadir* (nā′dēr), the lowest possible point.

PHILOSOPHY

1. **agnosticism** (ag-nos′ti-siz′əm): the doctrine that one cannot know about God or the hereafter, or of anything but material phenomena.

2. **amoral** (ā-môr′əl): neither moral nor immoral; having no connection with morality.

3. **animism** (an′ə-miz′əm): the belief that inanimate objects and natural phenomena, such as stones, sun, and rain, are alive and have souls.

4. **apologetics** (ə-pol′ə-jet′iks): the branch of theology which deals with the defense and proofs of Christianity.

5. **a posteriori** (ā′ pos-têr′i-ō′rī): reasoning from particular instances to principles or from effect to cause; inductive; empirical: opposed to *a priori*.

6. **a priori** (ā′ prī-ō′rī): reasoning from general principle to particular instances or from cause to effect; deductive; based on theory rather than experiment.

7. **Berkeleianism** (burk-lē′ən-iz′əm): the philosophy of George Berkeley, maintaining that ideas are real and that material objects do not exist.

8. **categorical imperative** (kat′ə-gôr′i-kəl): the doctrine of Immanuel Kant that one must do only what one would want others to do in the same situation.

9. **deism** (dē′iz-əm): a belief in God based on reason but rejecting biblical revelation.

10. **determinism:** the doctrine that every action is the inevitable result of a sequence of causes.

11. **dialectics** (dī′ə-lek′tiks): the practice of examining ideas logically, usually by the method of question and answer.

12. **eclectic** (i-klek′tik): selecting what is considered best from various sources; not following any one system but choosing from all.

13. **empirical** (em-pir′i-kəl): depending on practical experience alone, not on theoretical reasoning: as, an *empirical* discovery.

14. **epistemology** (i-pis′tə-mol′ə-jē): the branch of philosophy that investigates the nature, limits, and validity of human knowledge.

15. **fatalism** (fā′tə-liz′əm): the belief that all events are predetermined and inevitable.

16. **free will:** the doctrine that people have the power to choose between alternative courses of action: opposed to *determinism*.

17. **hedonism** (hē′də-niz′əm): the doctrine that pleasure or happiness is the main goal of life.

18. **materialism:** the doctrine that physical matter is the only reality; also, a concern for worldly goods rather than spiritual goals.

19. **monism** (mon′iz-əm): the doctrine that there is only one kind of ultimate substance.

20. **nirvana** (nir-van′ə): In *Buddhism*, the blessedness achieved by absorption of the soul into the supreme spirit.

21. **ontology** (on-tol′ə-jē): the study of the nature of reality or being.

22. **oversoul:** the universal spiritual element which unites all human souls, according to Emersonian transcendentalism.

23. **positivism:** the system of Auguste Comte based on positive facts of sense experience and rejecting speculation.

24. **pragmatism** (prag′mə-tiz′əm): the doctrine that ideas have value only in terms of their practical results.

25. **relativism:** the theory that truths are relative and that the basis of judgment varies according to persons, events, etc.

26. **subjectivism** (səb-jek′tə-viz′əm): the theory that all knowledge is subjective and relative, a reflection of one's own consciousness.

27. **syllogism** (sil′ə-jiz′əm): a formula for deductive reasoning, consisting of a major premise, a minor premise, and a conclusion.

28. **Thomism** (tō′miz-əm): the dogmatic theology of Saint Thomas Aquinas, which became the basis of thirteenth-century scholasticism.

29. **utilitarianism:** the doctrine that ideas and things ought to be judged strictly by their usefulness rather than by beauty, tradition, etc., and that conduct should promote the greatest happiness for the greatest number.

30. **volition** (vō-lish′ən): the act of willing; a decision of the will.

SOCIAL SCIENCE

1. **Abolitionist:** one who favored wiping out Negro slavery in the United States.

2. **acculturation** (ə-kul′chə-rā′shən): the process of adopting new cultural patterns.

3. **agrarian** (ə-grâr′ē-ən): relating to farmlands and their ownership.

4. **amnesty** (am′ni-stē): a general pardon, as to political offenders, extended by a government.

5. **Anglican** (ang′glə-kən): pertaining to England, particularly the Church of England.

6. **apartheid** (ə-pärt′hīt): discrimination and segregation enforced against non-whites, as practiced in the Republic of South Africa.

7. **authoritarianism:** a system involving unquestioning obedience to authority, rather than individual freedom.

8. **Benthamism** (ben′thəm-iz′əm): the utilitarianism of Jeremy Bentham, who judged the morality of an action by its production of happiness and who measured that happiness by such criteria as intensity, duration, purity, and extent.

9. **blitzkrieg** (blits′krēg′): a lightning-speed military offensive (WWII).

10. **bloc** (blok): a coalition of nations or factions for a common cause.

11. **Bourbonism** (boor'bə-niz'əm): extreme conservatism in political and social issues, like that of the Bourbons.

12. **bourgeois** (boor-zhwä'): middle-class; commonplace, conventional, respectable, and smug.

13. **bureaucracy** (byoo-rok'rə-sē): government by numerous bureaus and officials, marked by inflexible routine and red tape.

14. **capitalism:** an economic system in which the means of production and of distribution are privately owned.

15. **cause célèbre** (kōz sā-leb'r): *Fr.*, a celebrated legal case; notorious incident.

16. **civil disobedience:** passive resistance.

17. **civil rights:** the rights of all to enjoy life, liberty, and property and the equal protection of law.

18. **Communism:** a totalitarian system of government in which the state owns all means of production and which is characterized by suppression of political opposition and individual liberties.

19. **coup d'état** (kōo dā-tä'): *Fr.*, a stroke of state; sudden, forceful act of politics, such as an overthrow of government.

20. **despotism** (des'pə-tiz'əm): tyranny; government by an absolute ruler.

21. **documentary** (dok'yə-men'tə-rē): presenting factual material, such as news events or social conditions, objectively and without fictionalizing.

22. **egalitarian** (i-gal'i-târ'ē-ən): equalitarian; believing that all men should have equal political and social rights.

23. **espionage** (es'pi-ə-nij): spying to secure military and political secrets.

24. **ethics:** a system of moral standards; code of right conduct for a specific profession or group.

25. **ethnocentrism** (eth'nō-sen'triz-əm): the belief that one's own race, country, or culture is superior to all others.

26. **ethos** (ē'thos): the distinctive spirit or character of a people, group, or culture.

27. **free enterprise:** the economic policy of having private ownership of business with little governmental control.

28. **Gandhiism** (gän'dē-iz'əm): passive resistance to achieve reform, as advocated by Mahatma Gandhi.

29. **genocide** (jen'ə-sīd'): the systematic killing of an entire people or nation.

30. **geopolitics** (jē'ō-pol'ə-tiks): the application of politics to geography, and aiming, as in Nazi Germany, at aggressive expansion.

31. **ghetto** (get'ō): a section of the city in which many members of a minority group, such as Jews or Negroes, find it necessary to live.

32. **granary** (gran'ēr-i): a storehouse for grain; grain-growing region.

33. **greenback:** a piece of United States paper money, printed in green on the back.

34. **Gresham's law** (gresh'əmz): the principle that bad money tends to drive good money out of circulation.

35. **gubernatorial** (gōo'bər-nə-tôr'ē-əl): pertaining to a governor or his office.

36. **hinterland:** back country, remote from the coast and the cities.

37. **humanitarian:** a philanthropist; one devoted to human welfare.

38. **husbandry:** thrifty management; the business of a farmer.

39. **Jacobean** (jak′ə-bē′ən): pertaining to King James I of England and his period (1603–1625).

40. **Jim Crow:** *colloq.* discrimination against Blacks.

41. **junta** (jun′tə): a group of political schemers; a faction; a cabal.

42. **laissez faire** (les′ā fâr′): letting people do as they please; *econ.* the theory that the state should not interfere with business.

43. **lingua franca** (ling′gwə frang′kə): any mixed language or jargon such as pidgin English that is used in international trade.

44. **lobby:** a special interest group that tries to get legislators to vote for a bill.

45. **Malthusian theory** (mal-thoo′zē-ən): the theory of Thomas R. Malthus (1766–1834) that if population is unchecked it will outrun its means of support and lead to famine, war, disease, and other natural curbs on overpopulation.

46. **manifesto:** a public declaration of views and intentions.

47. **mediation:** friendly intervention to settle disputes.

48. **mercantilism** (mûr′kən-ti-liz′əm): the national policy of establishing a favorable balance of trade—that is, more exporting than importing—and of accumulating precious metals.

49. **miscegenation** (mis′i-jə-nā′shən): marriage between members of different races.

50. **monetary** (moni′i-ter′ē): pertaining to money or coinage.

51. **Montessori method** (mon′ti-sôr′ē): a system aiming at self-education of a child through guidance rather than enforced discipline.

52. **naturalization:** the process of becoming a citizen.

53. **nepotism** (nep′ə-tiz′əm): favoritism to relatives, especially in public appointments.

54. **nihilism** (nī′ə-liz′əm): rejection of customary beliefs in religion, government, morality, etc.

55. **oligarchy** (ol′ə-gär′kē): government by a few persons.

56. **opportunism** (op′ər-too′niz-əm): the policy of backing whatever furthers one's interests, regardless of basic principles.

57. **pacifism** (pas′ə-fiz′əm): opposition to all war.

58. **partisan:** one who supports a person, party, or cause.

59. **power politics:** international diplomacy backed by a threat of military power.

60. **progressive:** a political liberal; one who favors reforms in legislation or religion.

61. **protocol** (prō′tə-kôl′): the proper courtesies to be observed in diplomatic affairs.

62. **revivalism** (ri-vī′və-liz′əm): a movement to revive religious belief, usually marked by fervid preaching, public confessions, and emotionalism.

63. **scapegoat:** any person or thing that bears the blame for others.

64. **schism** (siz′əm): a split in a church or other organized group caused by differences of opinion.

65. **secession** (si-sesh′ən): formal withdrawal, as of a state from the union.

66. **sedition:** stirring up of rebellion against the government.

67. **Siegfried Line** (sēg'frēd): a fortified defense line constructed in west Germany to face the French Maginot Line before World War II.

68. **social register:** a book listing socially prominent people.

69. **soviet** (sō'vē-et'): any of various governing councils in the Soviet Union.

70. **spoils system:** the practice of distributing appointive public offices to party workers, after a political victory.

71. **standing army:** a permanent army ready for action in peacetime as well as in time of war.

72. **stereotype:** a fixed pattern; a conventional character typifying a special group.

73. **technocracy** (tek-nok'rə-sē): a proposed system of government in which technologists would try to control the industrial and social systems with maximum efficiency.

74. **tory** (tôr'ē): an extreme political conservative; reactionary.

75. **totalitarianism** (tō-tal'i-târ'ē-ə-niz'əm): one-party government, characterized by political suppression and cultural and economic regimentation.

76. **tycoon** (tī-kōōn'): *colloq.* a powerful industrialist; financier.

77. **ultimatum** (ul'tə-mā'təm): a final proposal, the rejection of which may lead to hostile action.

78. **Volsteadism** (vol'sted-iz'əm): national prohibition of liquor sales (1919–1933), named after Rep. Andrew J. Volstead.

79. **yellow journalism:** the featuring of cheap, sensational news to increase newspaper sales.

80. **Zionism** (zī'ə-niz'əm): a movement originally to re-establish a Jewish nation, now to aid Israel.

APPENDIX B

Supplementary Exercises

LATIN DERIVATIVES
CHAPTER 3: Supplementary Exercise 1

One derivative of each Latin root is given. Write three more derivatives. If in doubt about a word, check its etymology in a dictionary.

	ROOT	MEANING	DERIVATIVES
1.	*ac, acr*	sharp	acrimony, _____ , _____ , _____
2.	*aer*	air	aerial, _____ , _____ , _____
3.	*agr*	field	agrarian, _____ , _____ , _____
4.	*ali*	another	alias, _____ , _____ , _____
5.	*alter, altr*	change	alternate, _____ , _____ , _____
6.	*anim*	spirit	animosity, _____ , _____ , _____
7.	*apt, ept*	adjust	aptitude, _____ , _____ , _____
8.	*arm*	weapon	armistice, _____ , _____ , _____
9.	*art*	craft	artificial, _____ , _____ , _____
10.	*avi*	bird	aviary, _____ , _____ , _____
11.	*bel, bell*	war	rebel, _____ , _____ , _____
12.	*ben, bene*	well	benefit, _____ , _____ , _____
13.	*brev*	short	abbreviate, _____ , _____ , _____
14.	*carn*	flesh	incarnate, _____ , _____ , _____
15.	*cid, cis*	kill; cut	precise, _____ , _____ , _____

16. *civ*   citizen   civil, _____ , _____ , _____

17. *clam*   shout   exclaim, _____ , _____ , _____

18. *claud, claus*   close   closet, _____ , _____ , _____

19. *cogn*   know   incognito, _____ , _____ , _____

20. *cord*   heart   cordial, _____ , _____ , _____

CHAPTER 3: Supplementary Exercise 2

One derivative of each Latin root is given. Write three more derivatives. If in doubt about a word, check its etymology in a dictionary.

ROOT	MEANING	DERIVATIVES
1. *corp*	body	corpse, _____ , _____ , _____
2. *cruc*	cross	crux, _____ , _____ , _____
3. *dent*	tooth	indent, _____ , _____ , _____
4. *dign*	worthy	dignity, _____ , _____ , _____
5. *doc, doct*	teach; prove	doctor, _____ , _____ , _____
6. *dom*	master	domineer, _____ , _____ , _____
7. *don*	bestow	donate, _____ , _____ , _____
8. *du*	two	duet, _____ , _____ , _____
9. *ego*	I	egotist, _____ , _____ , _____
10. *err*	wander	error, _____ , _____ , _____
11. *fin*	end; limit	define, _____ , _____ , _____
12. *fort*	strong	fortify, _____ , _____ , _____
13. *fus*	pour	effusive, _____ , _____ , _____
14. *gen*	birth; race	progeny, _____ , _____ , _____
15. *grat*	please; favor	gratify, _____ , _____ , _____
16. *grav*	heavy	gravity, _____ , _____ , _____
17. *jac, ject*	throw	eject, _____ , _____ , _____
18. *junct*	join	adjunct, _____ , _____ , _____

| 19. *labor* | work | elaborate, _____ , _____ , _____ |
| 20. *leg* | law | legal, _____ , _____ , _____ |

CHAPTER 3: Supplementary Exercise 3

One derivative of each Latin root is given. Write three more derivatives. If in doubt about a word, check its etymology in a dictionary.

ROOT	MEANING	DERIVATIVES
1. *lev*	light; rise	levity, _____ , _____ , _____
2. *lib*	book	libel, _____ , _____ , _____
3. *luc*	light	elucidate, _____ , _____ , _____
4. *magn*	large	magnify, _____ , _____ , _____
5. *mar*	sea	mariner, _____ , _____ , _____
6. *medi*	middle	medium, _____ , _____ , _____
7. *min*	little; less	minimum, _____ , _____ , _____
8. *mon, monit*	warn	premonition, _____ , _____ , _____
9. *mor*	custom	moral, _____ , _____ , _____
10. *mut*	change	mutation, _____ , _____ , _____
11. *nav*	ship	navigator, _____ , _____ , _____
12. *nomen, nomin*	name	nominee, _____ , _____ , _____
13. *ocul*	eye	monocle, _____ , _____ , _____
14. *par*	equal	parity, _____ , _____ , _____
15. *pater, patr*	father	patron, _____ , _____ , _____
16. *rat, ration*	reason	rational, _____ , _____ , _____
17. *rect*	right	direct, _____ , _____ , _____
18. *simil*	like	simile, _____ , _____ , _____
19. *struct*	build	construct, _____ , _____ , _____
20. *ten*	hold	tenacious, _____ , _____ , _____

GREEK DERIVATIVES
CHAPTER 5: Supplementary Exercise

One derivative of each Greek root is given. Write three more derivatives. If in doubt about a word, check its etymology in a dictionary.

ROOT	MEANING	DERIVATIVES
1. *cosm*	world; order	cosmic, _____ , _____ , _____
2. *crac, crat*	power	plutocrat, _____ , _____ , _____
3. *gam*	marriage	monogamy, _____ , _____ , _____
4. *gen*	race; kind	genetics, _____ , _____ , _____
5. *geo*	earth	geometry, _____ , _____ , _____
6. *gon*	corner; angle	hexagon, _____ , _____ , _____
7. *gyn*	woman	gynecology, _____ , _____ , _____
8. *iso*	same	isobar, _____ , _____ , _____
9. *lith*	rock	monolith, _____ , _____ , _____
10. *mega*	great	megaphone, _____ , _____ , _____
11. *micro*	small	microbe, _____ , _____ , _____
12. *necr*	dead	necrosis, _____ , _____ , _____
13. *nom*	law; order	economy, _____ , _____ , _____
14. *onym*	name	antonym, _____ , _____ , _____
15. *ped*	child	pedant, _____ , _____ , _____
16. *phos, phot*	light	photograph, _____ , _____ , _____
17. *poli*	city	police, _____ , _____ , _____
18. *scop*	see; watch	episcopal, _____ , _____ , _____
19. *techn*	art; skill	technique, _____ , _____ , _____
20. *zo*	animal	zoo, _____ , _____ , _____

WORDS OFTEN CONFUSED
CHAPTER 9: Supplementary Exercise

Homonyms and often confused word pairs are listed below. Use each word correctly in a sentence. When in doubt about the meaning of a word, consult your dictionary.

1. addition, edition
2. aisle, isle
3. alley, ally
4. allowed, aloud
5. altar, alter
6. anecdote, antidote
7. angel, angle
8. ascent, assent
9. bare, bear
10. base, bass
11. beach, beech
12. beat, beet
13. berth, birth
14. board, bored
15. boarder, border
16. bridal, bridle
17. censor, censure
18. cereal, serial
19. chord, cord
20. coarse, course
21. council, counsel
22. costume, custom
23. dairy, diary
24. dammed, damned
25. dear, deer
26. deceased, diseased
27. device, devise
28. disinterested, uninterested
29. dyeing, dying
30. emigrate, immigrate
31. envelop, envelope
32. fair, fare
33. flea, flee
34. flour, flower
35. forth, fourth
36. foul, fowl
37. heal, heel
38. hear, here
39. hoarse, horse
40. hole, whole
41. holey, holy
42. incidence, incidents
43. knew, new
44. lessen, lesson
45. liable, libel
46. mantel, mantle
47. meat, meet
48. pail, pale
49. peace, piece
50. picture, pitcher
51. pole, poll
52. pore, pour
53. profit, prophet
54. prophecy, prophesy
55. respectfully, respectively
56. ring, wring
57. sail, sale
58. steal, steel
59. summary, summery
60. threw, through

DESCRIPTIVE WORDS
CHAPTER 10: Supplementary Exercise

Fill in the blank with the descriptive word that fits the definition. Although these words were not defined in Chapter 10, you should recognize most of them. Check your answers with the key at the end of the exercise. Use your dictionary to study any unknown words.

abstemious, articulate, auspicious, avid, bland

1. _____ mild; nonstimulating; insipid

2. _____ very eager; greedy

3. _____ temperate; eating and drinking sparingly

4. _____ favorable; propitious; of good omen

5. _____ able to express oneself well; clearly presented

caustic, compatible, coy, culpable, deferential

6. _____ able to get along well together

7. _____ very respectful; courteous

8. _____ at fault; deserving blame

9. _____ corrosive; stinging; sarcastic

10. _____ shy; bashful; coquettishly modest

delectable, delusive, derisive, disgruntled, disoriented

11. _____ ridiculing; mocking

12. _____ disappointed; displeased; sulky

13. _____ misleading; false; deceptive

14. _____ delightful; enjoyable

15. _____ confused; out of adjustment to one's environment

dissident, dormant, dyspeptic, erudite, exotic

16. _____ strangely beautiful; foreign and fascinating

17. _____ grouchy and gloomy because of indigestion

18. _____ as if asleep; inactive

19. _____ not agreeing; differing; dissenting

20. _____ learned; scholarly

heinous, illicit, immaculate, imperturbable, impotent

21. _____ pure; flawless; completely clean

22. _____ atrocious; extremely wicked

23. _____ powerless; helpless; without virility

24. _____ calm; unruffled

25. _____ unlawful; improper

Key

1. bland	6. compatible	11. derisive	16. exotic	21. immaculate
2. avid	7. deferential	12. disgruntled	17. dyspeptic	22. heinous
3. abstemious	8. culpable	13. delusive	18. dormant	23. impotent
4. auspicious	9. caustic	14. delectable	19. dissident	24. imperturbable
5. articulate	10. coy	15. disoriented	20. erudite	25. illicit

DESCRIPTIVE WORDS
CHAPTER 11: Supplementary Exercise

Fill in the blank with the descriptive word that fits the definition. Although these words were not defined in Chapter 11, you should recognize most of them. Check your answers with the key at the end of the exercise. Use your dictionary to study any unknown words.

inclement, indolent, indefatigable, insipid, luminous

1. _____ without flavor; tasteless; dull

2. _____ stormy; without leniency

3. _____ shining; clear; bright

4. _____ tireless

5. _____ lazy; idle

nomadic, morbid, ornate, precocious, ruthless

6. _____ overdecorated; flowery

7. _____ wandering

8. _____ cruel; pitiless

9. _____ maturing early; bright for its age

10. _____ excessively interested in gruesome matters

salutary, scurrilous, skeptical, spasmodic, squalid

11. _____ doubting; questioning; not easily convinced

12. _____ occurring now and then; fitful

13. _____ wretched; poverty-stricken in appearance

14. _____ foul-mouthed; grossly abusive

15. _____ beneficial; having a good effect

squeamish, staid, stalwart, suave, subtle

16. _____ strong; valiant; unyielding

17. _____ smoothly pleasant and polite; urbane

18. _____ oversensitive; prudish, easily disgusted

19. _____ cunning; crafty; delicately skillful

20. _____ sedate and settled

sullen, surreptitious, tepid, terse, voracious

21. _____ secret; stealthy; sneaky

22. _____ gloomy and resentful; glum; morose

23. _____ concise; to the point

24. _____ greedy; gluttonous; insatiable

25. _____ lukewarm

Key

1. insipid	6. ornate	11. skeptical	16. stalwart	21. surreptitious
2. inclement	7. nomadic	12. spasmodic	17. suave	22. sullen
3. luminous	8. ruthless	13. squalid	18. squeamish	23. terse
4. indefatigable	9. precocious	14. scurrilous	19. subtle	24. voracious
5. indolent	10. morbid	15. salutary	20. staid	25. tepid

ACTION WORDS
CHAPTER 12: Supplementary Exercise

Fill in the blank with the verb that fits the definition. Although these verbs were not defined in Chapter 12, you should recognize most of them. Check your answers with the key at the end of the exercise. Use your dictionary to study any unknown words.

atrophy, belie, browbeat, corroborate, covet

1. _____ to bully; to intimidate

2. _____ to confirm; to make more certain

3. _____ to prove false

4. _____ to desire what belongs to another

5. _____ to wither; to waste away

decry, deploy, dismantle, edify, emulate

6. _____ to instruct; to enlighten spiritually

7. _____ to imitate so as to equal or excel

8. _____ to spread out forces according to plan

9. _____ to denounce; to condemn; to disparage

10. _____ to strip of equipment; to disassemble

epitomize, equivocate, implicate, impoverish, jettison

11. _____ to represent the essence of

12. _____ to be ambiguous purposely; to hedge; to mislead

13. _____ to make poor; to reduce to poverty

14. _____ to throw cargo overboard in an emergency

15. _____ to show to be involved; to entangle

mollify, osculate, rankle, retaliate, retrench

16. _____ to kiss

17. _____ to cause resentment; to fester; to irritate

18. _____ to pay back injury for injury; to revenge

19. _____ to make less angry; to soothe; to appease

20. _____ to cut expenses; to economize

scrutinize, skulk, swelter, thwart, tipple

21. _____ to prevent from accomplishing a purpose; to hinder

22. _____ to drink liquor frequently

23. _____ to move about furtively; to lurk; to shirk

24. _____ to examine carefully; to look at closely

25. _____ to suffer or perspire from oppressive heat

Key

1. browbeat	6. edify	11. epitomize	16. osculate	21. thwart
2. corroborate	7. emulate	12. equivocate	17. rankle	22. tipple
3. belie	8. deploy	13. impoverish	18. retaliate	23. skulk
4. covet	9. decry	14. jettison	19. mollify	24. scrutinize
5. atrophy	10. dismantle	15. implicate	20. retrench	25. swelter

---

GENERAL LITERATURE
CHAPTER 15: Supplementary Exercises

In the following exercises, study the list of definitions; then do the quiz.

Exercise 1 (Fiction)

1. **existentialism** (eg'zis-ten'shə-liz'əm): a view of life which maintains that man is alone in a purposeless universe and that he must exercise his own free will to oppose a hostile environment. This *existentialist* theme of man's total responsibility to himself in the midst of conformist pressures is reflected in the fiction of Jean-Paul Sartre, Albert Camus, Franz Kafka, and others.

2. **protagonist** (prō-tag'ə-nist): the main character of a drama or fictional work. Hamlet, Ivanhoe, Huck Finn, and Brer Rabbit are *protagonists* of literary pieces.

3. **realism:** the presentation of everyday life as it is, in accurate, photographic detail rather than in a romanticized way. *Realism* began as a nineteenth-century literary movement that tried to reflect actual life, using commonplace characters and depicting their ordinary impulses, problems, and surroundings.

4. **satire:** wit, irony, or sarcasm used to ridicule abuses and follies. Outstanding *satire* has been written by Horace, Juvenal, Swift, Byron, Rabelais, Voltaire, Lewis Carroll, and others.

5. **sentimentalism:** excessive emotionalism, with emphasis on tender feelings and tears; called *sensibility* during the eighteenth century. Whereas *sentiment* is an expression of delicate, sensitive feelings, *sentimentalism* suggests a soft-heartedness that is gushy and insincere.

6. **setting:** the physical and spiritual surroundings or environment in which the story takes place. The *setting* of Sinclair Lewis's *Main Street* (1920) is a midwestern village.

7. **thesaurus** (thi-sô'rəs): a treasury of words, with synonyms and antonyms classified and arranged to help writers. A dictionary and a *thesaurus* are indispensable to an author. Talent helps, too.

8. **trilogy** (tril'ə-jē): a series, by a single author, of three related works, as in fiction or drama. Eugene O'Neill's *Mourning Becomes Electra* (1931) is a *trilogy*, a series of three plays, in which the ancient Greek playwright Aeschylus's theme of fate haunts an American household.

Quiz

Write the letter that indicates the best definition.

1. (h)	( ) 1. existentialism	a. portrayal of life as it is
2. (c)	( ) 2. protagonist	b. a word treasury for writers
3. (a)	( ) 3. realism	c. the main character or hero
4. (f)	( ) 4. satire	d. emotionalism in excess
5. (d)	( ) 5. sentimentalism	e. background of the action
6. (e)	( ) 6. setting	f. a witty attack on follies
7. (b)	( ) 7. thesaurus	g. three related works by an author
8. (g)	( ) 8. trilogy	h. Sartre's doctrine of man's responsibility to himself

Exercise 2 (Drama)

1. **conflict:** the opposition of forces, or the struggle, necessary to any drama. *Conflict* may be against oneself, against other men, against nature or fate.

2. **denouement** (dā-nōō-män'): the unknotting of complications and resolving of problems following the climax. Sometimes the *denouement* of a play reveals a hidden identity or looks to a future marriage.

3. **dramatis personae** (dram'ə-tis pər-sō'nē): the characters in a play; also, the list of characters. The *dramatis personae* are listed at the beginning of a play script.

4. **foreshadowing:** a hint of some coming event, possibly tragic. Dramatic *foreshadowing* may be provided by a prediction, a dream, blood on a picture, a stormy night.

5. **problem play:** a play that comes to grips with a social issue. The *problem play*, also called the *drama of ideas*, has dealt with many social problems, such as husband-wife relationships, racial integration, and the causes of war.

6. **properties:** any furniture or objects used in a play, excluding costumes and scenery. Tables and sofas are called *set props*; magazines and bottles are *hand props*.

7. **Stanislavski method** (stan'i-släv'skē): an acting technique whereby the actor first recalls a parallel emotional situation in which he was once involved and then relives that emotion on stage. The *Stanislavski method* has distinctly influenced American acting.

8. **unities:** singleness of time, place, and action in a drama. The three classical *unities*, as specified by sixteenth-century French theorists in their misinterpretation of Aristotle's doctrines, require that a play should involve a single plot, a single setting, and a single day.

Quiz

Write the letter that indicates the best definition.

1. (e)
2. (c)
3. (h)
4. (g)
5. (d)
6. (a)
7. (f)
8. (b)

( )	1. conflict	a. chairs, tables, lamps, etc.
( )	2. denouement	b. one time, place, and action
( )	3. dramatis personae	c. final clearing up of problems
( )	4. foreshadowing	d. a drama of ideas and issues
( )	5. problem play	e. struggle; opposition of forces
( )	6. properties	f. a reliving of emotions
( )	7. Stanislavski method	g. a hint of future events
( )	8. unities	h. characters in a play

Exercise 3 (Poetry)

1. **ars poetica** (ärz pō-et'i-kə): the art of poetry.

2. **imagery** (im'ij-rē): the various appeals to the senses made by a literary passage; any descriptive phrasing and figures of speech which make us feel, see, hear, smell, taste; for example, "fragrant hair," "gentle rain," "a swarm of golden bees," "The hare limped trembling through the frozen grass."

3. **internal rhyme:** rhyming within the line; for example, "And nations rush faster toward disaster."

4. **inversion:** a reversal in the natural word order to help out the rhyme or rhythm. *Inversions* are now usually considered undesirable: "And them behold no more shall I."

5. **light verse:** short, light-hearted poems. Witty, sophisticated *light verse* has been written by Dorothy Parker, Ogden Nash, Phyllis McGinley, and others.

6. **masculine rhyme:** a rhyme limited to the stressed last syllable; single rhyme; for example, "kiss" and "miss," "late" and "fate," "repent" and "consent."

7. **feminine rhyme:** a rhyme of two or three syllables, with the stress on the first syllable; also called double-rhyme or triple-rhyme; for example, "stranger" and "danger," "sleeping" and "creeping," "saddening" and "maddening."

8. **quatrain** (kwoʹtrān): a four-line stanza, variously rhymed; for example, "I never saw a moor, / I never saw the sea; / Yet know I how the heather looks, / And what a wave must be."

Exercise 4 (Poetry)

1. **scansion** (skanʹshən): the analysis of verse to show its meter and rhyme scheme *Scansion* marks include ˘ for an unaccented syllable, ʹ for an accented syllable, and | for a foot division.
2. **foot:** the basic unit of verse meter, consisting usually of two or three syllables of which ordinarily one is stressed. The number of feet to the line determines the meter.
3. **iamb** (īʹamb): an unstressed syllable followed by a stressed syllable; for example, "tonight," "deny," "and now," "my love."
4. **trochee** (trōʹkē): a stressed syllable followed by an unstressed syllable; for example, "faster," "damsel," "dying," "fling it."
5. **anapest** (anʹə-pestʹ): two unstressed syllables followed by a stressed syllable; for example, "of the men"; "to rejoice"; "interfere."
6. **dactyl** (dakʹtil): a stressed syllable followed by two unstressed syllables; for example, "sing to the"; "fleeing from"; "rapidly."
7. **tetrameter** (te-tramʹi-tər): a line of poetry containing four feet; example from Lord Tennyson of iambic *tetrameter:* "I come from haunts of coot and hern." The *pentameter* line contains five feet (see Chapter 15). Shorter lines are the *trimeter*, three feet; the *dimeter*, two feet; and the *monometer*, one foot.
8. **hexameter** (hek-samʹi-tər): a line of poetry containing six feet. Longer and less common than the *hexameter* line are the *heptameter*, seven feet, and the *octameter*, eight feet.

Quiz

Write the letter that indicates the best definition or example.

Answers			
1. (f)	( ) 1. scansion	a. a foot like "tenderly"
2. (h)	( ) 2. foot	b. a foot like "the stars"
3. (b)	( ) 3. iamb	c. a foot like "in her home"
4. (d)	( ) 4. trochee	d. a foot like "kissing"
5. (c)	( ) 5. anapest	e. a verse with six feet
6. (a)	( ) 6. dactyl	f. metrical analysis
7. (g)	( ) 7. tetrameter	g. a verse with four feet
8. (e)	( ) 8. hexameter	h. basic unit of verse meter

NAME DERIVATIVES
CHAPTER 16: Supplementary Exercises

In the following exercises, study the list of definitions; then do the quiz.

Exercise 1

1. **argosy** (är′gə-sē): a fleet of merchant ships (from Ragusa, a Dalmatian port).
2. **behemoth** (bi-hē′məth): a huge animal (alluded to in Job, 40:15–24).
3. **Boswell**: a friend and biographer (from James Boswell, who wrote *The Life of Samuel Johnson*, 1791).
4. **derrick**: crane; hoist (from Derrick, a seventeenth-century London hangman).
5. **draconian** (drā-kō′nē-ən): harsh, cruel (from Draco, a Greek lawmaker).
6. **galvanize**: to startle; to excite; to electrify (from L. Galvani, an Italian physicist).
7. **hector**: to browbeat; to bully (from Hector, the Trojan hero of Homer's *Iliad*).
8. **jezebel** (jez′ə-bel′): a shameless wicked woman (from II Kings, 9:7, 30).

Quiz

Write the letter that indicates the best definition.

Answers			
1. (e)	( ) 1. argosy	a. to bully; to annoy
2. (c)	( ) 2. Boswell	b. to electrify; to startle
3. (h)	( ) 3. behemoth	c. a biographer
4. (d)	( ) 4. derrick	d. a crane
5. (g)	( ) 5. draconian	e. a fleet of merchant ships
6. (b)	( ) 6. galvanize	f. a shameless woman
7. (a)	( ) 7. hector	g. cruel; inhumanly severe
8. (f)	( ) 8. jezebel	h. a hippopotamus-like animal

Exercise 2

1. **martinet** (mär′tə-net′): a very strict disciplinarian (from General Jean Martinet, a seventeenth-century French drillmaster).
2. **masochism** (mas′ə-kiz′əm): the obtaining of pleasure, particularly sexual pleasure, from being hurt (from Leopold von Sacher-Masoch, an Austrian author).
3. **mecca**: a place attracting many people; a goal (from Mecca, a holy city of the Moslems).
4. **mesmerize**: to hypnotize (from Franz Mesmer, a German physician).
5. **panjandrum** (pan-jan′drəm): an exalted official (from a character invented by Samuel Foote, English dramatist).
6. **pharisaical** (far′i-sā′i-kəl): self-righteous; hypocritical (from the Pharisees in the New Testament).
7. **pickwickian**: benevolent, naive, and blundering (from Mr. Samuel Pickwick in Dickens' *Pickwick Papers*, 1836).
8. **Portia** (pôr′shə): a female lawyer (from the heroine of Shakespeare's *The Merchant of Venice*, 1596).

Quiz

Write the letter that indicates the best definition.

1. (f)
2. (d)
3. (a)
4. (e)
5. (b)
6. (h)
7. (g)
8. (c)

( ) 1. martinet   a. the goal of many travelers
( ) 2. masochism   b. an official of lofty importance
( ) 3. mecca   c. a lady lawyer
( ) 4. mesmerize   d. the enjoyment of being hurt
( ) 5. panjandrum   e. to hypnotize
( ) 6. pharisaical   f. a rigid disciplinarian
( ) 7. pickwickian   g. good-hearted, naive, muddled
( ) 8. Portia   h. self-righteous, censorious

Exercise 3

1. **protean** (prō′ti-ən): changeable; readily taking on different shapes (from Proteus in Greek mythology).
2. **rodomontade** (rod′ə-mon-tād′): bragging; blustering (from Rodomonte, a boastful king in Ariosto's *Orlando Furioso*, 1516).
3. **sadism** (sad′iz-əm): the obtaining of pleasure, particularly sexual pleasure, from hurting others (from the author Count de Sade, who describes brutal sexual aberrations).
4. **sardonic** (sär-don′ik): scornful; sneering; cynical (from a poisonous Sardinian plant causing laughter-like convulsions).

5. **serendipity** (ser′ən-dip′i-tē): a knack for making lucky discoveries by accident (from the story, "The Three Princes of Serendip," whose heroes made lucky finds).

6. **Shylock:** a relentless creditor (from the usurer in Shakespeare's *The Merchant of Venice*, 1596, who wants his pound of flesh).

7. **titian** (tish′ən): auburn; reddish yellow (from the artist Titian, who often painted women's hair this shade).

8. **yahoo** (yä′hōo): a crude or vicious person (from the brutish Yahoos in *Gulliver's Travels* by Jonathan Swift).

Quiz

Write the letter that indicates the best definition.

1. (f)	( ) 1. protean	a. the enjoyment of inflicting pain
2. (h)	( ) 2. rodomontade	b. a hard-fisted creditor
3. (a)	( ) 3. sadism	c. reddish yellow
4. (g)	( ) 4. sardonic	d. a bestial person
5. (e)	( ) 5. serendipity	e. a knack for lucky finds
6. (b)	( ) 6. Shylock	f. changeable in form
7. (c)	( ) 7. titian	g. cynical; scornful
8. (d)	( ) 8. yahoo	h. boasting; blustering

Exercise 4

1. **Adonis** (ə-don′is): an extremely handsome young man (from Adonis, who was loved by Aphrodite but was killed by a wild boar).

2. **Amazon:** any tall, strong, or athletic woman (from the Amazon women who helped the Trojans fight the Greeks).

3. **Babbitt:** a smug, conventional, uncultured businessman (from George Babbitt, a character in a Sinclair Lewis novel).

4. **bacchanalia** (bak′ə-nā′li-ə): drunken parties; orgies (from Bacchus, god of wine).

5. **bedlam** (bed′ləm): a scene of noisy confusion (from Bethlehem, a lunatic asylum in London).

6. **gargantuan** (gär-gan′chōo-ən): huge; gigantic (from Gargantua, the enormous prince in Rabelais' *Gargantua and Pantagruel*).

7. **micawberish:** ever optimistic and cheerful (from the Dickens character Micawber, who keeps saying, "Something will turn up").

8. **Spartan:** brave, hardy, stoical (from the Spartan soldiers who practiced austerity and self-discipline).

Quiz

Write the letter that indicates the best definition.

( ) 1. Adonis   a. mad, noisy disorder
( ) 2. Amazon   b. hardy; lacking luxury
( ) 3. Babbitt   c. a handsome male
( ) 4. bacchanalia   d. drunken orgies
( ) 5. bedlam   e. enormous; very large
( ) 6. gargantuan   f. a female warrior
( ) 7. micawberish   g. a middle-class conformist
( ) 8. Spartan   h. optimistic

VOCABULARY EXPANSION

Keep a list here of interesting words from your college courses and your reading that you want to remember. Define each word and show how it was used.